The State

in Theory and Practice

Justice is a power; and if it cannot create, it will at least destroy. So that the question for the future is not, shall there be revolution, but shall it be beneficent or disastrous?

—G. Lowes Dickinson

Justice and Liberty (1908), p. 206.

THE STATE IN THEORY AND PRACTICE

BY

HAROLD J. LASKI

NEW YORK
THE VIKING PRESS
MCMXXXV

First Published February 1935

Printed in the United States of America by
The Vail-Ballou Press

To Marion Denman Frankfurter

with our love

F.

D.

H.

Contents

PREFACE

The purpose of this book is to discover the nature of the modern state. It seeks to explain that nature by an examination of its characteristics as these have been revealed by its history; and, in their light, it seeks to outline a theory of the state more in consonance with that history than the classic outlook. In some sort, it is a sequel to my *Democracy in Crisis* (1933), the philosophic implications of which it tries to develop further.

I owe much to friends who have helped me with criticism and discussion. Above all, I must thank my colleagues Mr. H. L. Beales, Professor M. Ginsberg, and Dr. W. I. Jennings. None of them, of course, has any responsibility for these pages. What it owes to my wife I only can know. But of this neither of us would speak.

Mr. Victor Gollancz has kindly allowed me to use several pages from a chapter contributed by me to *The Intelligent Man's Way to Prevent War* edited by Mr. Leonard Woolf.

HAROLD J. LASKI

London, October 24, 1934.

The State in Theory and Practice

I

The Philosophic Conception of the State

I

EVER since Plato denied that justice was the rule of the stronger, men have sought to justify the state by reason of the high purposes it seeks to protect. The human mind, indeed, revolts from the notion that the possession of coercive power can be defended regardless of the ends to which it is devoted. We argue, as with Aristotle, that the state exists to promote the good life. We insist, as with Hobbes, that there can be no civilization without the security it provides by its power over life and death. We agree, as with Locke, that only a common rule-making organ, to the operations of which men consent, can give us those rights to life and liberty and property without the peaceful enjoyment of which we are condemned to a miserable existence. Rousseau could find certain terms of statehood in which, by obeying its laws, men could be more free than in pre-civil society. "The state," wrote Hegel in a famous sentence,[1] "is the

[1] *Philosophy of History* (trans. Sibree), p. 41.

Divine Idea as it exists on earth"; and he argued that all the worth of the human being is derived from his immersion in its activities.

Few institutions have received panegyrics more splendid than the state; and it is important to understand the grounds upon which they rest. They are rarely panegyrics of actual states; though there are occasions when the panegyrist has found his ideal embodied in an actual society. More usually, they are the defence of a system of purposes which the thinker deems good, and conceives as capable of realization only through the peculiar form of association we call the state. These purposes, in the history of political philosophy, have a fairly constant character. They are a search for the terms on which individual men and women may most amply fulfil themselves. They are a recognition of the fact that, because individuals move differently to the attainment of conflicting desires, a common organ is necessary in society to define the terms upon which that movement may legitimately proceed. Views differ violently as to the form that organ should take. The basis upon which it should act, the ambit of its authority, are questions upon which no unanimity has been attained. But, the philosophic anarchist apart (and in political philosophy he has been a curiously infrequent creature), the necessity of a coercive authority in society to define the permissible rules of social behaviour has been almost universally admitted. Granted the nature of men, the alternative appears to be a chaos of individual decisions fatal to the emergence of settled ways of life. With the state there comes security; and security is the condition upon which the satisfactions men seek to secure are capable of peaceful attainment.

But to argue that there is need in society for a coercive authority which is commonly obeyed begins and does not end a problem. Men do not obey that authority for the sake of obedience. They obey it for the purposes they believe to be secured by its operations. They submit to orders for the sake of what they believe those orders to imply. They scrutinize those orders in terms of the satisfactions they seek from life, and, from time to time, they reject them upon the ground that they are a denial of those satisfactions. Obedience, that is to say, is the normal habit of mankind; but marginal cases continually recur in which the decision to disobey is painfully taken and passionately defended.

These marginal cases make it clear that men obey the state not merely for the sake of order, but also on account of what they deem that order to make possible. They are, in fact, judging the state from the angle of satisfactions they think it should provide. Their judgments, no doubt, vary with time and place. Expectations of what is legitimate are always born of experience; and the demands of one society at one period will differ from those of another society at another period. But the implication is the clear one that the exercise of coercive authority in a society is never unconditional. It must act by rules. It must realize those purposes which the citizens who live by its activities deem to be fundamental. Any inquiry, therefore, into the nature of states, is at least as much an inquiry into the realized intentions of power as into the announced purposes by which their operations are justified in theory. For its citizens, a state is what it does; it is not justified merely because it is a state. It secures their assent to its actions by the judgment they make of the consequences. They concern themselves not with the philosophic purpose of the state as such, but with the results of its actual processes as these are experienced in their daily lives.

The philosopher may, like Burke, think of the state as a partnership in all virtue and all perfection; the common man thinks of it as a way of being ruled which satisfies his expectation of legitimate satisfactions. The philosopher, that is, has, in the main, been satisfied to construct an ideal form of state and to transfer its implications to the actual experience of states. That ideal form has been, very largely, the philosopher's personal conception of what is desirable in the light of his experience; he has externalized his autobiography into a programme and criterion of reality. Hobbes's theory of the state is, at bottom, built upon the insistence, intelligible enough in an epoch of civil war, that order in itself is the highest good, without regard to what that order makes. Hegel's assertion that the personality of the state is incomplete without a monarch chosen by primogeniture is clearly less a universal truth than it is the elevation to that plane of Hegel's own preference for the Kingdom of Prussia as the highest form in which a state can clothe itself. Unless we take the view that, as Bosanquet argued, "the state is a brief expression for states *qua* states" [1]; that, therefore, the theoretic purpose is always being realized in living fact; that the failures we encounter are to be attributed not to the state as such, but to non-state sources which the state is seeking to purify; it is obvious that a theory of the state must be a way of valuing the achievement of actual states, a criterion of measurement, rather than a statement of reality. We cannot say, with Hegel, that the individual's "highest duty is to

---

[1] *Social and International Ideals* (1917), p. 274.

be a member of the state"[1] until we have judged the quality of the actual state of which he is a member.

I shall seek, in this book, to set out as best I can that philosophic justification of the state which has, I believe, exercised, in the last century, the main influence upon Western civilization. I shall then examine that justification in the light of the states we encounter in our daily lives. This will lead me to a formulation of a theory of the state more related, as I shall suggest, to the facts we know than that which is commonly accepted at the present time. Finally, in the light of that formulation, I shall seek to draw some practical inferences by which we may predict—since prediction is the ultimate test of a true social theory—the probable course of events in the future.

My argument throughout will be based upon a single assumption. I shall assume that the justification of coercive authority, the only title upon which it can claim the obedience of those over whom it is exercised, is in the measure of its satisfaction of maximum demand. It is not, that is to say, its intention merely to achieve this end that is its title to allegiance; a theory of intention can never be the basis of an adequate political philosophy. It is not the purpose announced, but the purpose realized, when this is set over against the reasonable possibilities of realization, that can alone be the criterion of value in human institutions.

II

We have to begin with definitions; not a little of the barrenness of political philosophy is due to the failure of men

[1] *Philosophy of Right* (Eng. trans.), p. 306.

to agree upon the meaning of their terms. We find ourselves living in a society with other men; that society, in relation to all other forms of human association, is integrated into a unity we call the state; as a state, its affairs are administered by a body of persons we call the government. What do these terms mean?

By a society I mean a group of human beings living together and working together for the satisfaction of their mutual wants. The basic wants they have to satisfy are economic in character; they must earn their living before they begin to live well. But, beyond bare economic need, there is every variety of want, religious, cultural, domestic, the satisfaction of which becomes possible through the social instinct of man. Theoretically, there is no reason why this group should not be equivalent to the totality of human beings; and, actually, as I shall show later, the implications of our methods of economic production make it necessary to regard that equivalence as having profound institutional significance. But for various historical and geographical reasons, into which it is impossible here to enter, the societies with which we are concerned are those such as England, France, Germany, the United States, and Russia—groups of human beings differentiated from other groups by sharing in certain traditions, political, psychological, linguistic, or whatever they may be, which separate them in an identifiable way from the rest of mankind. The societies with which we shall be here mainly concerned are those which, over a long period of history, have assumed the form of a national state.

By a state I mean a society of this kind which is integrated by possessing a coercive authority legally supreme over any individual or group which is part of the society. An examination of any national society will always reveal within its boundaries not only individuals, but also associations of men grouped together to promote all kinds of objects, religious, economic, cultural, political, in which they are interested. Such a society is a state when the way of life to which both individuals and associations must conform is defined by a coercive authority binding upon them all. The French state, for example, is a territorial society, divided into government and subjects, whether individuals or associations of individuals, whose relationships are determined by the exercise of this supreme coercive power.

This power is called sovereignty; and it is by the possession of sovereignty that the state is distinguished from all other forms of human association. A municipality is a territorial society divided into government and subjects; so, also, may be a trade union or a church. But none of them possesses supreme coercive power. Each must normally subordinate its habits to those defined as legitimate by that supreme coercive power. Its will is, formally, an unchallengeable will, since, otherwise, it could not be supreme. For the same reason, its will can suffer neither division nor alienation; as Bodin said, the state is sovereign because it gives orders to all and receives orders from none. Its orders are therefore law and, as such, binding upon all who come within the ambit of its jurisdiction.

It is important to realize that the attribution of sovereignty, in this fashion, to the state connotes merely a formal source of reference and nothing more. It is the description of a structure, not an inference of valuation. It says nothing of the wisdom or the justice that may or may not be inherent in the will of the state; it only says that the state is supreme over all other forms of association because it is formally competent to bind them to obedience without itself being bound. It may, in fact, be unwise or unjust in what it commands; but neither unwisdom nor injustice makes any difference to the formal legal right of the state to exact and enforce obedience to its orders.

The state, then, is a way of organizing the collective life of a given society. It is, indeed, legitimate to regard it not as the society itself in its manifold complexities, but as an aspect of the society in which the totality of its life is, at least contingently, embraced. For since the coercive power of the state is supreme, there is, in theory, no activity within its jurisdiction the character of which it may not seek to define. Anyone who considers for a moment the extent of the functions of the modern state will not be tempted to underestimate the reality of its sovereign power. Defence and police; the control of industry; social legislation, including functions so far-reaching as education and insurance against sickness and unemployment; the encouragement of scientific research; the operation, with all its immense consequences, of a system of currency; the power of taxation; the definition of the terms upon which men may, for their various purposes, associate together; the maintenance of a system of courts in which the state's own legal principles will be given effect no matter what person or body of persons may be involved; merely, it is clear, to take a rapid view of its outstanding functions is to realize the degree to which it pervades and permeates the individual life. The modern citizen is enmeshed at every turn in the network of its operations.

But it is vital to realize how the individual citizen encounters the state. All institutions must act through persons.

The power they exercise cannot operate in any other fashion. The state, therefore, needs a body of men who operate in its name the supreme coercive authority of which it disposes; and this body of men is what we term the government of the state. Now it is one of the fundamental axioms of political science that we must distinguish sharply between state and government. The latter is but the agent of the former; it exists to carry out the purposes of the state. It is not itself the supreme coercive power; it is simply the mechanism of administration which gives effect to the purposes of that power. It is not, we are told, sovereign in the sense in which the state is sovereign; its competence is defined by such authority as the state may choose to confer upon it; and if it oversteps that authority it may, where such provision exists, be called to account. The idea of a government responsible for the commission of acts beyond its allotted powers is the central idea of every state where legal rule has replaced arbitrary discretion as the basis of political action. Louis XIV could, not unjustifiably, identify his private purpose with the will of the state; but even a ruler so powerful as the President of the United States must find authority for the exercise of his will either in the Constitution or in some power legally granted to him thereunder by the Congress of his country. There are even countries, of which the United States is itself an example, in which the state expressly forbids its government, by the Constitution under which that government must act, to take certain types of power or to exercise others in certain ways.

The purpose, it is said, of the distinction between state and government is to emphasize the limitation upon the latter so to act that it pay proper regard to the end for which the state exists. That end, however variously defined, is the creation of those conditions under which the members of the state may attain the maximum satisfaction of their desires. The expedients of limitation—a written constitution, a bill of rights, the separation of powers, and so forth—are all methods which experience has suggested to prevent abuse of the state's sovereign power by the government which acts in its name. For every government is composed of fallible men. They may deliberately exploit the authority they possess for their own selfish purposes. They may, with the best intentions, but quite unreasonably, mistake the private interest of a few for the well-being of the whole community. They may be ignorant of the position they confront, or incompetent in handling it. Circumstances such as these have occurred in every political society at some period of its history. The value of the distinction between state and government is the possibility it offers of creating institutional mechanisms for changing the agents of the state, that is, the government, when the latter shows itself inadequate to its responsibilities.

Yet it must be said at once that the distinction between state and government is rather one of theoretical interest than of practical significance. For every act of the state that we encounter is, in truth, a governmental act. The will of the state is in its laws; but it is the government which gives substance and effect to their content. We say that the British state went to war with Germany on August 4, 1914; but those who brought the sovereignty of Great Britain into action on that day were its government. We say that the British state returned to the gold standard in 1925 and abandoned it in 1931; but in each case it was the government which made the decision. We say that the Russian state went communist in the November Revolution of 1917; we mean in fact that a body of men became its government who were able to use the sovereignty of the Russian state for the purposes we broadly call communist. Whenever a state acts in some given way, it is invariably because those who act as its government decide, rightly or wrongly, to use its sovereign power in that given way. The state itself, in sober reality, never acts; it is acted for by those who have become competent to determine its policies.

By those who have become competent; and here we have to ask what, again in sober fact, gives them their competence. We may say that their power derives from the law. But the law, after all, is only a body of words until men give it the substantiality of enforcement. We may say that it is the consent of those over whom they rule which gives them the power to get their will obeyed. There is a truth in this view in the sense that Hume emphasized when he insisted that all governments, however bad, depend for their authority upon public opinion.[1] But this cannot be regarded as the whole truth for the effective reason that there are times and places when men are ruled by a state from the policies of which their consent is actively withheld. It is hardly a proper use of language to say that the Tsarist state before 1917, or the state of Fascist Austria today, can be regarded as built upon the consent of their citizens; for, in each case, many of those citizens sought to change the policies of the state by revolt against the government responsible for them.

I think, therefore, that we have to say that, in the last analysis, the state is built upon the ability of its government to operate successfully its supreme coercive power. It is true

[1] *Essays* (World's Classics edition), p. 29.

(and it is, of course, important) that when the members of a state are fundamentally at one about the purposes embodied in its policy, the coercive aspect recedes into the background. It is even true that in a constitutional state which offers the critics of the government a fair chance of replacing it in power at the end of its allotted term, the coercive aspect will not appear predominant either. But at any critical moment in the history of a state the fact that its authority depends upon the power to coerce the opponents of the government, to break their wills, to compel them to submission, emerges as the central fact in its nature. A state of which the purposes are challenged has to respond to the challenge or change its purposes; and if it proposes to maintain them it must do so by the use of force. It must therefore have at its command coercive instruments, separate from the mass of the population, upon whom it can rely to enforce its authority. Normally, that is to say, the basis of state-sovereignty is the contingent power to use the armed forces of the state to compel obedience to its will.

For every critical challenge to law involves a threat to order; and every government, where order is threatened, will necessarily use the armed forces of the state to preserve it. Where it cannot use those forces, for whatever reason, it must either change the law or abdicate. And this is true not merely in an internal sense only. A state which quarrels with another state only imposes its will upon its rival—where settlement by consent is not to be had—as a function of the force at its disposal. In every society, national or international, there is conflict, whether actual or potential; and the armed forces of the state are there to protect, so far as may be, its sovereignty from invasion. Those, therefore, who control the use of the armed forces of the state are in fact the masters of its sovereignty.

From this angle the state may legitimately be regarded as a method of organizing the public power of coercion so that, in all normal circumstances, the will of the government may prevail. It is a power outside and above that of the people as a whole. It is in suspense so long as the will of government is unchallenged; it becomes operative immediately the effectiveness of that will is in danger. And it is the possession of this legal right to resort to coercion which distinguishes the government of the state from the government of all other associations. The authority of a trade union or a church over its members is never a coercive authority in the first instance; it can only become such when the state decides to support the trade union or the church. The sanction of that support is always, in final analysis, the same: it is the knowledge that behind the decision of the state is the coercive power of those armed forces upon whose services its rulers are legally entitled to rely.

Two facts in English history are worth recalling as an interesting commentary upon this hypothesis. The jealousy of a standing army until the eighteenth century was born of the realization that those whom it served were, in fact, the masters of the lives and liberties of English citizens. The limitation of the operation of the Mutiny Act, therefore, to the duration of a year is the expression of a fear, derived from the grim experience of Stuart misgovernment, that an executive in independent control of the army might easily be persuaded to usurp the functions of the legislature. Superficially, no doubt, the emergence of constitutional democracy has changed the normal attitude we take to these problems. But it still remains true that a government which can control the armed forces of the Crown would, for the duration of its control, be able to make its will effective. That was why, in the Home Rule crisis of 1913–14, the Conservative Party bent all its efforts to undermining the loyalty of officers to the Liberal government; as realists, its leaders saw at once that a government which could not rely upon the army in a period of crisis would be unable to remain in office. For to lose the army is to lose the power effectively to coerce an opposition. That was why, also, Hitler was compelled, in June of 1934, to purchase the support of the Reichswehr upon the latter's terms; his sovereignty had no meaning unless he could command the army for his purpose. And in general it may be said that, under modern conditions, no revolution has any serious prospect of success so long as the loyalty of the armed forces to the government has not become a matter of doubt. There is the heart of sovereignty.

This claim does not, of course, touch upon the view—which I shall deal with later in detail—that the state stands above all narrow interests in the society and uses its coercive power on behalf of the permanent and abiding interests for which men live together. It does not, either, touch the view, most strongly held by the Hegelian school, that whatever the abuses we may meet in practice, the state is nevertheless the "realization of the ethical idea." My discussion, so far, has not been concerned with the purposes the state announces itself as seeking to fulfil. It deals only with the fact that, whatever be its purposes, the state in daily fact is a power-organization relying upon its legal title to coerce for the ultimate enforcement of its will; and that, in the last resort, the armed forces of the state are the instrument of his enforcement.

My argument, so far, has no ethical implications of any kind. It is a neutral description of fact applicable to any state of which we have knowledge. I should even agree that the possession of this power is at once the condition of the state's survival, on the one hand, and the guarantee of law and order upon the other. For certainly it is obvious from feudal history that any society in which the armed forces are not concentrated in the government's hands, in which, so to say, coercive authority is multiple and not single, has little prospect of preserving the peace. The anarchy of Stephen's reign, the wars of the Roses, the tragedy of the religious wars in France, the numerous adventurers who took advantage of the breakdown of the Russian state in 1917 to do armed battle for its sovereignty, are all an eloquent commentary on what occurs in any society when the residence of coercive power is left in doubt.

Nor is the proper inference from my argument that the motive to obedience in the state is fear. That this is a motive is, of course, unquestionable; but as an explanation of the complex factors of obedience it is far too simple to cover the facts. Those who obey the signals of a traffic policeman—behind whom there stands the majestic panoply of the law—do so at least as much from a willing recognition of the convenience of his directions to themselves as from a fear of the penalties which may be incurred by disobedience. Those, again, who obey the law of compulsory school attendance are not impelled to its acceptance by a fear of fine or imprisonment if they neglect their legal duty. It may be doubted whether, save in times of passionate crisis, the vast majority of people ever think of fear in the contest of obedience to the law.

At this point, perhaps, it is worth while to say a word upon the relation between the state and law. The problem is not a simple one, for it does not exist upon a single plane. But, from a purely formal angle, once we accept the idea of the state as sovereign, law can be no other thing than the will of the state. For, granted the nature of sovereignty, law must be that, and that alone, which, in the last analysis, the state is prepared to enforce; and it can only be prepared to enforce that which it accepts as in conformity with its will. From the juristic angle, the content of the decision it enforces is wholly a matter of indifference. It may be unwise, or mistaken, or wrong. It is nevertheless law because the state enforces it. That which gives it its title to obedience is simply the source from which, in the last resort, it comes. For, were it otherwise, the state would not be a sovereign association. Could any will, on this formal plane, claim a title to obedience equal to that of the state, it would be equally sovereign with it; and in such a society there would either be no sovereign at all—in which case there would be no state—or sovereignty would belong to that organization, if there were one, entitled to resolve controversies of this kind, and able effectively to do so. But, again, such an organization of last resort, with the final say in the resolution of controversy, would be a state; for it would then be what, by our definition, the state is, an institution disposing of supreme coercive power.

This, at least, is the classic approach of the pure jurist to the problem of law. We must not make it mean more than it announces itself as meaning. It is, so to speak, an abstract conceptualism in which, for certain clearly defined purposes, law is divorced from justice and made simply a final term in a hierarchy of wills behind which it is impossible to go. The jurist here is engaged on a purely formalistic analysis. He excludes from his field of discourse all considerations of what is ethically right or socially expedient and considers only as law that which emanates from a will whose source may be traced to the sovereign. For him, as jurist, the only problem involved is whether the sovereign sanctions the particular form of behaviour which presents itself as legal. Any other question is, in Maitland's happy phrase, metajurisprudence, and so outside his province.

The human mind, it may be said, revolts from a jurisprudence as bare and as formal as this. It remembers the long mediæval effort to identify law with the will of God, the stoic notion of law as the voice of universal reason, the famous phrase of Ulpian which makes of law the science of distinguishing between right and wrong in human conduct. It rejects the idea of law as that behind which there is found the sovereign power of the state because, as the eminent Jesuit jurist Cathrein has said, "then one must regard every statute, however absurd, contrary to reason, or despicable, as a true statute, and one no longer becomes entitled to complain of injustice." [1] Law, to be law, it is widely felt, must correspond with something more valid than the will of an authority which grounds its claim to respect upon nothing more than the coercive power at its disposal.

There are two answers to this view. Any criticism of the pure theory of law, in the sense in which that theory has been set out here, is an endeavour to change its postulates be-

[1] *Naturrecht und positives Recht* (1902), p. 85.

cause of a dislike of the results to which they formally lead. This is, of course, an inadequate methodological procedure; one may prefer non-Euclidean geometry to that of Euclid, but the preference does not alter the fact that Euclidean geometry is a self-consistent system. And, in the second place, views like that of Cathrein are not so much a theory of what the state actually is, as a definition of the ends the state ought to pursue. They are, that is, a criterion by which to judge the practice of states, and, from that angle, of unquestionable value in their proper place. There is, no doubt, behind them the whole formidable history of the idea of natural law, the search for those universal conditions of justice the attainment of which is the condition of the state's satisfactory functioning. But, on the purely formal plane, they raise issues with which the jurist, as jurist, is simply not concerned. Any effort he may make to translate law into justice takes him at once from the pure theory of law directly into the realm of political philosophy. He has then to consider questions of value the answers to which are undiscoverable upon the plane of formal law.

On this view, therefore, a philosophy of the state need not concern itself, at least directly, with the problems in which the pure jurist is interested. It takes over from that realm of thought a body of facts which it must proceed to evaluate upon postulates derived not from law but from ethics. There, and there alone, can be found the standard by which all social relations must be judged. The criteria of ethics, of course, must be grounded in the experience we know. Conceptions of the good life, measures of value, must be sociologically attainable by human beings living in the kind of world we know; criteria of value which would work only in Utopia can hardly be treated seriously in a workaday world. Thus, it is not really helpful to make conformity with the will of God the criterion of right action in politics. For this is to omit from our equations the question of what god it is to whose announced will all questions of value must be referred. A Brahmin and a Roman Catholic, a Calvinist and a Mohammedan, answer these questions too differently for their views to be regarded as universal. The mediæval Christian commonwealth broke down exactly because the application of its criteria of value gave rise to varying interpretations about which men were prepared to kill one another.

That is why I assume in this book only that the object of the state must be to fulfil, at the maximum possible, the desires of its citizens. From this we may logically infer the bewildering variety of desires that we meet in the societies we know. We may infer, also, that the reason why, in the context of state-action, some desires go unsatisfied is that, on balance, the end of the state is best served by the result which then occurs. There must have been many slaves in ancient Athens who denied that their condition was compatible with justice; but we must assume, from the knowledge we have, that the Athenian state took the view that the basis of its civilization in slavery was the best method open to it of attaining its end; and it therefore put all the authority of its coercive power behind the system of slavery. So, also, with Hitlerite Germany. Its rulers exclude the Jews from citizenship of that state on the ground that the ends they deem good are not otherwise attainable. Rightly or wrongly, that is to say, the purposes of a state are always referred by those who operate its sovereignty to a criterion of good they are prepared to defend. The defence must be in terms of reason. For, if it is stated on other grounds, those of revelation, for instance, or force, it has no meaning for those who do not accept the revelation, or who deny that force merely can of itself make a rule of right.

If this be true, the inference surely follows that the state must aim at satisfying the desires of all its citizens, and satisfying them in equal measure, unless it can demonstrate by rational argument that the good of those who are excluded from equal treatment is served by their exclusion. That was the ground taken by Aristotle when he defended the Greek system of slavery. For by arguing that certain men are by nature slaves, he really sought to show that a system of slavery would, on the whole, best enable them to maximize the satisfaction they sought from life.[1] And this may be generalized into the view that, in any political association, equality of satisfaction must be the rule; and that exceptions to this rule can be justified only when it can be rationally shown that the exceptions themselves are a necessary part of the equality aimed at, a logical condition of its fulfilment.

For, otherwise, the action of the state is biased. Otherwise, it must be inferred that the object of the state is not the maximum possible satisfaction of all citizens, but of some part only in whose interest the sovereign power of the state is exerted. Those who operate the will of the state, who exercise, that is, supreme coercive power in its name, must argue that the greater satisfaction secured by the part so benefited results in a greater satisfaction for the remainder than could otherwise be secured. The case, for instance, for the maintenance by the state of the present system of private property in the instruments of production must be that this

[1] *Politics*, I, iv–v.

results in a greater total satisfaction to all who are affected by its maintenance than would be the case under such an alternative system of socialism, in which the instruments of production are publicly owned. When such a case can be made out, differentiation of treatment in the receipt of satisfactions is justified.

But it is important to note here the need for the state, when it maintains such a differentiation, to convince those directly excluded from it of its validity. It is not a sufficient defence of slavery, that the slave-owners think it for the ultimate benefit of the slaves. It is not a sufficient defence of the system of private property in the instruments of production that their owners think it a system which works to the ultimate benefit of those who do not so own. Hitler's view of the place of the Jews in Germany does not, it is significant, convince the Jews; and it is not wholly unreasonable to argue that the lawyers, doctors, and teachers in Germany who have welcomed his attitude do not take a wholly unbiased outlook in their judgment of his policy. Inequalities, that is to say, are not proved to be adequate because they secure the assent of those who benefit from them. In all matters of social constitution, the degree to which the judgment made is born of our personal relation to the result is fundamental to any objective assessment of it.

This has been well put by Hobhouse. "It is a standing temptation," he wrote,[1] "to overbear questions of right and wrong by confident predictions, which, in reality, rest more on the prepossessions of the prophet than on his insight into cause and effect." History is strewn with the wrecks of predictions made by men who, no doubt sincerely, mistook in-

[1] *Metaphysical Theory of the State* (1918), p. 15.

ferences from their private experience for the welfare of civilization. Macaulay told the House of Commons that universal suffrage would destroy the foundations of society [1]; Nassau Senior insisted that the legal limitation of the hours of labour was incompatible with the prosperity of British industry [2]; the bankers, in 1914, would have denied that the credit-structure of the modern state could withstand a great war that would last for a period of four years. We are all so much the prisoners of our experience that we are, usually unconsciously, coerced by it into identifying our personal insights with inescapable truth. Half the tragedies of social change arise from our inability to persuade ourselves that we may be wrong.

It is difficult, in a word, to be scientific about cause and effect in human affairs as we can be scientific about them in the material world. For into our judgment of the first there enter emotions and prejudices from which we can never wholly free ourselves. They affect our selection of postulates, upon which our conclusions depend, even when we believe ourselves objective in our analysis. The facts, that is, come to us coloured by the environment of which we are a part so that the objectivity we largely secure in chemistry or physics is unattainable in the world of affairs. We may seek with all our power to maintain a distinction between the facts and the ends that we approve. But the distinction is never complete. The bias of the personal equation may be a matter of degree, but it is always there. And it is there the more because the world of affairs is a seamless web in which we can never, as

---

[1] Speech in House of Commons, May 3, 1842.

[2] On the actual effects of the limitation see Hutchins and Harrison, *A History of Factory Legislation* (1908), App. A.

in the realm of science, isolate the factors in such a fashion as to make cause and effect a pure or absolute relation. The jurist may find it unnecessary to consider the purposes for which the state claims obedience from its citizens; not for a moment dare the statesman forget what those purposes may signify. The economist may insist that problems of welfare are wholly outside his domain; given scarcity, he is concerned only with finding the best means to maximum production.[1] But when he assumes as the constants of his equations the principles of the legal order, political stability, the psychology of men, all of which are becoming, rather than being, in an interrelated whole, he is simply constructing an intellectual geometry which, whatever its value as a discipline of the mind, is dangerously alien from the actual world in which we live. For though the statesman is interested in maximum production, the conditions under which things are made, the way in which they are distributed—both of them elements of welfare—cannot be divorced for him from the question of maximum production. His world is not a static world in which, for his convenience, certain bloodless constants remain perpetually fixed. His world is one in which the thoughts and judgments of men are vital agents in its unending transformation. His policy must be interwoven with those thoughts and judgments as facts not less formidable than the bank-rate or the volume of production if he is to be successful in the task of governing.

An illustration may make clear the purpose of this emphasis. In a brilliant book [2] Professor Robbins has discussed

---

[1] L. Robbins, *The Nature and Significance of Economic Science* (1932), pp. 22–44.

[2] L. Robbins, *The Great Depression* (1934), see especially pp. 160 f.

the causes of the great depression of 1929 and the subsequent years, and the ways by which we may recover from its disastrous consequences. He traces it to over-investment aggravated, especially in the United States, by a too luxuriant credit-policy. Recovery, he argues, depends upon our ability to secure political stability, and our willingness to abandon those policies of intervention, tariffs, quotas, subsidies, and the like, by which the "natural" functioning of the capitalist system is impeded. The assumptions of the argument are even more interesting than the remedies proposed. For, first, political stability, though in part a function of non-economic causes, is not less fundamentally incapable of being divorced from economic ones. To ask for political stability, in fact, is to ask for economic recovery, since there is hardly an element in the political situation today making for insecurity which does not find its roots in the economic position. The growth of Fascism and communism, the failure of disarmament, the menace of Japan in the Pacific, these, to take only the major causes of instability, are in large part economic in origin; so that to postulate their removal as a condition of revived well-being is to argue in a circle.

And what is meant by the "natural" functioning of capitalism? It is surely clear that Professor Robbins has in his mind what Mr. Lippmann has termed a "stereotype" of capitalism which has no relation at all to the system in being, but is born of an abstract conceptualism, the inferences from which are largely devoid of effective actuality. For the policies of intervention have been born, not from any desire in the statesmen responsible for them to destroy the capitalist system, but from pressures and tendencies inherent in the system itself. They are as "natural" to it as we have encountered it in history as the policy of non-intervention to which Professor Robbins invites us to return. The resort to intervention, whether mistaken or no, was the outcome of pressure from capitalists who were in a position to secure from the state action on their behalf. Their demand was born of that need to make profit which is the basic motive of the capitalist system itself. To make it impossible or unnecessary for the statesman to yield to the pressure of interests seeking for intervention Professor Robbins must alter the whole nexus of relationships in the modern state by which that pressure can be made effective. But, as he assumes the nexus as a given postulate in his argument, he deprives himself thereby of one of the main instruments for removing the error of which he complains.

But that is not the only difficulty in which Professor Robbins is involved by his postulates. At bottom, he is really urging a return to that "natural system of liberty" which Adam Smith defended so strongly, a system, that is, in which the main function of the state is to stand as aloof as possible from intervention in the economic conflict. It is heroic to preach a return to the conditions of the negative state; and we may waive on that ground the discussion of its practicability. For what is interesting in the thesis is less the question of whether it implies a practical policy than the assumptions upon which it rests. These are, first, that the unfettered competition of private interests will produce a well-ordered society; and, second, that, in life as distinct from theory, a competition which begins as unfettered will remain such. Neither assumption conforms to our experience. Historically, the development of intervention by the state arose from the fact that the social cost of unfettered competition became intolerable even to the spectator who was not involved in that cost. Historically, also, the outcome of unregulated competition has been, sooner or later, combination which looked towards monopoly. The evidence we have does not suggest that manufacturers are driven by the state to that trustification which alone, in their judgment, enables them to escape from the consequences of unregulated competition.[1] On the contrary, history seems to show that at a certain stage in industrial development the impulse to combine is just as strong and just as "natural" as the impulse to compete; and state-intervention becomes necessary to protect society from its consequences.

Thinkers who share Professor Robbins's view may argue that this history is the outcome of the abuse of capitalism; it is not inherent in the nature of capitalism itself. The particular answer, of course, is that, on the assumptions of the argument, we are given no means of discriminating between abuse and nature. Without it, we have to assume a causal sequence; and, even with it, we should have to call upon the state to intervene whenever a combination of capitalists threatened to prevent unregulated competition. That, as is well known, was the underlying principle of the famous Sherman Act in the United States; and I venture to doubt whether it is an expedient we are called upon to admire.

But there is a more general answer, the significance of which is the reason why I have examined the thesis of which Professor Robbins is the exponent. That answer is the need, at every stage of social investigation, to be quite certain of

---

[1] Cf. the *Report of the Committee on Trusts* (1918); R. Liefmann, *Trusts, Monopolies, Cartels,* (1930); L. D. Brandeis, *Other People's Money* (ed. cf. 1933); A. A. Berle and G. C. Means, *The Modern Corporation and Private Property* (1932).

what the problem is to which we are making a response; and, particularly, whether the problem dwells upon the actual or upon the ideal plane. A response to a solution which is relevant only to the latter plane can be transferred to the former only in terms of a full awareness of the initial assumptions upon which it has been built. We are not entitled, in order to make an ideal theory work, to argue that whatever contravenes those assumptions is, in some way, "unnatural," and that it must, therefore, be regarded as less real than the picture they require. If, in our experience of competition, it is always, at some stage of its development, followed by combination; if, further, combination in any vital phase of the industrial process is always followed by state-action in some form; then it is, I think, obvious that we must regard combination and state-action as inescapably connected with competition; and postulates which begin by regarding them as not so connected necessarily continue by perverting altogether the world of facts with which we have to deal. The "naturalism" which we attach to one line of action rather than another is definitely not in the facts themselves. It is simply a consequence of the postulates with which we have chosen to begin our investigation; and those postulates themselves are, however unconsciously, an index to a scheme of values we propose to defend, a method of attaining a result in social behaviour which, wisely or unwisely, we deem desirable.

The postulates of any social theory are, in fact, value-judgments born of the experience of the individual thinker who makes them. Hobbes's immense edifice is built, in the last analysis, upon the dual foundation of a belief that human nature is evil and that only an irresistible sovereign can maintain order against its inherent tendency to evil. Locke starts with a belief in the goodness of human nature, and the danger of any government which can act without regard to the wishes of its subjects. Rousseau sought a formula of state which, in its operations, would secure an equal interest for all citizens in the result of the social process. From Plato onwards, the more we know of the thinker's personal history the more fully we can explain the causes which led to the assumptions upon which he based his work; and those assumptions are always the result of the view he takes of what society ought to be like.

This does not mean that the assumptions are wrong. It does mean that there is in them the bias of a personal equation absent, for instance, from Mendelyeev's law, or the theory of the conservation of energy in modern physics. An economics which excludes welfare from its field of behaviour lacks, accordingly, the claims to recognition, say, of the etiology of scarlet fever; for once the cause of the latter is known we have the means of its control in our hands in a way that is completely different from the way in which we can control, say, the depressions of capitalism when we know their causes. In the case of scarlet fever, the activities of the germ which causes it follow a procedure independent of human will; in the case of a capitalist depression the wills of human beings, and the institutions which are the product of those wills, are fundamental to the decisions we make. In physical disease, that is to say, treatment is an objective process directly born of the nature of the disease, and largely independent of both doctor and patient. In social disease, the will of both doctor and patient—the state and its citizens—are decisive factors both in diagnosis and cure. The successful application of the remedy is a function of their consent to every stage of the treatment; and their consent depends, in the last resort, upon the view they take of what the society ought to seek to be. That view very largely determines their explanation of the etiology of social ills.

III

It is in this background that the philosophic conception of the state must be set. Historically, what the political philosopher has done is to take the jurist's theory of the state and to find for it a justification outside the lawyer's universe of discourse and, in his judgment, applicable to the practice of existing states. The philosophic theory then becomes a means of justifying the states we know. Their title to obedience is then grounded on their relationship to the ideal state and the purposes the philosopher has attributed to it.

The simplest way, I think, to show that this is the case is to take the idealist theory of the state (still the most widely accepted at the present time) and to examine it in its classic presentation. As a theory it defines the state as that organization of the community "which has the function of maintaining the external conditions necessary to the best life." [1] We therefore owe it allegiance on the ground that, when we obey its orders, we obey an association the function of which is clearly to promote a well-being in which our own well-being is involved.

Now it is obvious that the transference of what this definition implies to the life of actual states raises very difficult problems. Are we to say of the Hitlerite state, for example,

---

[1] But compare Bosanquet, *Philosophical Theory of the State* (1910), Chap. VIII, where other and not easily reconcilable definitions are given.

that it "has the function of maintaining the external conditions necessary to the best life"? If so, what are the grounds of that attribution? Is it because it so represents itself? In this case, then, are we to take announcement of function by those formally competent to make the announcement as a valid test of their purposes? Or is it because their announcement is accepted as valid by those to whom it is addressed? If the latter, what does "accepted" mean? Does it mean absence of effective resistance to the announcement? More, surely, it cannot claim. For Jews and socialists, communists and liberals, all insist that the Hitlerite state denies to them the "external conditions" they deem essential to the "good life." Everyone, indeed, is aware of states in which the attribution of a purpose such as this is a denial of elementary common sense.

As a criterion, in fact, of actual states the idealist theory would force us to argue that the state is the state when it is "maintaining the external conditions necessary to the good life," but that it is not the state when it does not maintain those conditions. The ambiguity of this view needs no emphasis. For it then leaves open the question of who are the judges between these two kinds of activities, and what rights they possess when, as judges, they decide that, by reason of the implications of their behaviour, those who claim to be acting in the name of the state are not the state at all. It is clear, I think, that either the definition of the state's function must enable us invariably to associate its performance with the actions of the body of men legally competent to exercise its power, or we are, by implication, back at Thrasymachus's definition of justice as the rule of the stronger. On that view the claim of the state to obedience is simply its possession of superior force. But, in fact, no idealist bases its right to be obeyed on this ground.

The same criticism applies to another definition with which the late Dr. Bosanquet has provided us. "The state," he tells us,[1] "is that society which is habitually recognized as a unit lawfully exercising force." Here, clearly, the validity of the definition turns upon the meaning we attach to the word "lawfully." If it is no more than an attribution of formal competence, then it is an accurate description of the nature of the state as we know it from the practice of actual states. But, if it is more than that, it must rest either upon the view that the actual is always the ideal, or upon a theory of the purposes of law to which the state must always devote itself. In the latter case, then, it follows that "lawfully exercising force" means exercising force for certain purposes deemed good for reasons outside the formal realm of law. The problem then becomes the twofold problem of (a) what those purposes are, and (b) who is to judge whether they are being fulfilled or no.

The idealist method of escaping from this dilemma lies in the special meaning it gives to the notion of freedom. Historically, until at least some such period as the time of Rousseau, freedom meant, for most thinkers, quite simply the absence of constraint. A man was free when he was able himself to determine his own mode of behaviour without being coerced into a particular line of conduct. Since the state was essentially an organ of coercion it followed that its actions implied some invasion, at any rate, of individual freedom. It was admitted that some invasion was necessary; the law against murder, the restraint of theft, the rule of the road,

[1] *Philosophical Theory of the State*, p. 186.

were all of them limitations of individual freedom; but it was generally admitted that, by reason of their consequences, they were justified invasions. Certain freedoms, most notably the freedom to speak and write without penalty, began slowly to be regarded as the tests of adequate government; and a state in which those freedoms were denied was held by the denial to contradict the purposes it was deemed to serve.

It is easy to understand the experience which underlay this view. Men who were struggling for the right to determine their own religion, or to shape the character of the civil legislation under which they lived, not unnaturally denounced a state as tyrannical which prevented them by force from realizing these rights. To them it was unimportant that the ground upon which the state defended its action was the good of the community, or the protection of religious truth, or the maintenance of order. They found, or thought they had found, that when the state denied them these freedoms it was debarring them from happiness; and they thought of the state, especially after the theological revolution of the sixteenth, and the scientific revolution of the seventeenth centuries, as essentially an organization to promote the happiness of individuals. It is not, I think, true to say that they placed the individual above the state. It is rather that they conceived it as bound by certain purposes to the realization of which its way of life as a state ought to conform.

This attitude to the theory of the state is, perhaps, best expressed by saying that men were regarded as possessing certain fundamental or natural rights, and that it was beyond the power of the state legitimately to invade them. By rights were meant those ways of behaviour without which happiness was regarded as unattainable. Their substance and their emphasis varied according to the time and place of different schools of thought. Sometimes it was religious freedom which was denied; and the individual thinker, Acontius, Castellion, Locke, would then explain why the right to religious freedom was a part of social good. Sometimes the evil complained of was arbitrary government by the Crown; and the individual thinker, again, as with Claude Joly in seventeenth-century France, or the Levellers in seventeenth-century England, would defend the right of the people to shape the policies of the government which determine the contours of its life.

We are less concerned with the details of the argument than with its general direction. That general direction was built upon the recognition of two basic principles. It was insisted, first, that unlimited power is always poisonous, both to those who exercise it and to those over whom it is exercised; and it was insisted, secondly, that the limitations upon power shall be so defined that certain activities and certain ways of action shall, at least under all normal conditions, be prohibited to the sovereign power in a community. The attempt—it is an impossible attempt—to find a legal basis for the right of revolution, as in 1642, 1689, 1776, 1789, was born of nothing so much as an effort to constrain the state to ways of behaviour which, at some given time, men deemed paramount. The theories by which they defended their views were always efforts to erect their sense of some particular need into a universal applicable to all times and places.

The state as an organization to promote the happiness of individuals; its authority as a power bound by subordination to that purpose; liberty as essentially absence of restraint and as an essential condition of happiness; rights as boundary-marks which traced out areas of conduct the state was not normally entitled to invade; these were the characteristics of the history of political philosophy roughly from the Reformation to the French Revolution. The tradition they represent was, of course, denied hardly less seldom than it was affirmed, and the acceptance of the tradition in any thorough-going way was hardly complete until the middle of the nineteenth century. What, here, it is important to realize is the fact that in its making the state was never itself an end, but always a means to an end; that the individual, finite, separate, identifiable, was always regarded as existing in his own right, and not merely as a unit serving the state to which he belonged. His happiness, and not its well-being, was the criterion by which its behaviour was to be judged. His interests, and not its power, set the limits to the authority it was entitled to exercise.

This tradition, which is broadly what we call the tradition of the liberal state, did not, of course, go unchallenged. It was brilliantly attacked by Hobbes in the seventeenth century, on the ground that its attempt to limit the claims of authority must necessarily result in anarchy; and his argument was repeated, though with a very different emphasis, by de Maistre at the end of the eighteenth. Indeed, as I shall show in a later chapter, the birth of the liberal tradition can be explained only by the shift in the residence of economic power which accompanied it. At bottom it was a way of justifying the transfer of political authority from a landowning aristocracy to a commercial middle-class; and, like all philosophies which seek to justify such a transfer, it stated its principles in terms of a logic wider in theory than it was prepared to admit in practice. The men who made both the

English and the French Revolutions announced themselves as the protagonists of the rights of man; but any analysis of the measures by which they gave effect to their principles, or, even more, any analysis of the claims they regarded as inadmissible, shows clearly that by the "rights of man" they meant in actual fact the rights of that limited class of men who own the instruments of production in society. The liberal tradition, in historical fact, was an intellectual revolution primarily made in the interests of property-owners in the new (and newly significant) industrial field.

No doubt it represented itself as more than that; for, otherwise, it could not have obtained, as it did obtain, the passionate support of men too poor to own property. Yet what is interesting in each revolutionary phase of the liberal tradition, whether it be the Cromwellian reaction in England, or Thermidor in France, is the disappointment it engenders when it is realized that the extension of privilege actually effected is much narrower than the formal basis from which it was made; hence, for example, Lilburne and Winstanley under Cromwell, and Babeuf and his followers under the Directory. The liberal tradition, in short, divorced from the actual purposes of the men who exploited it, is a perpetual challenge to the state. So long as those excluded from its benefits feel themselves so excluded, and move to act upon their feeling, the liberal tradition gives them a strong title to do so. Its theory of obedience, therefore, is defective to the extent that it emphasizes the contingent nature of the state's authority.

The idealist theory of the state came to remedy this defect. The view it sought to maintain was based upon four connected propositions. It denied, in the first place, that liberty meant absence of restraint. That conception it regards as too negative; absence of restraint may be a condition of freedom but it is not the essence of freedom itself. This, it affirms, is self-determination. I must rule myself. If I do not obey others in order to escape slavery, then I must obey myself in order that there may be creative purpose in my freedom.

But self-determination does not mean obedience to any chance desires that pass through my mind. To be the slave of immediate impulse is the worst form of bondage. Freedom in the sense of self-determination must mean that I am controlled by that permanent system of desires which is my real self. That is where I most truly find myself; that is where I have the largest possible chance of fulfilling myself at my best. I am most truly free when I obey rules that I have made for myself in terms of a high purpose that I seek to attain. That purpose is my real good, and it is in obedience to its dictates that I find my freedom. For without this goal at which to aim I am like a swimmer tossed to and fro on an uncharted sea. I move without direction, the slave of forces that I cannot control. To be truly free, I must do not what blind impulse commands, but what my real self ordains. It is in doing what I ought that I find the conditions of freedom.

But what ought I to do? The idealist's answer is the vital one that my real will is identical with the purposes of the general tradition of the society to which I belong. My purpose in life is not of my own making; it is made for me by the system of purposes in the society in which I find myself. Taken in isolation, I am incapable of high aims; I become that of which I am capable by virtue of the social relations which give meaning and direction to my life. My will which, otherwise, would seek no more than the irrational satisfaction of immediate impulse—which, in isolation, would be indolent and selfish and devoid of permanent objectives—becomes transformed by its social context. It finds, in Bosanquet's phrase, "objects which have power to make a life worth living for the self that wills them."[1]

And, as rational beings, we cannot escape from the obligations embodied in this context. They represent the highest part of our existence. They constitute, whether we recognize them or no, the permanent ends of the search to realize which gives meaning and colour and beauty to our lives. Since, further, society can live only when obligations having this objective are enforced, the institutions which embody them have an obvious claim upon our allegiance. For when we obey them, we are most free. When we obey them we are fulfilling that real will which enables us to discipline ourselves for our own highest satisfaction. We surrender slavery to impulse as unworthy of rational beings. We receive in exchange the obligation to obey a rule of conduct, loyalty to which is the condition of the higher life open to man. We find our freedom in obedience to this social morality.

But what defines its content? Amid all the conflicting claims to man's allegiance which he encounters in his normal existence, how is he to know that which embodies his real will? He is a member of countless associations, family, village, trade-union, church, which, often enough, move in incompatible directions. What is the rock upon which he may set his feet in the secure knowledge that, having done so, he has chosen freedom? The idealist answer is the vital answer that the real will of the individual is identical with the will

[1] *Philosophical Theory of the State*, pp. 148–9.

of the state. By obeying the state, he is obeying the best part of himself. By obeying it, he gives his allegiance to the authority which protects the permanent and total interests of the society against the partial interests represented by all other associations within the ambit of its authority. For the state is the supreme and all-inclusive association within which all other associations find their meaning; it is "the sole organizer of rights . . . the guardian of moral values." [1] The more fully, therefore, our will is identified with its own the more likely we are to realize those rights and moral values in our own lives; and this realization is, after all, the true end of a rational freedom.

In fairness to this view, one of its emphases must be noted before we proceed to its examination. The idealist does not contend that the state is the master of the individual conscience. If I believe that I ought to rebel against its commands, I have the duty to do so. I must be moved, indeed, to rebellion by something more than private desire. I must remember that "the nearer I approach to being myself, the more I approach identification with the communal mind" [2]; and since this communal mind is the state, I am entitled to rebel only upon the public conviction that I represent its permanent interests better than do its legal representatives. I must remember, that is, first, how likely I am to be mistaken in such a view; and, second, the danger I run in sacrificing the permanent values of social organization to some immediate, practical gain. In general, it is the habit of the rebel to attribute to the state defects which are owing to the action of its gov-

---

[1] Bosanquet, *Social and International Ideals*, p. 284.

[2] *Ibid.*, p. 281.

ernment. When he seeks to overthrow the latter, he jeopardizes the permanent good to promote which the state exists.

This emphasis, I remark at the outset, is itself fatal to the whole idealist theory. For once it is admitted that there is a right, indeed a duty, of rebellion, however rarely to be exercised, it follows that my allegiance is due not to an institution, but to the purposes that institution exists to promote; and I am asked to obey it clearly only insofar as it is in actual fact promoting those purposes. I cannot know whether it is promoting them except by examination of its operations; and if, after conscientious examination of them, I decide that it is not, my duty is obvious. My real will, that is, is identifiable with the will of the state only when the latter is truly acting as the "guardian of moral values." Either the idealist has to argue that all states automatically act as the "guardian of moral values," or that those who posssess the sovereign power and yet do not so act are not the state. But, in the first case, there can be no ground for admitting a right to rebel; and, in the second, since rebellion, if it comes, is not rebellion against the state, it cannot give rise to the strictures upon which the idealist lays so much emphasis.

The truth, in short, is that the idealist theory of the state has not satisfactorily solved, at least in its most notable modern formulation, the essential problem of the relation between the ideal and the real. For the state of which he speaks dwells, Dr. Bosanquet has insisted,[1] solely in the realm of concepts, and it is not, therefore, one with actual states but merely a method, a measuring-rod, by which to judge their performance. As such, it does not solve the problem of political

---

[1] *Ibid.*, p. 276.

obligation in the real world. It merely tells us what constitutes the title of a state to our allegiance. But it still leaves us with the problem of whether the state in the real world fulfils the conditions upon which its title depends.

If, indeed, we go the whole way with Hegel, and affirm that, the real being the rational, whatever is ought also, by the fact of being, necessarily and desirably to be, it can only be said that we are thereby denying the patent experience of mankind. For he would indeed be courageous who affirmed, for example, that the French state before 1789, or the state of Tsarist Russia, was worthy of the allegiance of its citizens. Any view of the state which led to conclusions so perverse seems, at least at first sight, too paradoxical to be worthy of credence. It is either a statement built upon the affirmation that whatever is is right, which no one believes; or it is (what I believe it in fact to be for most people who accept it) an argument that the way of change should lie through persuasion rather than force, a contention that the way of revolution as the mechanism of social change is always more costly than the value of its product.

But, even apart from all this, the idealist theory is profoundly unsatisfactory. It is psychologically inadequate in its analysis of the nature of will. The fact that I choose to do things which I regret having chosen is no more a ground for regarding the later regret as more essentially myself than it is a ground for regarding the original choice as more real. I am my will with all its limitations and imperfections; these constitute that personality which identifies me as different from the rest of mankind. The ascription of reality to that part of my will which is free from the imperfections which mark another part is a device of rhetoric merely; for I must be taken as I wholly am to be myself. To suggest, as the idealists do, that I can be wholly myself only when I will what is willed by the constituted society to which I belong is to mistake altogether the nature of personality.[1]

It is a further weakness in the idealist view that it fails to understand the nature of individuality. It finds its essence not in that ultimate isolation which all of us daily experience but in the contribution that isolation makes to the life of the whole in which the individual shares.[2] It is therefore able to argue that my isolation is unreal, that, in fact, it forms a unity with the isolation of all who share in the common experience in which I am immersed. But the point neglected here is the vital point that this common experience does not present itself to one man as it presents itself to another. Karl Marx and Mr. Gladstone did not draw the same inferences from the social life they shared in common. Unity does not arise from sharing in a common world. It arises from taking the same kind of view about the action which the meaning of that common world seems to render desirable. And history becomes wholly meaningless unless we assume that men can legitimately differ, as they have differed, about the import of the facts in that world. Unity is not there as something given; it is made as men discover it by seeking similar ends. But the discovery is always a voyage made in isolation. It is private to me in a sense which means that no other person can be aware of its meaning save as I report upon it.

The importance of this view lies in the fact that it enables us to reject the idealist view of liberty. For once selfhood is

---

[1] For a full and brilliant exposition of this view see L. T. Hobhouse, *The Metaphysical Theory of the State*, *passim*, but especially Chap. II.

[2] Bosanquet, *Philosophical Theory*, p. 178.

regarded not as real by reason of its isolation but in terms of its unity with other selves, constraint is not the use of force by the state against the individual, but only its imposition upon him of the will which his real will desires. From that angle, indeed, there is no problem of liberty, since when the individual is constrained in this way he is in fact willing only what his true self desires. Yet most of us, I think, would argue that the revolutionist is never conscious that the government which imprisons him is giving his true self freedom. What he experiences is constraint; and he regards that as a denial of his liberty. To tell him that he is made free when he is prevented from fulfilling the purpose he regards as the *raison d'être* of his existence is, I would suggest, to deprive words of all their meaning.

It is not a satisfactory answer to this view to say, with Bosanquet,[1] that the rejection of idealism makes it impossible to explain the paradox of self-government. I feel free in a society which exercises compulsion over me to the extent that I accept the purposes for which the society compels; and I may even forgo my right to challenge compulsion, in some given instance, cheerfully because, on balance, I take the view that the good of the general objects the society seeks to attain outweigh the evil of the particular end I dislike. But that is not to say that I welcome the compulsion because I find in it, on analysis, the real purposes towards which my will is striving. The Nonconformist who paid his education rate under the Act of 1902 did not do so because his real will approved of the Act. He did so because he took the view that, on balance, it was better to put up with one bad law than to

[1] *Social and International Ideals,* p. 271.

challenge the authority from which all laws derive. The decision did not make him feel more free; its main effect was to convince him of the need to change those who exercised the authority of the state for the making of bad laws.

One other aspect of the idealist theory needs examination. It grounds its defence of political obligation on the notion of a common good shared in by all members of the community and realized through the state because in the latter is the institutional embodiment of the real wills of all those members. But it is clear (1) that this view is based upon a theory of the real will which we have already rejected. The common good, moreover, (2) is a phrase which covers a number of different conceptions, each of which must be carefully distinguished from the other. It may mean (a) the good which is achieved by definition in the ideal state. This leaves unsolved the problem of the common good in actual states. It may mean (b) those principles of well-being at which states ought to aim. This, even if we can secure agreement upon them, does not, of course, decide the question of whether some given state is actually trying to achieve them in practice. The phrase may also (c) mean those habits, traditions, purposes, which a given society is seen from its history to aim at preserving. We associate the idea of England with notions of this kind. We feel that we all, as Englishmen, share in their quality even if we are uncertain of their precise definition. We expect the state to use its sovereign power to preserve the spirit which informs them with the peculiar quality we recognize as English. We feel, also, that their violation, in some fundamental way, would at least weaken, and possibly destroy, our allegiance to our conception of what the English state is seeking to be; and, *mutatis mutandis*, this is true of all other countries which share in a national heritage to which they cling.

What the idealist theory fails sufficiently to realize is the significant fact that each of these conceptions of a common good is a function of what men think about them as they meet them in daily life. They do not judge the state by the intentions it announces, though this may play a part in their judgment; in all marginal cases, and these are the really important ones, they judge it by their view of the import for themselves of its actual behaviour. The thing they ultimately ask of the state is that what of common good it achieves should be something each citizen feels he demonstrably shares in a way and to a degree that leaves him satisfied with its performance. It is not enough to tell him, in this context, that the ideal is really the actual. In the marginal case, he must really believe it for himself. No theory of the state can even begin to claim adequacy unless it satisfies this need to convince the individual, taken as a separate and isolated human being, that his good is inherently involved in the common good his actual state is establishing.

This, it may be pointed out, was seen by Rousseau, and, in a lesser degree, by T. H. Green. For though Rousseau's theory of the general will made him, in some sort, the modern founder of the idealist school of politics, in him, quite decisively, the stage of its operation is set upon principles scrupulously devised to prevent the perversion of its purposes. For the whole informing spirit of his conception is the idea of equality. It is to protect equality that, in the formation of civil society, men surrender their all to the state. It is to protect equality that the law, to be law, must always be general and affect men equally. It is to protect equality that the state must always be small, so that the general will may be shaped by all the members of the community. It is to protect equality, finally, that a civil religion is established, that men may be trained passionately to safeguard the spirit of the constitution. Rousseau's sovereign can claim the obedience of members of the community because it is, and can only be, the community itself. The idea that the sovereign power can be exercised upon the community's behalf by an organ such as the government cuts at the very foundation of Rousseau's conception of the legitimate state.

And something of this perception underlay the attitude of T. H. Green. That is why he could write that "the claim or right of the individual to have certain powers secured to him by society, and the counter-claim of society to exercise certain powers over the individual, alike rest on the fact that these powers are necessary to the fulfilment of man's vocation as a moral being, to an effectual self-devotion to the work of developing the perfect character in himself and others." [1] Here is the basis of his famous definition of the state as "a body of persons recognized by each other as having rights, and possessing certain institutions for the maintenance of those rights." [2] My rights, clearly, as an individual, are not, in this conception, independent of the state; but the title of the state to my obedience is, equally clearly, a function of its recognition of them. A state, therefore, which failed to recognize them would fail, on Green's view, to be a state at all, since it would be void of the moral quality which gives it its title to the loyalty of its citizens. That is why Green could

[1] *Principles of Political Obligation*, p. 347.
[2] *Ibid.*, p. 443.

insist that will, not force, is the basis of the state. For him the use of force is justified as it supports the realization of the conditions of the good life; and he was emphatic that a political society which maintains itself only by coercion cannot possess moral authority over its citizens. "We only count Russia a state," he wrote,[1] "by a sort of courtesy on the supposition that the power of the Tsar, though subject to no constitutional control, is so far exercised in accordance with a recognized tradition of what the public good requires as to be on the whole a sustainer of rights." He doubted, that is, the title of the Russian state to obedience because the character of its actions seemed to him inadequately related to the purposes a political society must fulfil. There is no effort in Green to equate the real with the ideal.

It is, I think, worth while to notice the different emphasis in these views from that to be found in the Hegelian presentation of the idealist theory. Both for Green and Rousseau the title of the individual to the enjoyment of rights is a function of his status as a moral being. His title to them is an equal one with that of other human beings. The state is not entitled to pick and choose among its citizens, to confer rights on some, to deny them to others. What it does must be done so as to bear with equal incidence upon all members of the society; they are taken, as moral beings, to have an equal interest in what it can secure of welfare. And they are taken, accordingly, to have an equal title to judge its operations. For each of them its sovereignty is always an essay in the conditional mood. It becomes, for them, a valid exercise of authority by realizing the conditions of that good life in

[1] *Principles of Political Obligation*, p. 443.

which, again to quote Green, the individual's "vocation as a moral being" is made possible of fulfilment.

There is nothing of this temper in Hegel. It is not merely that he denies that ethical criteria of state-action are applicable to it. "The state," he wrote,[1] "is the self-certain absolute mind which recognizes no authority but its own, which acknowledges no abstract rules of good and bad, shameful and mean, cunning and deceit." Even more his attitude appears in his identification of the actual state with the nobility, which alone rises high enough in the scale of virtue to be treated as fully human. He has little use for either the worker or the employer; they have too narrow an ideal, severely limited by the scope of their work. To make money and win respect from the little circle to which they belong is the measure of their ambition. They cannot understand the temper of the soldier. They are too obsessed by money-making to be capable of patriotism. For the peasant, Hegel has a higher regard. He is capable of fidelity and loyalty; but it is always to a person, never to an idea. The peasant has shrewdness; but he lacks that wide-ranging intelligence which enables him to rise superior to the particular interests in which he is involved.

To Hegel, therefore, the organic totality of the nation-state is shown by its formation of these three orders. Manufacturers and industrial workers may have intelligence, but they are sunk in a narrow and selfish particularity. The peasant may have loyalty to the whole, but, through lack of intelligence, it is a blind and silent trust; it makes him a healthy element in the state, but it shows his unfitness for the exercise

[1] *Die Absolute Regierung*, in *System der Sittlichkeit*, p. 32.

of those qualities which government demands. It is only the nobility which can rise above the selfish interest of their class to the plane where private duty becomes identical with public; and an order capable of this insight is alone fitted to give orders in the name of the state. For such an order, by its power to rise above the particular, exhibits by its disinterestedness the social virtues in their highest form. It alone is capable of bringing to full expression the immanent ideal which, in the nation-state, is ever struggling to be born.[1]

It is not difficult to see the sources of this attitude. In part, it is born of enthusiasm for that Greek outlook which denied a capacity for citizenship to those dependent upon effort for their livelihood. It took Burke's view that men who are free from the need to think of the morrow are thereby freed from subjugation to narrow personal interest and capable, accordingly, of a full public devotion. In part, also, it represents the passionate reaction of Hegel from the confused experimentalism of the revolutionary age in which he lived; his desire, on almost any terms, to find the conditions of an equilibrium in which Prussia could be reborn as a great state worthy of itself and no longer subject to the French conqueror. Like all of Hegel's political writing, it is full of insight into the weaknesses of those classes whom he dislikes; but, not less characteristically also, it has the same blindness that Burke revealed for the inadequacies of those to whom he looked for political regeneration.

For, in essence, the result of Hegel's approach is to deny the capacity for effective citizenship to all save a tiny minor-

[1] This summary is based on (1) the *System der Sittlichkeit,* (2) the *Philosophie des Rechts,* and (3) Part III, Section II, Sub-Section III of the *Encyclopädie.*

ity of the state. They are excluded from the operation of its sovereignty because the nature of their vocation condemns them always to that narrow view which sacrifices the common good to their selfish interest. They are to trust for the realization of that common good to the self-sacrifice of an aristocracy which, as Hegel himself said, is to receive its subsistence from them in return for the contribution of political direction to the community. Obviously, the assumptions are vast upon which this attitude rests. It shows none of the caution which Rousseau and Green showed in their outlook. For it starts by excluding the major part of the human race from the capacity to be moral beings. It continues by assuming that an aristocracy can be trusted to identify, and not to mistake, private welfare and public good. It does both these things despite all the evidence of history that political capacity arises quite independently of vocation, and that all aristocracies, however high the ideal with which they start, always fail, in the end, by taking too narrow a view of the objects of public policy. And that narrow view, invariably also, is the result of the fact that they too, like the mercantile class, or the workers, or the peasants, are necessarily the prisoners of an experience they are unable to transcend. Hegel had read with full effect the *Reflections on the French Revolution* of Burke; it is a pity he had not realized how final a commentary on its implied principles was the *Thoughts on the Present Discontents*. Whig practice was a sufficient answer to the Whig ideal.

At bottom Hegel's view, and, indeed, the whole idealist theory, rests upon an assumption about social organization the implications of which are of major importance. The whole, it is argued, is greater than its parts; the interest of the nation-state must therefore be regarded as greater than the interest of any one, or any body, of its members. Those, therefore, who control the sovereignty of the state have, by reason of the superior interest for whose care they are responsible, a higher claim to obedience than can be made by any charged with the care of a lesser interest.

But such an assumption is heavy with problems that it does not solve. Unless the state is identical with society—and this the idealist view affirms without a shadow of proof—the interests of the nation are not identical with the interests of the state. The latter, as Bosanquet has said, is simply "that society which is habitually recognized as a unit lawfully exercising force." As a sovereign body, it is, of course, true that every other association within its territorial ambit comes under its jurisdiction. But that is not to say that they are part of it. The Roman Catholic Church in Russia could not admit that it was part of the Soviet state; and the rise of the "German Christians" is due to the logical attempt of the German Evangelical Church to deny the validity of its identification with the Hitlerite state. We cannot, with justice to the facts, look upon the state as containing within itself all social purposes and defining their legitimacy. It defines their legality; it can legally seek to coerce them into submission to its requirements. But to assume that subordination to legality is anything more than a formal and conceptual inference from the defined nature of sovereignty is altogether to mistake its nature. Legitimacy is a matter belonging to a wholly different universe of discourse.

And, in any case, to say that the state, as a whole, is greater than the sum of its parts does not decide anything at all. For, first, this is true of all associations—churches, trade unions, political parties, and what not—and, second, it still leaves unsolved the question of the inferences to be drawn from it. Clearly enough, we are warranted in saying that the good of the state, where this truly implicates the good of all its members, is greater than the good of any single member, individual or corporate; but then this still leaves unsolved the major question of whether the action proposed by the state is in fact for the good of all its members. More: we have to remember that "action proposed by the state" means, in sober fact, action proposed by the government which acts in its name. But nobody in his senses suggests that government action is legitimate because it is government action. It is no more than an attempt by a body of men to fulfil some purpose which may seem to them satisfactory, which may even be made with the highest intentions of good. But it is not a right purpose merely because it seems to them so; and it is not a right purpose merely because it was made with high intentions. Some of the worst mistakes in history have been committed by men with no other motive than the achievement of right.

Metaphysical difficulties apart,[1] the fallacy of this idealist view rests upon a continuous confusion between the ideal purposes of the state and the actual policy of the government. The state is an organization exercising coercive power for social good. But it can only act through persons who speak in its name. It is assumed that when they so speak they do so for the purposes for which the state is constituted. Their acts claim the credit of the majestic penumbra which surrounds the philosophic conception of the state. But no Marxist or

[1] These are well discussed by Hobhouse *op. cit.*, p. 27; and cf. my *Grammar of Politics* (6th ed.), pp. 29 f.

Jew or liberal would give that credit to Hitler when he acts in the name of the German state; and no opponent of communism would give that credit to Stalin, either, when he acts in the name of the Soviet state. In each case we say that the action must be judged by what we deem to be its congruence with the policy we ourselves deem right in the given situation; and we do not regard the judgment of the state itself (which is simply the judgment of those who exercise its sovereignty) as entitled, because it is the judgment of the state, to take the place of our own.

When, moreover, we say that the state is an all-embracing unity, we must be careful to remember that this is a unity of conceptual ideal and not of fact. It is made so by abstract definition; it becomes realized as men will to make it real. And we can, by seeking to learn the lessons of history, affirm with some confidence what are the conditions upon which it will become real. It will not be real so long as any considerable body of citizens is excluded from participation in what of good the state is able to make; in the long run, in any political community, exclusion from political power is also exclusion from the benefit of its operations. It will not, either, be real where the mind of the citizen is not allowed to express itself freely upon affairs of state. For wise policy is always the outcome of reflection upon experience; and, where the reporting of experience is prohibited, in the measure of its prohibition also the materials for the making of a wise policy are absent. That is why, in general, dictators have never been able to build up a stable dynasty. By confining the experience to which they allow expression to that which expresses satisfaction with their effort, they deprive themselves of access to the minds of their subjects. Only in a state where the opportunity to criticize is free is the use of force, at any rate over a period, likely to appear justified in any society.

Nor is this all. The unity of any state is always a function of its ability to satisfy the established expectations of its citizens; and there is no sphere of its operations in which it is exempt from this rule. To deprive a people of its political freedom, as in Hitlerite Germany, is to deprive it of stability; for men who do not know what to expect on the morrow become the prey of those fears which are incompatible with a willing allegiance. Few states, moreover, can endure, over any space of time, a serious reduction in the standard of living unless it can be shown, first, that the reduction is necessary, and, second, that it bears with approximate fairness upon the different strata of society. Once, that is, the members of the state become convinced that its action is biased, they do not feel their previous obligation to regard its authority as legitimate; and that moment is always the beginning of one of those epochs of criticism which precede a revolutionary age.

The ability to satisfy established expectation does not require any particular form of constitution; in the past, every type of state, from dictatorship to direct democracy, has achieved successfully the unity which results from this satisfaction. What, indeed, is notable in the history of the forms of state has been their relative instability; and it has been one of the weaknesses of philosophical theories of politics that they have offered no satisfactory explanation of this phenomenon. For, on reflection, it is sufficiently remarkable, to take only one example, that the British parliamentary system, which, only a generation ago, not only received the eager loyalty of its own subjects, but was also widely regarded as a model for the whole world, should, today, be regarded, equally widely, either with doubt or with dislike.[1] Or, in another realm, it is striking enough that the use of the state-power to support the legal foundations of capitalism, which, in 1914, were hardly challenged in any country save by a little band of zealots, should today be questioned upon a wider front, and more profoundly, than at any period in the history of its devotion to this end.

Before we examine the causes of this phenomenon, it is worth while to start with a generalization. The members of a state are not interested in the preservation of its unity for the sake of that unity as such; they seek to preserve it for what they believe that unity makes. Their conception, that is, of the right to exercise the power of the state depends upon their view of what results to them from its exercise. The Tsarist state fell because its rulers could not satisfy the masses of the adequacy of the results obtained by their policy. The Weimar republic fell because a section of its citizens significant enough to be able to seize its sovereignty were persuaded of its impotence to secure for them the conditions of the good life. In either case, the grounds upon which this view was taken are relatively unimportant; certainly, in the German case, they seem to the outside observer to have been largely fantastic. What is important is that in both cases the unity of the state was destroyed, and a new unity was made, in the belief that its sovereignty could, in the new circumstances, be devoted to better purposes than before. The state which was destroyed was held, at least by a section of its citizens powerful enough to seize its sovereignty, to have failed to satisfy their legitimate expectations.

[1] Cf. my *Democracy in Crisis* (1933), esp. Chap. I.

The classic theories of the state in general, and the idealist theory in particular, make no adequate explanation of such situations as these; or, where they deal with them, as in the famous fifth book of Aristotle's *Politics*, it is rather as *Politik* than *Staatslehre*. Yet the situation is one of a recurrence so notable and perpetual that keen observers like Machiavelli could insist upon a cyclical view of history in which each form of state is bound, in an inevitable sequence, to decay and pass into some other form. The unity of the state in history, in short, so far from being a unity, is always breaking down; the allegiance it exacts for its purposes is always being withdrawn upon the ground that those purposes, at least in an adequate degree, are not fulfilled. The state of theory and the states of practice bear a resemblance to one another too transient to be recognized as valid by those affected by their operations.

It may be said that this transience is, at bottom, not a criticism of the state at all, but essentially a revelation that the governments of particular states do not fulfil their functions adequately.[1] But the citizen can reach his state only through the government. He is compelled to insist, at every point of crisis, upon their identity, for the simple reason that, since governments act in the name of the state, their purposes become its own as its sovereignty puts them into effective operation. He infers, that is, the nature of the state from the character of its governmental acts; and he cannot know it otherwise. That is why no theory of the state is adequate that does not make the governmental act central to the explanation it offers. A state is what its government does; what any given theory requires that government should do to fulfil the ideal

[1] Cf. Barker, *Political Thought since Herbert Spencer* (1915), p. 80.

purposes of the state is merely, as I have said, a criterion for judging it and not an index to its actual essence.

I shall discuss in the next chapter of this book what seems to me the explanation of the historic phenomenon I have just described. Here it is sufficient to discuss the relation of the fact to philosophic theory. That relation, I suggest, is built upon the constant drive of human impulse towards the establishment of greater equality in society. This emphasis, it may be remarked, is almost as old as political philosophy itself. It was noted by Aristotle[1]; and it is significant that it is the central element in the approach of men so different as Rousseau and Tocqueville. Men take the view that differences in the state require justification; their exclusion from some privilege always leads to a demand for either its abolition or its extension to themselves. They will bear with inequality so long as they are convinced that society offers them the best that can be obtained from its processes. But so soon as they begin to believe that there is a significant margin between what they have and what they are entitled to expect, it is to the existence of some inequality which the state protects by its sovereignty that their attention immediately goes. Broadly speaking, that has been the history of religious toleration; it has been the history of the suffrage; it has been the history of the intervention of the state in economic processes. Indeed it is of peculiar significance that the wider the basis of the franchise, the profounder, also, should have been that intervention. It is not too much to say that the conference of the right to vote upon the working-class has transformed the state into an organization able to satisfy its citizens only in the degree that it is also able to correct the major contrasts provided by an unequal

[1] *Politics*, III, 8; V, 1.

economic society. There is hardly a function of social welfare undertaken by governments today which is not an effort to provide the poor with some, at least, of the amenities that the rich are able to provide for themselves.

The state, that is, seeks to convince its citizens that its action is unbiased by organizing for them the material conditions of an adequate life, and especially for those of its citizens who cannot afford these conditions for themselves. The range of this organization, especially since 1919, is remarkable enough. Health, education, housing, social insurance, the regulation of hours and wages in industry, the control of factory conditions, the provision of meals for poor school children, are only outstanding examples of the range. We may explain the change on various grounds. We may say that it is the outcome of a profounder social conscience. We may argue that it is the price the rich have to pay to the poor for their security. We may think that it is a proof of the Hegelian thesis that history is the revelation of a freedom that constantly widens. Whatever our view, the fact remains that, at least since the Industrial Revolution, the continuous tendency of modern legislation, not less in the new world than in the old, has been to soften by governmental action the harsh contrast which would otherwise obtain between the lives of the rich and the poor. And, on any long view, the ability of the state to win the loyalty of its citizens depends upon its power continuously to soften the contrast. Attainment in one sphere is invariably followed by demand in another.

The significance of this experience for the philosophical theory of the state is, I think, clear. It must start from the assumption that the state is to act without bias in the interest of all its citizens. It cannot fulfil its end, as a state, if it differentiates between them, unless it can establish the right to differentiate upon a basis which proves that those so differentiated are equally benefited thereby. So far, in history, no such proof has been forthcoming. We have had differentiation of pagan against Christian, of Christian against pagan, of rich against poor, of white against black. On the evidence, they have all been proof not of a search for total good, but of a partial and selfish good which excluded those differentiated against from equal consideration. It is unimportant that men have always been able to convince themselves that the differentiation was justified; there is no error, either in the physical or the social sciences, which men have not been able to persuade themselves was truth, if it has been to their interest to do so.

The state, therefore, must postulate the equal claim of its citizens to the benefits which accrue from its exercise of power. But if it wills that end, it must, logically, will also the conditions upon which the fulfilment of that end depends. Philosophic theory must judge the behaviour of actual states in terms of the degree to which they establish these conditions. In the past, it has sought to do so in various ways. Most usually it has inferred the need for a system of rights which it regards as the conditions necessary to attain the good life for its citizens; and it has judged the actual behaviour of states in terms of its relation to the system of rights which ought to be recognized. There are, of course, exceptions to this general tendency. No small part of the history of political philosophy is occupied by elaborate attempts to prove that particular groups of men are unfit for the privileges of citizenship; and their exclusion from the field of consideration has therefore been justified. But any careful examination of these exclusions, whether they are built upon the possession of too small an amount of property, or membership of some race or creed or party, will always be found, at bottom, to rest upon the thinker's desire, an ultimately emotional prejudice, to defend some transient equilibrium of power which he would wish to make permanent. Aristotle's defence of slavery, Locke's defence of the exclusion of Roman Catholics, Hitler's defence of the exclusion of the Jews, from citizenship, are all attempts to erect private prepossessions into universal principles of reason. None of them stands examination by a thinker who does not accept the particular emotional prejudices upon which they are based.

Any analysis, moreover, of the system of rights put forward by any given thinker will be found, on examination, to be historically conditioned. Granted his environment, it would have been remarkable if Aristotle had not attempted to justify slavery; granted his environment, also, Locke's exclusion of Roman Catholics from citizenship is easily explicable. Men's conceptions, that is, of what they may legitimately expect are born of the experience they encounter and the needs they infer from that experience. A theory like that of the indirect power of the papacy, Bellarmine's for example, is the natural product of a mind which accepts the political consequences of the Reformation, but seeks, in that acceptance, to save as much for Rome as it can.[1] Locke admitted, with the frankness characteristic of him, that the purpose of his *Two Treatises* was to defend the title of William III to the throne.[2] The difference between the communism of Mably and Morelly

---

[1] On Bellarmine and the indirect power of the papacy cf. his *De Romano Pontifice*, V, 1–8.

[2] *Two Treatises on Government*, Preface to the Reader.

and the communism of Marx and Engels is set by the intervention of the Industrial Revolution between their intellectual constructions. The pragmatic element in all philosophic conceptions of politics is always integral to their understanding.

The significance of this relationship between theory and the historical environment is manifold. But here attention must, above all, be drawn to one element in the relationship which has a special bearing upon men's attitude to the behaviour of states. Their condition leads them to expect certain satisfactions from its functioning, and they judge the state by its response to those expectations. It is no use to tell an English workman today that his level of real income is four times as great as that of an English workman during the Napoleonic epoch,[1] if he is meant to infer therefrom the duty to be satisfied with his condition; for the vital postulate he makes in estimating his condition is built, not upon a comparison of this kind, but upon his judgment of what he is entitled to now. There is hardly a material element in the life we lead which does not show immense improvement upon the standards of a century ago; but it is not less important to realize that our expectations of benefit are also immensely greater. Every advance we may make in technical progress only increases our sense of what is due to us by reason of the achievement. The slums of a century ago aroused no such indignation among the men who built them as they do among ourselves.[2] The denial of educational opportunity was not, in the age of Bentham,

---

[1] L. Robbins, *The Great Depression* (1934), p. 2.

[2] J. L. and B. Hammond, *The Town Labourer* (1918), gives a description of what they were like.

felt so widely as a denial of right as it is at the present time.

Political philosophy, therefore, cannot content itself with a static theory; it must take account of how its conceptions function if it is to hope for any authority that endures. When we say, therefore, that the state must secure to each citizen the conditions under which he can fulfil himself as a moral being, we must realize that those conditions are not permanent, but relative to an environment perpetually changing; and the level at which the conditions must be secured is invariably a function of that environment. We can never arrest, as it were, some given moment of time, and make its possibilities a criterion of reasonable expectation. Dynamic experience plays havoc with our standards of fulfilment.

Any system of rights, that is, must be prepared for new emphases at every epoch of its application. In the time of the younger Pitt a bill like the Sedition Bill [1] would hardly have caused a ripple on the surface of public opinion; but the Victorian age, with its security and tolerance, supervened to give a new content to the standards of free expression, and the bill evoked, during its discussion, an indignation which would have been unintelligible to most of Pitt's contemporaries. Unemployment insurance may introduce rigidities into our wages-system incompatible with the flexibilities which the free functioning of the price-mechanism requires [2]; but once the workers in any state have experienced the benefits it confers, the statesman who proposes its abolition does so at his peril. Half a century ago most economists thought that

---

[1] Cf. *The Sedition Bill* (1934) by W. I. Jennings, published by the *New Statesman* (1934), for a full account of this measure.

[2] Robbins, *op. cit.*, p. 84.

the free functioning of the price-mechanism was a part of life's unalterable good; today a defence of its habits on this ground is the rare exception and not the general rule.

It is, then, the obvious inference from all this that the philosophic conception of the state gives us, at best, a measuring-rod by which to test the conduct of states. It gives us no more than this. It still leaves the adequacy of that conduct a matter upon which, however imperfectly, we must make up our own minds. There is, outside the purely formal realm, no obligation to obey the actual state. Our obedience is, and can only be, a function of our judgment upon its performance. That judgment, moreover, is never one which each citizen can make upon the same postulates, intellectual or emotional. What he decides will be the product of the place he occupies in the state, and the relation of that place to his view of what he ought to attain. He may be wrong in the view he takes; but he has never any rational alternative to action in the light of his own certainties.

IV

Upon this attitude there hinges a view of law the implications of which are important. It regards the validity of law as unrelated to the source from which it comes. Law becomes law as it goes into application; it is made law by being accepted. That is not to say that accepted law is right law; for law may be accepted by the might which is behind it. We have, in fact, to distinguish between three different senses in which the idea of law can be used. There is the formal juristic sense, which is no more than an announcement, ultimately dependent upon the sovereign authority, of the will to enforce certain decisions. There is the political sense, in which the formal announcement is validated by the acceptance of it by those to whom it applies. There is, finally, the ethical sense, in which the decision announced ought to be obeyed because it is morally right that what it proposes should be done.

Now it is clear that in the first two of these three senses the citizen has no inherent duty to obey. Few people would seriously claim that the juristic sense is always to be equated with the ethical; certainly, to take an obvious example, no Quaker could admit that a state whose government ordered its citizens to make war had, for this purpose, a title to their obedience. Nor can it, I think, be seriously claimed, either, that the political and ethical senses are identical; the commands of the Hitlerite state on June 30, 1934, were law in the sense that they went into effective operation, and were accepted by the population over whom it ruled; but most people in a position to make an independent judgment would, I suggest, regard them as ethically outrageous. Might, however profound, does not make right; effective operation of law still leaves undecided the question of ethical adequacy.

Neither formal competence, then, nor political power can confer a just title to obedience. With what are we left? Only, I think, with the insistence that law to be ethically valid must conform with the requirements of the system of rights the purposes of which the state exists to maintain. And since law is a command seeking to control my behaviour in some particular way, I must judge that conformity for myself as the test of its ethical adequacy. The roots of valid law, that is, are, and can only be, within the individual conscience. I make law legal, so to say, by giving to its operation the consent of my conscience.

If it is said that such a view, by justifying refusal to obey, opens the door to anarchy, the answer is that the accusation is true. But it is not a serious accusation. In the life of states the door to anarchy is always open because men are never willing to admit the unconditional conference of power. If, further, it be said that the individual conscience is at least as likely to be wrong as the consciences of those who rule the state, the answer, again, is that, while this may be true, the citizen who yields his conviction on the ground that he may be mistaken will soon cease, in any meaning sense, to be a citizen at all. There is no way of making a state active in the fulfilment of its function except the knowledge that men will refuse to obey its commands where they regard them as a violation of that function. That was the truth that Pericles saw when he told the citizens of Athens that the secret of liberty was courage. Unless men are prepared to act by the insights they have, even when these insights are erroneous, they are bound to become no more than the passive recipients of orders to whose moral quality they are indifferent. When they do that, they poison the foundations of the state. For they then cease to be moral beings in any sense of the word that has meaning. They associate truth and justice and right automatically with the possession of physical power. No people prepared in that fashion to abdicate its humanity is likely to be long capable of creative achievement. For so to abdicate the duty of moral judgment is to sell oneself into slavery.

It is said that the individual is powerless, and that he wastes his energy by acting upon his judgment. But there are at least two answers to this view. A moral obligation is not less compelling because it may end in failure. To adopt that canon of effort is to accept the view that justice is the will of the stronger—a doctrine against which, as I have pointed out, the whole history of humanity is a protest. And to argue, secondly, that the individual is powerless is, on the record, quite untrue. He is powerless only when his perceptions are so completely unshared that he fails to arouse any note of response among his fellow-citizens; and he has always to remember that the shift of events may cause them to be shared at a later stage. The early Christians must have appeared singularly futile to their own generation when they challenged the majesty of Rome; but their steadfastness conquered the Western world. Luther's recalcitrance must have appeared akin to madness to a church which remembered its successful emergence from the stresses of the Conciliar revolt; but he changed the history of the world by his courage. Even so liberal a mind as Emerson could write of the American abolitionists that they were "narrow, self-pleasing, conceited men, and affect us as the insane do" [1]; but it was hardly a generation afterwards that so respectable an observer as Oliver Wendell Holmes, not given to extreme views, could say of his friend's judgment that "it would have taken a long time to get rid of slavery if some of Emerson's teachings in that lecture had been accepted as the whole gospel of liberty." [2]

History, indeed, abounds with such instances. The individual who protests against the law he deems unjust is far less alone than he is likely to imagine. He is acting in a mental climate in which the experience borne in upon him is likely to be shared by others; and the gesture he makes may awaken

---

[1] Quoted in V. F. Calverton, *The Liberation of American Literature* (1932), p. 330.
[2] *Ibid.*, p. 331.

others to the understanding of their obligations. No one who looks back upon their history can doubt that the suffragettes, who for eight years defied the law, awakened the British government to a sense that their claims were serious in a way that altered the whole perspective of those claims. No one can doubt either that the unbreakable will of Lenin was central to the success of the Bolshevik Revolution in 1917. That we must fight for our philosophy if we believe in it seems to me the inescapable implication of the record.

Against this view two considerations are urged, in both of which there is, unquestionably, considerable force. It is said that to challenge the government is to weaken the authority of all law, and that to do so is to open the floodgates to chaos. It was the sense of this danger which made T. H. Green, who admitted, in the last resort, the right to revolution, insist that we must approach the state in fear and trembling. But it is surely not less important to realize that respect for law must always mean respect for what the law does; and, if the individual, whether alone or in concert with others, judges what the law does to be ethically intolerable, he must act upon the basis of his judgment. To decide otherwise is to argue that the highest duty of the individual is to maintain order, without regard to the quality of the order that is maintained. I do not find this argument compatible with the notion of the individual as a moral being.

It is said, secondly, that this view admits the right of any doctrine to support itself by force, if it can. Men have only to announce that they are moved by some profound conviction to be justified in using violence to attain their ends. Such an attitude, it is argued, is utterly destructive of the foundations of social well-being.

But the answer is surely that no doctrine, however evil, moves to the use of force unless it is rooted in a profound grievance which it sees no other way to remedy. We may believe the Bolshevik Revolution to have been wholly evil; but it is clear that the previous conditions of the Russian state alone account for its origin and methods. We may argue, with the communists, that Hitler has been no more than the agent of finance-capitalism in Germany [1]; but it is also clear that his victory was built upon the profound grievances of millions of Germans who saw no adequate redress for them in the habits of the Weimar republic. The truth is that men in general are so accustomed to obey that their departure from the normal canons of political behaviour is always an index to grave disease in the state. They have, as Burke said, "no interest in disorder; where they do wrong it is their error and not their crime." We need not argue that a doctrine which arms itself is wise or right to do so. But, on the facts, we have to argue that no doctrine ever does successfully arm itself unless the government it attacks has failed to deal with the grievances it expresses in a reasonable way.

That is, I think, apparent in the history of most revolutions. Certainly the student of the English civil wars, of the revolutions of France and of Russia, will note as not the least remarkable of their features the patient efforts of the common people to await reform before they turned to violence. And in any society violence is unlikely if the conviction is widespread that the state is seriously attempting to fulfil its obligations. Violence comes when the facts persuade men to believe that the bona-fides of their rulers is no longer to be trusted. They may be mistaken in that belief. There

[1] Cf. E. Henri, *Hitler over Europe* (1933).

have certainly been occasions in history when the members of a government which has been overthrown have been well-intentioned men struggling with adverse circumstances it has been impossible to conquer. There have been other occasions, also, when the ends sought by men who resisted the state could not be attained within the framework of existing institutions. The overthrow of Dr. Brüning is, I believe, an instance of the first; the history of the French Revolution is a clear instance of the second.

But, not seldom, the use of violence to defeat the law is the outcome of a clash of values between which compromise is impossible. What is the situation when this arises? No one, at least, can say that the problem is a simple one. It is no answer to it, for example, to argue that the duty of a minority whose values are denied is the simple one of becoming a majority, and so using constitutional processes to obtain power by persuasion. For, in the first place, those constitutional processes may not exist. It is no use telling the citizen of one of the European dictatorships today that he should use the methods of peaceful persuasion to get his views accepted; for, *a priori*, the right, legally, to use those methods has been abrogated. He, at least, has no alternative save revolution if he seeks the realization of his purposes. The German socialist cannot be asked to hope for the peaceful conversion of Hitlerite Germany.

The situation, it is said, is different in a state of which the form is a constitutional democracy. There, at any rate, freedom to criticize exists; and provision is deliberately made for those who differ from the government of the day to take its place if they can persuade a majority of their fellow-citizens to vote with them. There is, I think, a vital truth in this view.

In general, it is impossible to condone the use of violence in politics except as a weapon of last resort; it must be shown that all alternative avenues of action have been exhausted before violence is resorted to. But it is, I think, important to realize that even in a constitutional democracy dependence upon reasonable persuasion alone is a function of certain conditions, upon the realization of which the minority concerned must be able to count. First among those conditions is the right to expect the unbiased operation of state-institutions; they must weigh with equal incidence upon all parties to the political equation. In a state even so free as Great Britain that equal incidence does not obtain. For the House of Lords is an instrument in the hands of a single party in the state; and its authority can be deliberately exercised to flout the will of its opponents even when they possess a majority in the electorate. And if it is said that the House of Lords will always give way when the will of the electorate is decisively known (after a general election, for instance, which is fought upon some special issue), the answer surely is that, even if this be the case, it subjects one party in the state to grave disabilities from which its rival is wholly free; and the consequence of those disabilities may render abortive the effort of a party which has won its electoral majority, by reason of the technical conditions under which it may seek to make its purposes effective.

Nor is this all. It is important that the incidence of state-institutions should be unbiased. It is important, also, that those who operate them should be able to assume that the principles of constitutional democracy will be observed by their opponents. It would be facile to argue that this assumption is justified as even approximately an invariable rule.

We may say, with some assurance, that in a society long accustomed to those principles departure from them will be less likely than in one where habituation to their exercise is novel. But, even there, it is, I suggest, a reasonable generalization that they will be observed only when the interests which an important minority deems, rightly or wrongly, to be fundamental, are not in jeopardy. That is the implication of the Ulster crisis in Great Britain in the spring of 1914; it is the implication, also, of the attitude of American employers like Mr. Ford and the steel magnates to that section of the National Industrial Recovery Act [1] which guarantees to labour the right freely to choose the organizations by which it will be represented in the settlement of industrial conditions. Unless, in a constitutional democracy, a government can be certain that its decisions will be respected, one can be certain that the assumptions of such a system will not be long preserved.

It is argued from this that it leads to the obligation, incumbent upon the governments of all such states, not to outrage the fundamental sentiments of an important minority. There are, that is to say, limits to the rights of a majority whose representatives are exercising the sovereign power. That is a platitude which has not even the merit of being profound. Anyone can see that, if the King in Parliament prohibited the exercise of the Roman Catholic religion, those who professed it would break the law rather than obey the law. Anyone can see, also, that, if the King in Parliament were foolish enough to declare trade unions illegal organizations, the trade unions would fight rather than give way. No one ever takes the legal right to exercise the powers of sovereignty as equivalent to the moral right to do anything one pleases.

---

[1] Section 7a.

But to say that there are limits to the rights of a majority is not to define those limits; and that, after all, is the real core of the problem. We cannot seriously argue that no government is entitled to take any decision which may outrage the conscience of a significant minority. A significant minority of American opinion was outraged by the decision to abolish slavery; but that did not render unjustifiable the decision to abolish it. A significant minority thought the Reform Act of 1832 an outrage; but, again, we should not attempt to justify a decision to withdraw it on that ground. A significant minority in Great Britain today thinks the "Means Test" in connexion with unemployment insurance outrageous; that is not held to justify its withdrawal. There is hardly, indeed, a single social expedient of any magnitude, adversely affecting an important interest involved, which has not been deemed, at some time or other, "outrageous" by the minority so affected. Even the death duties imposed by Sir William Harcourt were suspect; and the land taxes imposed by Mr. Lloyd George were denounced as outrageous by those to whom they applied.[1]

Are we then to say that the point at which the limits of majority rule become apparent are defined when the minority proposes to fight rather than to give way? This raises several issues. Does a proposal to fight mean actual conflict in the streets, or is it sufficient that action like a general strike, in which the use of some violence at least is pretty inevitably inherent, should be attempted? But it is impossible to conduct the process of ordered government upon the terms that a majority must not use its power when a minority threatens re-

[1] Cf. Gardiner, *Life of Sir W. Harcourt* (1923), II, 282, for an account of the moderate resentment provoked by the death duties.

sistance. In a situation, for instance, like that of Ireland in 1914, the will of the government would have been completely paralysed. For there the Ulster extremists threatened to fight if the Home Rule Bill went into operation, and the Irish nationalists threatened to turn out the government if the bill was withdrawn; and the Asquith solution, which was to enact the bill, but suspend its operation, effectively resulted in a complete victory for the Ulster extremists.

There are, no doubt, occasions when it is wise for a government so threatened to compromise rather than to seek the maintenance of its prestige without regard to the price that may have to be paid for it; Lenin's adoption of the New Economic Policy in 1921 is a classic instance of a wise surrender of principle made to critical circumstances. But it is certainly not a method which can be made a general rule, for the simple reason that it would make majority government invariably impossible. Normally, a government that is challenged is obliged, so long as it feels confident that it has public opinion behind it, to meet the challenge; for it is the primary thesis of constitutional democracy that it can be overthrown only in ways specifically provided for by law. The limits of majority rule, therefore, cannot really be defined with any precision in terms of principle. They rest upon felt insights rather than exact measurements of what particular situations involve. Certainly a government which estimates their meaning must always remember that any consistent series of surrenders to the clamour of interest will rapidly prevent it from being able to embark upon any measures of serious importance.

What seems to emerge from our historic experience is the lesson that a government can impose its will upon the citizens of a constitutional democracy so long, but only so long, as those citizens are in fundamental agreement about the actual purposes of the state. Whenever a deep fissure in opinion appears, the fragility of all constitutional structures becomes apparent, and, in those circumstances, movement towards dictatorship is easy and rapid. This, moreover, is most notably the case in times of economic insecurity. Men who have much to lose by far-reaching changes of the wisdom of which they are unconvinced will not lightly be convinced, either, of the right of the government to make them. They will generalize their sense that their own interests are in jeopardy into the principle that the welfare of the community is at stake; and, not seldom, they will move to what they represent to themselves as its defence even at the cost of seeking to overthrow law and order. They will do this with complete sincerity; no one, to take the classic instance, doubts the sincerity of Lord Carson and his followers in 1914. We may think their actions morally wrong or politically unwise; but it is impossible to doubt, on the evidence, that occasions will arise when the decision will be made to take action of this kind.

We may think them morally wrong or politically unwise; but it is of the first importance to realize that we do not always pass this judgment upon their actions. Few people now take the view that the resistance to Charles I by Parliament, with all its cost in blood and suffering, was unjustified; fewer people still deny that those who resisted James II in 1688 were justified in what they did. Most Frenchmen now will defend the events of the French Revolution; and it is still possible for our generation to remember the almost universal satisfaction which acclaimed the Russian Revolution of March 1917. But this is to say that some resistance is justified; and, since there is no tribunal to which reference may be made for a decision upon the problem, it follows that the decision to embark upon resistance must always be left in the hands of men. All that we can ask of them is that they should judge their own actions by the same relentless tests they apply to the government they oppose.

The bearing of this upon a philosophy of law is, I think, straightforward. It makes the limits of effective legal action dependent upon the consent of citizens. The consent, of course, may be exacted by indifference or coercion; it is clear that there are millions of citizens in Hitlerite Germany from whom obedience is, so to say, exacted only at the point of the sword. But a philosophy of law which does not test the principles upon which it rests by constant reference to its roots in the minds of those affected by the result of its application can never produce a working theory of the state. Valid law, we must affirm, is law judged adequate by men as it seeks for their consent. It has no final title to acceptance because it emanates from the sovereign power. It has no title to acceptance, even, because it presents itself as an effort to realize the right. Its claim to be obeyed is in the decision men make about the legitimacy of its pretensions. It becomes valid law by its power to satisfy the demands they make upon the institutions whose will it represents.

One other remark it is important to make in this context. The argument in this chapter has been based, essentially, upon the denial of two propositions. On the one hand, I have denied that a purely positive theory of law can give us an adequate philosophy of political obligation; no framework of fact can, of itself, make just law. On the other hand, I have denied the idealist view that the actual law can, at any given time, be necessarily identified with the law as it ought to be. The Hegelian identification of the real and the rational in politics is, I have suggested, incapable of leading to a satisfactory philosophy of history. And, at bottom, all theories of political obligation are seeking to be such a philosophy.

Because there is no *a priori* connexion between law and justice, between the law that is and the law that ought to be, I have argued that the judgment of the individual citizen is the basis in which law must find its title to consent. If it be said that the individual's liability to error makes this a fragile basis inadequate to the burden it is asked to bear, there are, I think, two things which may be fairly said. First, the individual judgment is all that we have. If we reject its right to make decisions, we are driven to assert one of three things. We must argue that order is the highest good, that, therefore, it is in all cases wrong to break the law; this is an impossible position which no one takes. Or we must argue that positive law is always entitled to be obeyed by reason of the purposes it is seeking to fulfil; this argument I have rejected on the ground that there is no inherent reason to suppose that any given positive laws are in fact seeking to fulfil these purposes since this is a question always to be decided by an examination of the relation between them and our sense of what they ought to be. Or, thirdly, it must be held that law, which is the will of the sovereign state, is right simply because it is the will of that association. This, broadly speaking, is the idealist view, and I have given reasons here why it seems to me untenable.

If it is said that, amid difficulties so profound, the part of the wise man should be scepticism, it is, I think, sufficient to reply that we cannot escape the need to decide what is right and what wrong in politics. And we shall be led, I think, to a rejection of the sceptical position upon several grounds. We shall note that the different views of political right taken by men are largely born of their different positions and unequal claims in society; the more fully we can find a plane of relationships in which those differences are eliminated, the more possible does it become for law to seem just to those to whom it presents itself as obligatory. It is significant that the periods of history when men are most satisfied with the law are those periods of expansion when the multiplication of opportunities offers the largest prospect of fulfilling the claims of individual personality to satisfaction. Such expansion makes for security, and in periods of security reason has always the best chance of establishing its empire over the minds of men. From this angle, it appears that law is most likely and most widely to appear as just where its operations make possible the fullest use of the instruments of production in society. Where there is a contradiction, which social institutions maintain, between potential and realized productive power, those who suffer from the operative results of the contradiction are likely to regard the working of social institutions as inherently unjust.

It is, moreover, important that, because man is a rational being, those who make law are always eager to defend it to him on the ground that it is in fact equated with justice. They offer arguments, that is, to prove that the law which is may be regarded as the law which ought to be. Now it is clear that once we admit that there is, in some given situation, a law which ought to be, we are admitting the existence of natural law. I myself take the view that, despite all the difficulties in the way of natural law, the need to postulate it as an essential part of the philosophy of political obligation cannot be avoided. None of the arguments by which its critics have so far sought to destroy it have so far been successful. The historical attack on natural law has broken down simply because an issue which dwells in the normative realm cannot be decided upon the issue of fact alone. The attack of the positive lawyers broke down simply because it became clear that positive law cannot provide for all possible cases; and once an unforeseen case occurs the judge or legislature must seek to meet it by introducing notions of what is just or reasonable in the given case. This has been well put by Sir Frederick Pollock. "Our courts," he writes,[1] "have to go on making a great deal of law, which is really natural law, whether they know it or not, for they must find a solution for every question which comes before them, and general considerations of justice and convenience must be relied on in default of positive authority." Indeed it is notable that many of those most anxious to repudiate the idea of natural law, Duguit, for example,[2] are building upon its concepts in the view they take of political obligation.

Nor is the metaphysical attack in better case. It is argued that all questions of justice are relative. Time and place can alone give meaning to their substance. In a world in which freedom of testamentary dispositions seems "natural" to Englishmen, while, twenty miles away, a Frenchman thinks it equally "natural" for testamentary disposition to be strictly regulated by the Napoleonic code, it is said that it is useless to seek a science of justice which claims universal validity. The metaphysical attack may even take the form, widely popular

---

[1] *Expansion of the Common Law* (1904), p. 112.

[2] Cf. my paper in *Modern Theories of Law* (1934), Chap. IV.

in an epoch of rapidly changing moral standards, of the insistence that justice is a question of individual opinion before which any attempt at an objective criterion is inadmissible.

This view, however, is far less satisfactory than appears at first sight. To begin with, as Professor Cohen has pointed out,[1] it is built upon a simple misunderstanding of the logic of science. "The objection," writes Professor Cohen,[2] "ignores the difference between a substantive code and a science of principles, a distinction which ought to be as clear as that between the directions of the engineer to the builder, and the science of mechanics." The variety of opinion we encounter about justice no more renders impossible a science of justice than the variety of farming practice renders impossible a science of agriculture.

And we must be careful not to exaggerate the variety we do in fact encounter. It is clear, to take the example of testamentary disposition, that we can easily exaggerate the differences between French and English habits in this field of law. For an English testator who left his family destitute to the advantage of some special cause in which he was interested would be regarded by most people as having made a patently unjust will; and the main reason why, historical reasons apart, freedom of testamentary disposition remains in England lies in the fact that most testators do in fact leave the bulk of their property to their families.[3] Notable as are our differences in value-judgments, at least equally notable are our agreements. That murder, unemployment, starvation,

---

[1] See his *Reason and Nature* (1931), Bk. III, Chap. IV, esp. pp. 412 f. My debt to this remarkable book will be obvious to the reader.

[2] *Op. cit.*, p. 411.

[3] And an attempt has recently been made in Parliament to compel them to do so. See *Hansard* (fifth series), Vol. LXXI (1928), 37–61.

sweated labour, the traffic in women and noxious drugs, are all bad is a matter of fairly universal consent. Most of our differences in judgments of value are, in fact, a function of the different social conditions that we confront; no one would expect Aristotle today to defend the institution of slavery. And it is not irrelevant that the whole process of politics is built upon the assumption that reasoned discussion will secure effective agreement about what there is of justice in any proposed arrangement. Were it otherwise, a collective social life would be clearly impossible.

This is not, of course, to say that we have today even an approximation to an adequate science of natural law. The obstacles in the way are enormous. It is not only that the naturally just must be sociologically possible. It is not only, either, that the choice of postulates is, in this realm, an immensely more complicated adventure than it is, say, in physics or chemistry. It is not only, finally, that, as a matter of pure logic, universal propositions do not give us a simple rule for specific cases; there are always "ifs" and "buts" dependent upon the facts of concrete situations.[1] There is the difficulty which springs from our ignorance of what our proposals will in fact do; the authors of the Prohibition experiment in the United States certainly did not foresee that gangster rule which we now realize was inevitably implied in the attempt. There is the difficulty, further, that our proposals too often assume identity of interest between the group making law and the group receiving it. There is the difficulty that a law, the Workmen's Compensation Act of 1896, for example,[2] may be

---

[1] It is upon this issue that all formalistic attempts at a theory of law, like those of Kant and Stammler and Kelsen, have broken down.

[2] Cf. my *Studies in Law and Politics* (1932), Chap. XII, esp. pp. 286 f.

made by one set of men with one body of purposes, and applied by another set of men with a different body of purposes; and there is the related difficulty which arises from the fact that in the modern nation-state law is made not by the masses but by a small group which tends, at least, to assume that their conception of its necessity will be shared not less intensely by the rest of the community. The frequency of this error is one of the most pathetic facts in the history of legislation. As long ago, for instance, as the time of Spinoza, it was possible to insist that sumptuary laws always fail to attain their end; but that does not prevent us from attempting to enact them again in each succeeding age.[1] The Hitlerite regime has even sought to prescribe what men shall eat for their dinner.

One final difficulty needs emphasis because it lies at the root of many fallacies in the social sciences. Any principles of natural law must be stated in an abstract way and in universal terms. This creates problems in the application of the principles of which it is impossible to over-estimate the magnitude. We say, for instance, that it is a generally accepted principle that all men should be equal before the law. But we can give no individual meaning to the application of the principle unless social conditions admit of its realization. There is no equality before the law, for example, as between Negro and white in Georgia. The problem of cost makes the ideal of equality difficult to realize as between rich and poor in England in all civil, and in most criminal, cases. In the first year of the Hitler regime members of the Brown Army received specially favoured treatment from the courts. Moreover, the principles of natural law, being built upon a uniformity which is abstract, and therefore artificial, need constant correction in

[1] *Tractatus Politicus,* X.

terms of equity, if they are not to work injustice. But the inherent idea of equity is the adjustment, outside the formal rule, to the individual case; and it is, therefore, so to say, an invasion of the idea of natural law on grounds not legal in character. It therefore prevents certainty, itself one of the desirable ends of law, and it denies the formal equality of treatment in terms of principle, which natural law is supposed to secure indifferently to persons. We know, in short, that the rigid application of law will only too often defeat the ends of justice. Our principles must be flexible in application if they are to win respect over any period of time by reason of the widely varying situations they will encounter. We seem caught in the dilemma that, if we apply the rule invariably, we may, on occasion, do grave injustice; while, if we do not apply the rule, we use a discretion which escapes the categories of law.[1]

Difficulties of this order should, I think, make us humble before the needs the idea of natural law must meet before it becomes available as a recognized criterion of political action. But I do not think this recognition of necessary humility ought to reconcile us to the abandonment of the search for adequacy. The gain in knowledge, particularly in the last century, has been immense. The difference between the juristic material at the disposal, say, of Lord Eldon or Mr. Chief Justice Marshall and that utilized by Mr. Justice Holmes and Mr. Justice Brandeis represents a progress almost as great as that between the physics of the Middle Ages and that of the seventeenth century. The same is true of historiography and anthropology. We have the right to believe that increasing

[1] On all this see a brilliant paper by M. R. Cohen in his *Law and the Social Order* (1933), pp. 259–67.

knowledge can, if we will, make for increasing wisdom in the rational disposition of human affairs.

If we will it so: the limiting condition is all-important. Every approach to objective tests of social good, all the groundwork, therefore, of political obligation, is ultimately a function of increasing equality in society. For it can never be said too often, especially of that material basis which is decisive in determining social relations, that men think differently who live differently, and that the unity which gives endurance and stability to a society is therefore unattainable where they live so differently that they cannot hope to see life in the same terms. It is the poison of inequality which has wrought the ruin of all great empires in the past. For what it does is to break the loyalty of the masses to the common life, and, thereby, to persuade them, not seldom rightly, that its destruction alone can clear the path to more just conceptions of statehood. In the long run, the exercise of power for ends unequally shared always breeds envy and hate and faction in a society; and no fabric can survive the circulation of these evils in its tissues.

The weakness of the classical conceptions of political philosophy has been their failure to pay serious attention to this truth; or, where attention has been paid, to make it of a superficial and fragmentary character. It should be incredible to ourselves that a philosophy so laborious and powerful as that of Hegel should end in the cul-de-sac of adoration for the Prussian monarchy as a supreme achievement of human skill. It should be a warning to us of the degree to which our private environment is the preceptor of our ideology that a mind so strong and agile as that of Bosanquet should have neglected altogether the economic foundations of politics.

Even in our own day, where events in Russia serve as a warning not less clear to our generation than the French Revolution was a warning to the men of the early nineteenth century, distinguished thinkers can still weave their systems in terms of that "natural system of liberty" which so tragically failed to understand how void is the concept of freedom once it is divorced from the context of equality. Until Marx, it is true to say that most political speculation was inadequate because it failed to understand the dominating influence of the property-relation in determining the purposes of the state. It is in the proper grasp of that influence only that an adequate theory of political obligation can be found.[1]

---

[1] For the effect of Marx on the study of economic history, for instance, cf. R. H. Tawney in *Economica*, Vol. XIII, p. 1 (1933).

II

State and Government in the Real World

I

THE claim of the state to obedience, I have argued, rests upon its will and ability to secure to its citizens the maximum satisfaction of their wants. To present this claim as valid there must be an absence of bias in the performance of this function. Where the effort of the state is seriously perverted to the interest of some special group within the society it controls, sooner or later revolution is likely to occur. Revolution may be defined as an attempt by the use of force against the government legally in power to compel a change in what are held to be, by those using such force, the actual purposes of the state.

That there is a bias in state-operations will be denied by no one who scrutinizes the historical evidence. The Greek city-state was biased against the slave. The Roman empire was biased against the slave and the poor. States in the mediæval world were biased in favour of the owners of landed property. Since the Industrial Revolution, the state has been biased in favour of the owners of the instruments of production as against those who have nothing but their labour power to sell.

This is, of course, a wholly excessive simplification of a process so complicated in its details that two historians would hardly tell the tale in exactly the same way. But the implications of the record are always the same. Allegiance to the state is constantly withdrawn by some group which takes the view that the state is biased against its interests. For the moment, we need not concern ourselves with the question whether it took that view rightly. What is significant is the permanent presence, latent or overt, of conflict in the state which has, thus far, always broken out into open conflict, for the right to use the sovereign power.

The purposes of the struggle have been as various in appearance as the groups we encounter in society. Sometimes the struggle has been waged on religious grounds; the civil wars of sixteenth-century France were avowedly fought to secure religious toleration for the Huguenots. Sometimes, as in the English civil war of the seventeenth century, the revolutionists have announced their aim to be the establishment of a constitutional system in place of the monarchical despotism they challenged. The aim of the Bolshevik Revolution of 1917 was the establishment of a socialist society. That of Hitler in 1933 sought to regenerate the German state by removing from influence within the society it controlled men and women of Jewish blood or Marxist ideas.

Whatever be the announcements of revolutionary intention—and these seldom coincide with revolutionary achievement—political philosophy must take over from history the results of the actual processes discovered there. It is not what men conceived themselves to be doing, but the meaning of what they actually did, that is important. Ways of state life are continually changed for other ways. The new mode of behaviour induces a temporary exhilaration in the community. A new unity is established upon the basis of the new mode of behaviour which lasts until we observe again the emergence of those signs of discontent which signalize the coming of a new revolutionary temper. Can we discover any general principles which explain this phenomenon?

Two centuries ago both Montesquieu and Rousseau observed in governments an inevitable tendency to degenerate; and Thomas Jefferson, who had himself observed two revolutions at first-hand, thought that there was need of them in every generation that governments might be compelled to recall the purposes for which they were constituted. That the exercise of power is only too often poisonous to those who exercise it has been a common theme among political philosophers; it led the elder Mill to remark that all the reasons which justify the conference of power are also reasons for the creation of safeguards against its abuse.[1] We have such safeguards and to spare. Written constitutions, Bills of Rights, the separation of powers, fundamental laws—none of these, to take only the outstanding techniques, has worked sufficiently well to persuade men that their objectives can be attained without violence. The roots of our problem lie deeper than constitutional processes can reveal. If Montesquieu and Rousseau are right, we still want to know what it is that causes governments to degenerate. If James Mill was wise in his caution, we still need to know what it is that causes governments to abuse their power.

The proper basis of a political philosophy, that is to say,

---

[1] *Essays in Government* (1824), p. 8.

is a philosophy of history. When we can explain the causation of historic events, we have the materials upon which to build the postulates of a satisfactory theory of the state. There is, no doubt, no lack of such philosophies. History is the record of the unfolding of the will of God, or, as with Hegel, it is the march of the Absolute. Or social change is explained in terms of climatic change; we are to expect democracy in the temperate, and despotism in the torrid, zones. Or we are to take history as the biography of great men, and find in Nero's will, in Cæsar, Luther, Napoleon, Lenin, the causal sequence of the events which occur.

The trouble with all such theories is a simple one. They do not enable us to predict the probable future of events. They leave us blindfold before our fate. To explain history as the unfolding of the will of God is to leave us without knowledge of the next stage in that will. To make it the march of the Absolute is to leave us still uncertain in what direction the Absolute is marching; and if, with Hegel again, we say that it is towards a greater realization of freedom, we then have to explain how that notion is compatible with that break-down of security (an essential condition of freedom) which seems likely to make our epoch an age of dictatorships not always benevolent. The theory of climate as the cause of change is not by any means devoid of truth; but there have been no fundamental changes in European climate conditions in the known historical period, while the forms of government and culture have profoundly changed in the same period. Great men have undoubtedly exercised an influence upon history; but the causes which led to the possibility of their influence are unexplained if we regard them as the key to social change. Washington did not cause the American Revolution, even though he was an important factor in its success; and the application of electric power to industrial uses, which is changing the character of our civilization, is due neither to one, nor to a collection, of great men. It is in other directions than these that we must search.

II

The basic factor in any given society is the way in which it earns its living; all social relations are built upon provision for those primary material appetites without satisfying which life cannot continue. And an analysis of any society will always reveal the close connexion between its institutions and culture and the method of satisfying material appetites. As these methods change, so also will the institutions and culture of the society change. A society in which the main work of satisfaction is performed by slaves will have quite different conceptions of life from those in which that work is done by free men. Its attitude to women, law, education, even religion, will be determined by the fact of its division into a class of slaves and a class of free men. Its laws, most notably, will be necessarily directed to maintaining the obligation of the slaves to labour. Its religion will lend the sanction of its authority to the enforcement of the obligation.

Changes in the methods of economic production appear to be the most vital factor in the making of change in all the other social patterns we know. For changes in those methods determine the changes of social relationships; and these, in their turn, are subtly interwoven with all the cultural habits of men. We cannot write the history of law without looking at its roots in the methods of economic production. We cannot explain the history of religious doctrines without relating them to the social background in which they evolved; and the key to that social background is always to be found in the relationships built upon the methods of production. Our educational systems seek to prepare the child for life; but the kind of life for which it is to be prepared is a function, once more, of the material relations of the productive system which obtains in a given society. Our styles of architecture, the forms of our literature, the character of our science, the basic framework of all that we call civilization, is, at bottom, determined by these productive relationships.

We are urging that the social superstructure is rooted in these economic foundations; that, accordingly, to change the relations of the latter is to change the relations of the former. We are arguing, accordingly again, that any given system of economic relationships will require political and social forms to develop all that is inherent in it. The law, for example, will define the property-relations that correspond to its implications. Education will be so organized as to train men for the performance of the functions their place in the system implies. Law in a feudal age will express the characteristics of a society in which the economic relations of men are primarily determined by their connexion with the ownership of land. Education in such a society will adjust its methods to the needs implicit in the relations such a society requires to maintain. For, clearly, if the society is unable to effect this adjustment, its power to produce, its capacity to satisfy the effective needs it will encounter, suffers an injury which may go deep enough to threaten its existence.

Any society, that is, must seek to sustain some stable relations of production in order to continue as a society. It has to put behind those relations the force of law. It needs, that is, a coercive instrument to secure the continuance of those relations simply because, otherwise, it will not continue to earn its living. They are, indeed, as relations, largely independent of the wills of those involved in them. In the societies we know changes in the relations are infrequent; they are individual rather than general in character. Studies of social mobility have decisively shown that, as groups, slaves remain slaves, employers remain employers, wage-earners remain wage-earners, from generation to generation.[1] The conditions of wholesale change are not possible in any society at a given moment without a disruption in its life. Since such a disruption would threaten the foundations of the existing order, the society has need of an instrument to prevent, if necessary by force, the emergence of that threat to peace the disruption involves. This instrument, historically, has been the state. Its primary function is to ensure the peaceful process of production in society. To do so it protects the system of productive relations which that process necessitates. Its function is to evolve, under coercive sanction, the legal relations by which the society maintains its life in terms of the way in which it earns its living.

Now the state, as we have seen, must act through persons—the body of men we call the government. It follows, therefore, that the control of legal relations in a society is in the hands of those men who, as the government, have the formal right to exercise sovereign power. To determine the way in which it shall be used is, accordingly, to determine how the fruits of the productive process shall be distributed; and it is impossible to make this determination save by having the right to

[1] Ginsberg, *Studies in Sociology* (1932), Chap. IX.

exercise sovereignty. Those, therefore, in a society who seek to alter the character of the distributive process in any fundamental way, who want, that is, to alter the productive relations of the system under which they live, must do so by altering the legal foundations of the society. This they can achieve only by possessing themselves, either peacefully or by violence, of the state-power; for that is the instrument through which alone essential legal relations can be changed.

From this there follow conclusions which are, I think, vital to any political theory. Any group which possesses the sovereign power in society will be guided in its use of it by the way in which the maximum satisfaction of wants can be secured by its exercise. But its conception of that way will necessarily be coloured by its special relation to the process of production. In a slave-owning society, slave-owners will think that slavery is for the good of the whole society; and they will use the state to enforce the relations which a slave-system necessitates. But, clearly, their conception of good will not be identical with that of the slaves themselves. Men's attitude to good being born of their experience, once the interest in the state is different, different experiences will lead to different conceptions of the uses to which the state-power should be put. These conceptions will struggle with one another for survival; and survival in this contest means the right to determine the uses to which the state is devoted. In any society, therefore, in which there are groups whose relation to the productive process is fundamentally different, conflict is inherent in the foundations of the society.

It is a conflict of two kinds. In part it is a conflict between the groups themselves; in part it is a conflict between the ideas each group puts forward as the expression of its idea of good, which is born of the experience it infers from its position. Groups, in short, produce value-systems which are a function of their social relations. Those value-systems will always claim universality; they will represent themselves as valid for persons beyond the group, just as the Southern slave-owners in the United States claimed that slavery was good for the slaves themselves. But, in fact, the values will always be limited by the width of the actual experience from which they arise. And the values which go into actual operation will always be those of the group which, at some given time, control the machinery of the state.

This attitude, it must be noted, does not assume, on the part of the dominating group, any conscious or deliberate identification of its private interest with the total well-being of the society. It does not, either, argue that they are insincere in seeking to give universal form to their conception of what the state should seek to do. The ideological processes of any society are far more subtle and complicated than so simple a theory of motivation would suggest. It is natural for a man to take on the colour of his environment. That is the experience he knows. The values it provokes come to him coloured with emotions, hopes and fears, which persuade him, without his knowing it, to regard them as necessary to social good. A child trained in the Roman Catholic tradition accepts the values of the Roman Church as part of the ultimate order of things; so does a Mohammedan in Mecca accept the values of the Koran; so, also, a child in Soviet Russia today regards the communist outlook as involved in the true nature of social relationships. Those who control an environment set the ideological quality of its life in a way, and to a degree, which involves hardly less those over whom they rule than it involves themselves. The rarest social type is the man who can transcend these familiar habituations.

But they are transcended; and the causation of this transcendence is of the essence of the theory I am outlining. We find slavery regarded as natural in one period, and as indefensible in another. Plato's defence of equality for women seemed to the early nineteenth century no more than a great philosopher's genial eccentricity; it seems elementary common sense to ourselves. William Windham could warn the House of Commons against the dangers inherent in a national system of education [1]; half a century later the warning of Robert Lowe was the need to educate our masters.[2] Interference by the state in every phase of the productive process seemed wholly natural in the seventeenth century to all save a little handful of thinkers; by the end of the eighteenth century the dominant note of economic thought was the insistence that that government is the best which governs least. The "just price" to the mediæval thinker was a quasi-theological concept derived by logical analysis from certain postulates of natural law; the "just price" to the modern economist is a function of secular demand and secular supply in a market wholly uninfluenced by theological prepossessions. There are not a dozen pamphlets in the vast political literature of eighteenth-century England which question the title of the House of Lords to its place in the framework of government; in the twentieth there is none in which it is not on the defensive and few which do not demand either its abolition or fundamental changes in its constitution. Fifty years ago few Eng-

---

[1] April 24, 1807. *Speeches*, Vol. III, p. 17.

[2] For Lowe's view of the working-class cf. his speech in the House of Commons, March 13, 1866.

lishmen of any sort, and fewer still who sought a place in political life, would have dared to profess unbelief in religious matters; today, it is at least doubtful whether such a profession would exercise any influence upon the result outside a small handful of cathedral cities. How can we explain developments of this kind?

The thesis for which I am arguing here is that they are caused by changes in social relationships which, in their turn, are caused by changes in the material forces of production. Men cease to regard slavery as "natural" as it becomes difficult, by its means, adequately to exploit those forces. The rights of women are transformed from a philosopher's eccentricity into claims socially recognized by the law when the relations of the productive process require that recognition. Education becomes a state-matter instead of one of purely private concern as soon as industry requires a corps of workers who can read and write. The degree of state-interference in industry depends on the degree to which that interference is held to promote a fuller productivity of the material forces upon which the society depends. Our attitude to the House of Lords is governed by the view we take of its relationship to the legislation we think desirable; this, in its turn, is involved in our conception of social good, which is born, in predominant part, of our place in the scheme of social relationships. But the scheme of social relationships is, in its turn also, a way of exploiting the utmost possible from the material forces of production.

We need not labour the point. It follows from it that epochs of rapid change are those in which the methods of production change rapidly also; and epochs of relative stability are those in which men pursue their wonted methods of production without notable differences. We should, on this view, expect an epoch of geographical discovery like the Renaissance, or epochs of great scientific change, like the nineteenth and twentieth centuries, to be, as they appear, ages of great social and intellectual creativeness. They breed instability in the state because changes in the productive system are necessarily reflected in the whole superstructure erected on the necessary relationships to which that system gives rise.

But we can say more than this. Epochs of instability are those also in which changed methods of production render inadequate the existing system of property relations. The legal principles maintained by the state, that is, do not permit the society to obtain the full result made possible by the methods of production. Some group in the society takes the view that relations it once deemed natural now so operate as to inhibit the full satisfaction of its demands. It seeks to change those relations. But unless the group which controls the sovereign power is prepared, for one reason or another, to acquiesce in the changed relations sought, the group claiming new relations must seek to capture the state in order to use the coercive power of the community to re-define them. Any group, that is, which regards itself as standing to gain by a change in social relationships will, when that change is denied by the existing order, become revolutionary, in order, if it can, to enforce the changes it desires.

History, in a word, is the record of a struggle between groups whose purpose is to defend claims to which they regard themselves as entitled by reason of the implications they see in the development of the productive process. Their denial, at a point where it is argued that their recognition is necessary in order that the forces of production may realize their full potentialities, leads always to a revolutionary movement. The claims, of course, will not be presented in this way. Men will seek to present them in the form most likely to give them a universal appeal, and their denial will proceed upon a similar basis. The English Revolution announced itself as the defence of constitutional principle and the Protestant religion. It was defending these things; but behind them was the basic fact that a quasi-feudal state, founded, like that of the Stuarts, upon the divine right of kings, was no longer compatible with the claims of the trading classes to a full share in the sovereign power. So, too, with the Revolution of 1789. Fought in the name of universal principles of right, its real result was to free middle-class owners of property from subjection to a state serving the privileged interest of the landed aristocracy. It is not even necessary to argue that the revolutionary group is insincere in the profession of its objectives. Certainly one can still feel in the hostility of Cromwell and Ireton to doctrines like those of Colonel Rainsborough a feeling as genuinely passionate as that which took them out into the field against Charles I.[1] The importance of an ideology lies, not in its profession of what it is, but in the transformation of the social relationships it proposes to effect.

These groups who thus contest with one another for the possession of the state-power always express, at bottom, the contradiction in a given society between its property-relationships and the potentialities of the productive system. The basic struggles, that is to say, are always struggles between economic classes to secure control of the sovereign power. An economic class may be defined as a group of people whose special place in the productive process is differentiated sharply from that

[1] For these debates see the *Clarke Papers* (ed. Firth). Four vols. 1891–1901, esp. I, 227–35.

of other groups.[1] That place is defined by the system of economic relationships which the state maintains. The state puts at the service of any dominant class in the society that supreme coercive power which is its essence; unless it possesses this, no class can alter fundamentally its position in the society. A class, therefore, which seeks such a fundamental alteration is bound to capture the state.

It follows from this that the state is never neutral in political struggles of this kind. It does not stand over and above the conflicting groups, judging impartially between them. By its very nature, it is simply coercive power used to protect the system of rights and duties of one process of economic relationships from invasion by another class which seeks to change them in the interests of another process. For, on analysis, the state appears as a body of men issuing orders to fulfil purposes they deem good. Their conception of good is the outcome of their place in the process which is challenged. To alter it, they must yield their place; and while, of course, such abdication is possible, it is also one of the rarest phenomena of history.

I shall deal later in this chapter with the implications of this historical process, the basis of which I have here sought to explain. At the moment, it is important to make clear what my argument is not intended to imply. It is not an argument that technological development is the clue to social change. Technological development is, of course, important; but it rather grows out of, than determines, social needs. In a system like our own, for example, the choice of the inventions to be selected for exploitation depends, at least predominantly, upon

---

[1] For an illuminating discussion of the problem of economic classes, together with abundant reference to the relevant literature, cf. T. H. Marshall in the *Sociological Review*, Vol. XXV, p. 1.

their capacity when used to show a profit; for that is the motive made essential by the economic relationships characteristic of our society. If technological considerations alone prevailed, John Stuart Mill would never have had to write his famous lament over the failure of machinery to improve the social lot of man.[1]

Nor am I arguing that the state is always subordinated to the private advantage of the class which dominates it; that their selfish desire for personal gain is, therefore, the clue to its policy. I admit fully that statesmen at any given time are likely to be as sincere as their critics in the belief that they devote the machinery of the state to the highest ends they know. My point is the wholly different one that what they can know is set by the economic relationships the state exists to maintain; that these give birth, in each of their historic phases, to a special body of ideals the virtue of which consists in their supposed power to maximize the possibilities of production; and that these ideals wax and wane as the relationships they express are deemed to fulfil that purpose. History is meaningless when read as a struggle between competing selfish interests; so to regard it is to defame the quality of human nature. It is rather the competition of ideals for survival, the character of which is determined by their power to exploit productive potentialities at any given time. Those ideals compete because the relation of classes to productive possibilities creates claims of right which seek for realization. These claims are "implicated" in the class-relation; and as soon as the proportion between claim and satisfaction is felt to be gravely impaired men move, in the nature of things, to attempt its read-

---

[1] *Principles of Political Economy* (1848), Bk. IV, Chap. VI, § 2. Mill here, of course, was uttering a warning against the results of over-population.

justment. This, I have argued, they can only do by conquest of the state since it is through the special coercive power of the state that class-relations are adjusted. New class-relations in any society mean, accordingly, the victory of new ideals. The characteristic ideology of nineteenth-century France was different from that of the eighteenth century because the French Revolution had intervened to alter the class-relationships of that society; and the road to that alteration led through the conquest of the state-power by the middle-class from the hands of the aristocracy which previously possessed it.

It is no part of my case to argue, either, that all historical change is necessarily determined by the economic factor whose significance I have been discussing; I argue only that the economic factor is the predominant element in that determination. I fully admit the influence of personality, tradition, logic, as factors in the making of change. English habits of freedom, for example, make resistance to dictatorship much more feasible than resistance in Russia where there were no such habits. Our lives would be definitely different if Luther or Napoleon or Lenin had never lived; and it is at least probable that, without Lenin, the Russian Revolution of November 1917 would have been different in character. In the operation of law it is quite clear that the effort of professional jurists strives towards a formal consistency for its own sake which frees it from any sole dependence upon the economic factor. It is not less true that tradition, personality, and logic, while predominantly shaped by the economic factor, also shape it in their turn. There is a reciprocity of influence between the factors of social change which no serious observer can reasonably deny.

But the admission of pluralism in historic causation is not

the same thing as a denial of the primacy of the economic factor. I am concerned only to insist that the part any other factor will play depends upon an environment the nature of which is determined by its system of economic relationships. The character these give to the society will enter into and shape, however indirectly, all the forms of its cultural life. Traditions will shape themselves to their necessities. Great personalities will realize themselves in terms of the opportunities these relationships create. The foundations of a legal system will be set by their requirements; and it is only as these have been settled that the search for formal consistency by the lawyer will begin. Anyone can see how the requirements of the new economic relationships of Russia have broken the tradition of the dreamy, mystic, pessimistic Slav who was our "stereotype" from the previous century of its history; how, also, its art, its literature, its philosophy, are in process of slow adjustment to what is implied in the new economic nexus. We may agree that Lenin seriously altered the history of the world; but it was the break-down of the class-relationships upon which Tsarist Russia was founded that gave him his opportunity. The canons of statutory interpretation developed by the courts in Common Law jurisdictions follow logically from the basic thesis of the Common Law that the protection of the interests of private property is the main assumption upon which it rests; but if Great Britain or the United States were to become a socialist commonwealth, the courts would require quite different canons to assure that self-consistency which is an essential legal ideal. For what determines the nature of self-consistency is the postulates from which we start; and these will be fixed, once more, by the economic relationships whose purposes they exist to protect.

III

The economic factor, then, is the bedrock upon which the social superstructure is built; and the way in which it mainly operates is through the struggle of economic classes to possess the state-power. I have argued that the different place occupied by different classes in the process of production gives rise to different needs and interests which, at a given point, come into antagonism with one another. That point is defined by the contradiction between the relations of production and the forces of production. The contradiction becomes significant when the relations prevent the expansion of the productive forces. For it leaves the class (or classes) disadvantaged by such prevention with a sense of frustration. Doubts of the validity of the existing order arise; a change in the legal principles upheld by the state is demanded; an ideology develops critical of, and hostile to, the ideology which defends the existing order. As the contradiction grows more complete, the hold of the new ideology grows more intense. There comes a moment when the old system is so riddled by attack that its only choice is between surrender and overthrow.

We can see an evolution of this kind very clearly in the slow downfall of the France of the *ancien régime*, or, again, in the century-long evolution of Russia to catastrophe from the outbreak of the Decembrists in 1825 to the victory of the Bolshevists in 1917. In each case, the general similarity of the phenomena is remarkable. We have a critical attitude, which pervades the whole society, to existing values and institutions. Authority seeks to arrest by forcible measures the growth of this critical spirit. In each case it is unsuccessful in the effort;

and, again in each case, the growing weakness of the state-power alarms it into the offer of concessions. But, in each case, also, the concessions come too late. Their price alarms the class in possession of power, and it seeks to preserve the old order by their peremptory cancellation; we get, as it were, a temporary revival of the older decisiveness. But the Indian summer of authority does not last; and in the next crisis it is discovered that the foundations of the state have been decisively undermined.

We have to discuss, in the light of these tendencies, the nature and implications of the class struggle in society. That struggle exists in every community marked by two features: (1) the division of labour, and (2) the private ownership of the means of production. It was the view of Marx that the development of capitalist industry would, more and more, divide society into two great and hostile classes, a bourgeoisie which owned the instruments of production, which used the power of the state, therefore, to protect the advantages it enjoyed by reason of that position, and a proletariat which could live only by the sale of its labour, which was disadvantaged by that position so soon as capitalism ceased to expand, and was therefore driven to capture the state-power in order to alter class-relations by which it deemed itself unjustly injured. Marx did not deny the existence of other classes than these in society; or that there would be contexts in which they were significant, landowners, the professional classes, small shopkeepers or business men, the official bureaucracy, and the like. But he argued that the role of none of them in the production process was profound enough under capitalism to make it their historic task to define new class-relations. That, essentially, would be the work of the proletariat, as it was the historic task of the bourgeoisie to complete the previous great revolution which destroyed the feudal state. In the final crisis, these relatively less significant classes would have to make their choice between the mightier interests in conflict.

The first question to which we have to address ourselves is whether class-antagonism is real. We are often told that it is the outcome of error in governmental policy, or that it is due to a failure to perceive the real unity of interest which pervades society beneath the superficial appearance of antagonism. It is true, for example, that strikes continuously occur; but a wise technique of arbitration can always find a just solution for them. Employers and employed, again, have a common interest in promoting the maximum production of the firm; for that makes possible increasing sales at a profit out of which better standards of wages and conditions become possible. Wise administration, in fact, can discover in any society the conditions of a reasonable and continuous harmony.

This is, of course, an idealist interpretation of the social pattern which omits most of what is elementary from the account we have to give. Let us confine ourselves to the kind of industrial society we know, remembering only that, *mutatis mutandis*, a similar picture can be drawn for the previous types of economic organization. We find a society in which the control of the instruments of production is in the hands of a small class, and that its interest in the total social product is different, so far as distribution is concerned, from the interest of the masses over whom it rules. For since the total social product is limited, it follows, to take an obvious instance, that the more there goes in wages to the masses, the less there will be in profits, rent, and interest for those who control the instruments of production. Since, moreover, upon the postulates of our society, the motive to production is the capacity to make profit, it follows that the level of wages will always be set, the power, indeed, to obtain employment will be set, by its relation to that level of profit sufficient to induce the owners of capital to use it for the purpose of production. Given the postulates of capitalism, in short, a failure to make profit must either mean unemployment or a reduction in wages. Clearly, there is therefore implicit in the private ownership of the means of production a basic antagonism between the interests of capital and labour.

It may be said that there are other social antagonisms, too; and that these do not necessarily lead to the political consequences I have discussed above. There is antagonism of interest between the owners of coal and the owners of oil, between the owners of railroads and the owners of motor-transport, between the private shopkeeper and the co-operative societies. There is the historic opposition between town and country, between the churches, between different trade unions catering for the same type of worker. We do not expect, say, the owner of coal to fight the owner of oil for the possession of the state; somehow we know that their interests are likely to be adjusted reasonably. Why, then, should we argue that the position is different when the antagonism considered is that of capital and labour?

The answer is pivotal to the thesis I am defending in this chapter; for it lies at the heart of the philosophy of the state I shall put forward. It is the answer that, in any society where the instruments of production are privately owned, their use and, therefore, the distribution of the product, necessarily involves the continuous disadvantage of the working-class simply because it does not share in the control of those instruments. In general, we can reach agreement about all other social antagonisms. Competing capitalists or competing trade unions combine or disappear. Conflicts between churches are not the exploitation of one class by another in any enduring way. The opposition, indeed, between town and country is more profound; and it is interesting to note that where it assumes serious proportions, as in Eastern Europe today, it becomes a struggle for the state-power. But the pacification of agrarian discontent can be achieved, as has been demonstrated in recent English history, without any alteration in the legal postulates of capitalist society. The distinction, which is ultimate, between all other social antagonisms and that between capital and labour is that the resolution of the latter can be achieved only by an alteration of those postulates.

It may be said that there are other antagonisms, that, for instance, between Negro and white in the United States and South Africa, which are not less profound than those we are discussing; or the hostility of Catholic and Protestant workers in Dublin. We need not deny their profundity; and we need not, either, deny that, wherever they exist, they will operate to prevent the emergence of that class-solidarity which specialized function and its relationships develop. American employers have long been accustomed to divide their workers by playing skilfully on the racial and national differences which characterize them.

But the existence of these antagonisms does not destroy the unique character of the antagonism between capital and labour in modern society; it only postpones its full expression. The Russian Revolution makes it clear that class-consciousness can, under certain circumstances, rise above differences of race or creed or nationality which operate to prevent its clear emergence. We cannot, indeed, define those circumstances with precision. We can only say that whenever the system of production so operates as to prevent the working-class receiving the return to its effort it regards as reasonable, it will seek the means to alter the fundamental structure of the society.

Its sense of a right to make this effort will, of course, depend upon a complex variety of conditions. The political maturity of a people, the quality of the government under which it lives, the authority of religious organizations, the psychological effects of racial divisions, will all make a difference. A society which is expanding economically, like the United States before the great depression, will feel the strain of class-struggle far less profoundly than one which, like Great Britain since the war, begins to find its opportunities of economic expansion checked and challenged. But such differences will never ultimately postpone the issue. So long as the system of private ownership in the means of production produces a continuous improvement in working-class conditions which satisfies the workers' established expectations, the latter will accept, even if doubtfully, the state as it is. But immediately that improvement fails over any considerable period, the workers will develop a revolutionary consciousness. They will always seek to improve the satisfactions they secure from the process of production; and if they cannot improve them under one system of property-relations they will seek for another system. The alternative to reform is always revolution.

I am not, it will be noted, arguing that the alternative is successful revolution. That is a problem in historical strategy with which I am not, in this immediate context, concerned. I am dealing only with the implications of this economic evolution so far as they throw light upon the nature of the state.

The critic of the view here put forward must, if he rejects it, be able to prove two things. He must show that the modern capitalist system, differently from all its predecessors, can expand indefinitely despite the property-relations upon which it is built; and he must show, further, that this expansion is always great enough to enable the workers to satisfy their established expectations. He must show this, not for the conceptual capitalism of an ideal world from which the frictions we know are absent, but for the world of the competing economic imperialisms we have to deal with, the world of inflation and deflation, of the hectic struggle for markets, of the quotas and tariffs and subsidies by which the trader retains control or seeks control of the markets into which he has penetrated. He has to show that the existing property-relations can rapidly overtake the grave gap which now exists between productive power and the power to consume; that the thirty millions or more who are unemployed today can either be pretty quickly re-absorbed by a revived demand for labour or can be maintained at a decent level by the state through its use of the taxing-power. And he has also to show that the state can not only maintain its unemployed in decent conditions, but that it can, under the inherent conditions of profit-making, also preserve and develop those social services which the workers have come to regard as essential to the proper performance of its function.

It is worth while, particularly, to note the conditions under which this proof must be forthcoming in a capitalist democracy.[1] Such a society is built upon the basis of universal suffrage. It seeks a reconciliation between the concentration of economic control in a relatively small number of persons, and

[1] I have discussed this problem at length in my *Democracy in Crisis* (1933).

the widest possible diffusion of political power. It is inevitable that the masses, in such a society, should use their political power to secure increasing material well-being; and, granted the assumptions of capitalist democracy, that always means, sooner or later, the presence of a government in office which is pledged to that end. It is easy to see that the fulfilment of the pledge offers no special difficulties in an age of expanding capitalism. The concessions that the government can then offer do not seriously invade the established expectations of those who control the means of production. They are prepared to pay the price involved in the assumptions of the system. But the situation is wholly different when capitalism is in a phase of contraction. The price of the concessions expected by democracy then appears too high. The assumptions of capitalism then contradict the implications of democracy. If the phase of contraction is prolonged, it becomes necessary either to abrogate the democratic process or to change the economic assumptions upon which the society rests.

That this is an accurate analysis is surely proved by the rise and development of the Fascist movement. The liberal phase of capitalism, when it made its marriage with democracy a universal ideal, corresponded with its phase of expansion. So long, that is, as the power of capitalism to extract their full potentialities from the processes of production was clear, so long also it could afford to concede democratic demands. The contradiction between its economic and political assumptions was concealed by satisfaction with the success of its operations. But as soon as capitalism ran into difficult weather the policy of concessions appeared dubious. The profit-making motive demanded lower wages, inferior general conditions of industry, a diminution of the charges imposed upon capital by taxation, a consequent contraction of the social services. But democracy had led the masses to expect the reverse of all this. They had come to believe that they were entitled to use their political power exactly for the material benefits implied in advancing wages, better general conditions of industry, continuous expansion of the social services; these things they had come to equate with the democratic process of the state. It might be possible for capitalism in difficulties to secure a temporary postponement of the demand for their fulfilment. But, if the postponement was prolonged, the logical result, so long as the marriage of capitalism and democracy continued, would be the transformation of capitalism.

Fascism came to rescue capitalism from this dilemma. By the abrogation of democracy, in one form or another, it has entrusted unlimited political power to those who own and control the means of production. Its methods have followed a fairly uniform pattern. All political parties which deny its purposes have been suppressed. The free trade unions have gone, and, with them, the right to strike. Wages have been reduced either unilaterally by the employers, or with the approval of the state. The right to free criticism has been suppressed; and the power of the electorate to change its government has been withdrawn. It is, moreover, significant that the main Fascist parties have built their authority in part upon an agreement with the armed forces of the state—which, as I argued in the previous chapter, are the centre of its supreme coercive power—and, in part, by arming their own partisans. Since, further, under modern conditions, liberty is largely a function of a supply of true news,[1] the press, the wireless, the publishing trade, the cinema, and the theatre have all come

---

[1] Cf. my *Liberty in the Modern State* (1930), Chap. II.

directly under government control. In Hitlerite Germany, there is even an effort to subordinate the churches to this purpose. Those, moreover, who attack the new dispensation find their way, relentlessly, to prison or to the scaffold. The neutrality of the civil service—an essential concept of capitalist democracy—was frankly abandoned; in a critical time, explains one of the intellectual protagonists of the new order, the bureaucracy must be staffed "with trustworthy and tried fighters of the national front." [1] And the judiciary is similarly subordinated to the service, not of legal principle, but of Fascist ideals. An eminent lawyer can defend even the grim massacre of June 30, 1934, as the embodiment of justice.[2]

In these circumstances, Fascism can rely upon the maintenance of capitalism so long as it can rely upon the loyalty of the armed forces of the state. While these are dependable, it can crush all internal discontent it encounters. It offers the capitalist a position in which the satisfaction of the profit-making motive is the first consideration of state-policy. The problems of capitalist democracy are solved by the simple process of eliminating the democratic element in that union. It is unimportant that Fascism professes the same anxiety for popular well-being as capitalist democracy. We have been told by Herr Hitler that propaganda must utilize any ideology, no matter how deceitful, which furthers Fascist purposes [3]; and Mussolini has explained that the individual fulfils himself in the fulfilment of the state-end.[4] Once we examine the actual character of that end in Fascist communi-

---

[1] Hans Seel, *Der Beamte im Neuen Staat* (1933), p. 9.
[2] Professor Carl Schmitt, cf. *The Times* (London), July 28, 1934.
[3] *Mein Kampf*.
[4] Cf. his *Political and Social Doctrine of Fascism* (1933), *passim*.

ties, it becomes clear that it implies the sacrifice of the ordinary worker to the capitalist need to make profit.

It is, I think, significant that the suppression of democratic institutions both in Italy and Germany should have been accomplished without any alteration in the economic relationships of classes in either country. Nothing could show more decisively the difference between these revolutions and that of Russia than this fact. In Germany and Italy the contradiction between the appearance and the reality of power was solved not by a change in the legal principles which determine the relations between classes but by suppressing the institutions, social and political, through which, in the previous regime, the workers sought to secure the concessions to which they deemed themselves entitled; in Russia the legal relations between classes was fundamentally altered by making the state, instead of private individuals, the owner of the means of production. The true effect of the new regimes in Italy and Germany is to take from the workers the legal right to deny that the purposes of the state are adequate for them. The distribution of the social product proceeds upon the same principles as before the change. The effective difference is that no struggle and no free discussion is permitted upon the principles which should govern the distribution.

And if it be said that these principles are determined by the independent arbitration of the state, the answer we must make is a simple denial of its neutrality. The Fascist state, like any other, must obey its fundamental postulates; and these, by the fact that the private ownership of the means of production is maintained, imply subordination of its habits to the motive of private profit. It was the threat to private profit in the first year of his regime which compelled Hitler to move to the right and abandon those policies which had a socialist emphasis. It was the threat to private profit, also, which has made the Fascist state in Italy acquiesce continually in the reduction of wages.[1] Once capitalist postulates are assumed, that is to say, the incidence of state-action must necessarily be biased in favour of the owners of capital. To resort to different principles would be incompatible with the inherent nature of Fascism.

That is the vital lesson of Fascism. No other historic experience of recent times has thrown so revealing a light upon the nature of the state. Its coercive power must be used to protect the stability of a given system of class-relations; it cannot be used to alter that given system. And this means that, whenever social institutions operate so as to threaten that stability, the state will move to attack them in the name of law and order. But by so moving it is, necessarily, also moving to protect the vested interests involved in the class-relations of the particular society. It cannot remain neutral between them by the law of its own being. It is compelled to choose just because it is a state. Its government must act as the executive committee of the class which dominates, economically, the system of production by which the society lives.

An American illustration will perhaps make this clear. The abuses connected with company unions in the United States, the overwhelming power, moreover, exercised by the great employers in industries where labour was badly organized, led to the enactment of a section in the National Industrial Recovery Act of 1933 whereby in each industry labour was

[1] Cf. L. Rosenstock-Franck, *L'Expérience corporative en Italie* (1934).

entitled to choose those by whom it would be represented in negotiations with the employers; it being an inference from the Act that labour was entitled to be represented by the ordinary trade unions if it so desired. It is well known that the opposition of the employers led to immense difficulties in the application of this section; and, on the Pacific Coast, the refusal of the dock and shipping companies to "recognize" the transport unions, after their employees, by large majorities, had chosen this form of representation, led to the outbreak of a general strike in San Francisco in July 1934.[1]

The strike collapsed after four days; and it collapsed because, in the name of law and order, all the energies of the state government were devoted to defeating its objectives. It did not matter that the strikers were seeking to secure a right deliberately conferred upon them by law. It did not matter, either, that by refusing to recognize the transport unions the employers of San Francisco were, quite consciously, evading an obligation imposed upon them by law also. It did not matter, finally, that it is the thesis of American law that it is applied equally and indifferently to all persons, whether employers or employed, since the courts of the state are, by definition of the state-purpose, neutral between them.

Once labour withdrew its services from the community of San Francisco, it threatened their continuity; that is the objective of a general strike. It is an attempt, by the use of the pressure involved in the withdrawal of labour, first to make the employers give way, and, second, to compel the government to use its influence with the employers to this end.

---

[1] For a vivid account of the strike see *The New Republic* of August 1, 1934.

Again, it must be noted, the objective in the San Francisco case was the realization of a right legally conferred. But a general strike, by its nature, is a threat to public order because it involves the cessation of the services essential to the life of the community; and it is the object of the state to protect public order. To do so, therefore, it must assure the functioning of essential services, must, that is, render inoperative the purposes of a general strike. "A general strike," said Mr. Hugh Johnson, the administrator charged with the application of the National Industrial Recovery Act,[1] "is a threat to the community, a menace to the government, civil war, and bloody insurrection." He therefore urged the "responsible elements" in the San Francisco labour movement to purge their ranks of the subversive forces in their midst who willed a general strike.

What, then, became involved in the situation? The employers had only to continue to refuse recognition to the transport union, that is, to evade their clear legal obligation, to ensure that the government would intervene to break the strike. The workers were left with the alternatives of surrender or conflict with the government; and the latter, of course, would have been a revolutionary act which the workers at no time had in view. The inference, I think, is the clear one that where, in any state, essential services are privately owned, and their continuity is threatened, the government will intervene, with all the coercive power at its disposal, to assure the maintenance of that continuity; and it can be challenged in its intervention only at the price of revolution. The intervention of the state is, of course, made in the name of

[1] *The New Republic,* August 1, 1934, p. 309.

the community; but its effect is, obviously, to place its power at the disposal of private ownership. It maintains, this is to say, a system of class-relations which, in actual operation, makes null and void an essential right which it has itself legally conferred upon the workers, the validation of which, therefore, upon the thesis of neutrality, they are entitled to expect. It is significant that in the San Francisco strike—which is by no means a solitary instance—the state took no steps whatever towards that validation. Rhetoric apart, as soon as the employers were challenged, it went into action as their agent. Nor could any other action by it be conceived as possible upon the assumptions within which the American state must work.

The San Francisco situation is only one illustration of a general thesis. This is the simple one that wherever a class-struggle exists in a society the power of the state will be manifested on the side of those who own the instruments of production in the society which it controls. Sometimes the processes of the struggle are implicit in character; the courts of law may be asked, for example, to issue an injunction restraining workers from picketing a factory where there is a strike. Sometimes, as in San Francisco, they are explicit; the power of the state is made manifest in machine-guns and bayonets. Whether implicit or explicit, the ultimate purpose of the class-struggle can be realized only by the conquest of the state. For there is no other way in which its power can be used to effect a decisive change in property-relationships. If, therefore, in a society the instruments of production are owned by the few, the power of the state will be used to protect them in that ownership; for this is then the thesis of the law, and law, by definition, is the will of the state.

IV

The conclusion we have reached is the grave one that in a society where the instruments of production are privately owned the main fact of significance is the struggle for the possession of the state-power between the class which owns those instruments and that which is denied access to the benefits of that ownership. The conclusion implies that the state is always biased in the interest of the former; and those in whose interests its authority is exercised will not surrender their advantages unless they are compelled to do so. They do not, let me emphasize again, take this position on merely selfish grounds. They act in this way because their position in the class-structure of the society drives them to identify their special privileges (which they rarely see as special privileges at all) with the well-being of the whole.

The view here taken is one that naturally disturbs many generous minds. It postulates the inevitability of revolution as the midwife of social change; and it admits that there are phases of human evolution in which men cease to settle their differences in terms of reason, and resort to force as the ultimate arbiter of destiny. They remember the horrors that accompany civil strife, the tragedies of the Puritan Rebellion, the sufferings of the French and Russian peoples during their revolutions, the hatred, the envy, the cruelty invariably evoked by the use of violence. They emphasize to themselves the immense improvements, especially since the Industrial Revolution, which have taken place in the material lot of man. They think of the profound effort made by the more fortunate members of the community to alleviate by charity the sufferings of the less well-placed. They think of that increasing sensitiveness to the infliction of unnecessary pain so widely characteristic of our times. They point to the growth of a deeper social conscience, as witnessed by our new attitude to the functions of the state, the high level of taxation the rich are prepared to impose upon themselves, the widening opportunities of the age. If these things can be achieved peacefully, why have we to assume that violence is not less essential an instrument in contemporary civilization than it was in less enlightened days? Why cannot we argue that men have come so increasingly to see the dangers of violence that they will accept the verdict of reason as the final arbiter?

The answer, I think, is an obvious one. It is that, historically, the important changes that have been made peacefully have always been made by an expanding economic system. Where there is expansion, there is security; and, where there is security, there are the time and the opportunity for men to give reason its right to empire. For where there is expansion of this kind, the established expectations of privilege do not suffer erosion when the demands of the masses are conceded. Accommodation is always possible in a society where new material benefits can be continually conferred. It is in jeopardy in those periods where economic contraction has reached the point where the demands cannot be conceded without a revolution in the class-relations of the society. For changed class-relations mean changed systems of ideas. They are denials of conceptions of good which represent the whole meaning of life for those who are asked to surrender them. Men may abdicate positions they do not deem fundamental. So far in history, at any rate, they have not abdicated peacefully, as a class, from any position they deemed vital to their well-being.

This, surely, can be seen from the most elementary examination of the facts. No civilized person now defends the economic institution of slavery; but it took a war to convince the Southern states of America that it was an indefensible institution. No civilized person now defends intolerance in matters of religious belief; but the religious wars are a commentary on the price we have had to pay for that realization. The British Commonwealth of Nations is built upon the principle of equality of status between its different members; but it took three civil wars to establish the recognition of the principle. There are few vital principles of social justice, in fact, for which their protagonists have not had to fight, even where their admission seems to us too obvious to have been denied. The right to the suffrage, equality before the law, the emancipation of women, the limitation of the hours of labour, the establishment of decent conditions in the factories, all of these, to take only the simplest illustrations, have had to be won at the cost of human life. We are still fighting to establish the right of free association in the industrial field. We are still fighting for the right of the Negro races to legal equality. On the plane of reason, we largely admit the futility of war; but even repudiations like those implied in the acceptance of the Covenant of the League of Nations and the Paris Pact imply a belief in the just exercise of force where the "honour" or "vital interest" of the signatories is held by them to be involved.

And when we say that we must trust in reason, what precisely do we mean? In whose reason is it in which we are to trust for the settlement of differences? Is it the reason of the government, a reason that we know is often biased and frequently mistaken? Is it the reason of that *major et sanior pars* of the community which mediæval thinkers so respected? But what is the *major et sanior pars* at any given time? Is it simply the will of the majority? Are we to take the view which, as I have already argued, men simply refuse to take, that a minority must always unconditionally submit? If it is not the majority merely, how do we discover the *sanior pars* where sanity is, in social matters, so largely a function of the experience we deem relevant to judgment? A *sanior pars* can hardly be the decision of the experts at any given time; for not only are the experts frequently wrong, but decisions in matters of social constitution are never wholly matters of *expertise.* Is it not, in fact, inescapable that the exclusion of the right to use force from human affairs means always, in ultimate analysis, the acceptance of the *status quo* until such time as those who operate the will of the state are prepared to change it?

It is said that there is a difference between the obligations of men to reason in a state where a dictatorship prevails from those obligations in a state where men accept the normal assumptions of political democracy. For, in the latter, the people may, by majority-decision, change the principles of government, the purposes, therefore, to which the state-power is devoted, at any time they think fit. The business, there, of the proponents of change is to secure that majority for their view by the persuasion of argument. They are not entitled to the use of force because they do not need to use it.

All this is obviously true; but those who build their whole philosophy upon this argument beg the entire issue involved in the thesis I have been urging. It is not a great discovery to insist that solutions made in terms of rational consent are always to be preferred to those made by violence. It is not even a great discovery to argue that men should, in a democratic society, patiently endure what they believe to be great evil, because they have the legal right, if they can secure a majority to support them, to change the law to which they take objection. Of the wisdom of these views no one who supports the thesis here laid down has, so far as I am aware, any doubts at all.

The issue involved must be settled on a different ground. My point has been the wholly different one that democratic institutions are judged valid in a capitalist society so long as they do not so function as to destroy the essential implications of capitalism, that is, the class-relations which the private ownership of the means of production involve. I have been arguing that, when the political democracy seeks to transfer that ownership to the community, the capitalist class will, if it can, use the state-power to suppress democratic institutions. I have therefore urged that, at this stage of economic development, the difference between classes can only be settled by force. I have argued that the maintenance of political democracy is not, as the experience of Italy, Germany, and Austria makes manifest, an inherent purpose of the state as such. It is a form of government able to maintain itself only so long as it does not contradict the implicit needs of the class-relations a capitalist system requires. It can be associated with a capitalist system only when the latter is successful enough to be able to satisfy the demands of the workers for increasing material benefits. So soon as capitalism ceases to maintain that success sufficiently long to make it clear that the kind of expansion it enjoyed in its hey-day is no longer available, it confronts the dilemma of having to choose between the suppression of the class-relations it implies, and the suppression of democratic institutions.

Now it is no answer to this argument to say that men should accept the postulates of democratic government because these make possible rational, instead of violent, solutions. Of course they should; but the question is whether they will in fact accept them. It is not very difficult to show that a democratic state has a better chance of realizing social justice than any possible alternative. But the state with which we are concerned here is not the democratic state pure and simple; it is the state of capitalist democracy. It is a state, therefore, the political implications of which are the equal claim of each citizen to the material benefits of the society; of which, simultaneously, the economic implications, by reason of its capitalist foundation, limit the equality of claim to material benefit by the needs of profit-making. And the problem then is not whether it is wise or just to abandon political democracy, but whether, in the period of capitalist contraction, democracy can be maintained.

The real answer, therefore, to the view here put forward would be the proof that such maintenance is probable. Any general proof of such a proposition would have some ugly facts to overcome. It would have to explain the erosion of belief in the validity of democracy among the sincere and honest men who have welcomed Fascism in, to take the most notable examples only, Italy and Germany and Austria. It would have to explain, also, the erosion of that belief simultaneously with economic crisis in capitalism. It would have to explain, further, why Fascist states seem able to preserve themselves only by terrorist methods, and why the suppressions upon which it depends are directed almost wholly against working-class institutions. It would have to explain, moreover, why the coming of Fascism has almost invariably involved the decline or suspension of the social services, the lowering of working-class industrial standards, the forcible repression of all criticism which denies the validity of these. Until such explanations are forthcoming, it is difficult to doubt the validity of the analysis here made.

It is sometimes said that, after all, the attack on political democracy has succeeded only in those countries where experience of its institutions was comparatively recent. In countries where the habituation has been more profound, Great Britain, for example, the United States, France, Belgium, Scandinavia, the attack on democratic institutions has been so far unsuccessful. That is, of course, true; but we must inquire carefully into what is involved in the truth. It is at least significant that all of them are witnessing a grave *malaise* of democratic institutions. It is significant, also, that in all of them the curtailment of liberty in recent years has been a striking feature of their administration. It is above all significant that none of them has experienced a government in office which has sought to use democratic institutions for the redefinition of class-relations. This, after all, would be the real answer to the implications of my argument. If a socialist government in Great Britain or France or the United States were peacefully to transform the basis of the property-system from private to public hands, the argument that fundamental changes could be accomplished by democratic means would be immensely strengthened.

That evidence does not exist, and what there is for consideration, even in the democratic countries, raises doubts the other way. The threat of Fascism to the French Republic is profound; and the events of February 1934 have had the effect of driving further apart the parties of the Right and of the Left. In the United States labour is as yet too unorganized politically to constitute a serious threat to the existing system of class-relations; but what is chiefly remarkable in the Roosevelt experiment, undertaken, it must be remembered, for the restoration of capitalism to health, and not for its supersession, is the inability of the President to prevent the great employers from sabotaging those of his measures which seek to confer material benefit upon the working-classes.[1] In Great Britain, even a minority Labour government, which attempted no socialist legislation, was held to threaten the foundations of economic stability; and it was followed by the National government, not only built upon a fairly complete fusion of the political parties which upheld the validity of the capitalist system, but also proceeding upon the assumption (politely termed equality of sacrifice) that the crisis which brought it to power justified suspension of, or economy in, the conference of that increasing material benefit political democracy seeks to secure.

Nor is that all. Capitalist democracy in Great Britain remains because, so to say, the validity of the marriage upon which it rests has not yet been tested in the courts. What we have to note is the fact that events since 1931 have driven the Labour Party increasingly towards a thorough-going socialism, and that, *pari passu* with this evolution, members of the

---

[1] On the Roosevelt experiment see Charles A. Beard and G. H. E. Smith, *The Future Comes* (1933); C. L. Dearing, *The A.B.C. of the N.R.A.* (1934); George Soule, *The Coming American Revolution*, (1934).

Conservative Party show a significant tendency to question the assumptions upon which the British Constitution has long rested. The reorganization of the House of Lords that it may be able authoritatively to delay the passage of socialist legislation by a Parliament in which there is a Labour majority in the House of Commons; the revival of the Royal Veto, now obsolete for over two hundred years; the emphasis, in relation to the power of dissolution and the right to create peers, that the monarch need not act upon the advice of his ministers if, by going to the Opposition, he can win assent to his invocation of delay; these suggestions are of the highest interest.[1] For in each case they suggest a technique which would operate against the Labour Party only, and not against its rival. In each case, they assume that constitutional barriers may be placed in the path of socialist legislation which would not impede the purposes of an anti-socialist government.

Two further remarks about the British position may be made; for they lead to a general inference of some importance. We are constantly told [2] that an alliance between the Liberal and Labour Parties is desirable because, since both are committed to the maintenance of democracy and might win electoral power by such an alliance, they would thereby safeguard democracy from invasion by the extreme Right. But it has been constantly explained by the leaders of the Liberal Party that, while they favour a wide extension of state-function, they are opposed to socialism; they would not, that

---

[1] Cf. my *Labour and the Constitution* (1932) for a detailed discussion of these proposals.

[2] Cf. the reports of the discussions of an address by Mr. A. L. Rowse at the Liberal Summer School in 1934. *The Manchester Guardian*, August 18, 1934. This is symptomatic of an argument that has been made for many years.

is, use the power of the state to alter the fundamental basis of class-relations. To organize the proposed alliance, therefore, Labour would have to put its socialist faith in abeyance and concentrate upon the Liberal programme of social reform. That, in its turn, is not a step which the bulk of the Labour Party is likely to approve, since the whole burden of its experience since 1924 has been the inadequacy of any policy which leaves untouched the fundamental basis of class-relations.

But let us suppose the Labour Party were prepared, at least temporarily, to put its socialist faith in abeyance in order, by an alliance with the forces of Liberalism, to secure an electoral victory. Under the conditions we confront, how far could such a victory realize its aims? Unless, after its assumption of office, there was a rapid economic recovery, it would not be in a position to embark upon any large schemes of social reform; for the cost of these would quickly lead to a position similar to that which led to its defeat in 1931. If Labour, in fact, is to work the capitalist system, it must frankly accept the assumptions of capitalism; and it is inherent in them that the state cannot embark upon costly social reforms in an epoch of commercial depression. It is difficult to see how such a government could long retain the confidence of its supporters since the conditions it confronted would prevent the realization of the purposes for which it won power.

And even if it came to office with the advantages of a rapid trade recovery, it is not easy to see that it could go very far. By the terms of its alliance with Liberalism, it could not embark upon a socialist policy. It would have, therefore, to confine itself to extracting from the capitalist system the largest possible benefit for the working-class. We need not underestimate the value of a policy which, if effectively pursued, means better housing, better conditions of employment, an improved educational system, a more intense trade-union activity, and so on. But unless the trade recovery was permanent, the only result of resuming the policy of concessions would be to create a new level of established expectation among the workers which would be certain of disappointment when the next slump came. Whether, in fact, we assume recovery or continuing crisis, for the Labour Party to accept as given the assumptions of the existing order means its acceptance of the contradiction between capitalism and democracy which, as I have urged, is sooner or later fatal to the one or the other. I do not believe it could maintain itself on these terms. As the electorate itself rightly inferred from its experience of the Labour government of 1929, it is in the long run better that the administration of a capitalist state should be in the hands of men who believe in its principles. It is as foolish to ask the Labour Party to administer a capitalist society as to ask a Nonconformist to be Pontiff of the Roman Catholic Church.

Such a proposal, therefore, does not really meet the central problem here raised. That is, let us insist once more, whether the transition from capitalism to socialism, with all the changes in class-relationships that it implies, can be accomplished peacefully in a democratic community. I am not arguing here that it cannot be so accomplished if the owners of the instruments of production are prepared to abide by the implications of democracy; but that is only saying that if democracy works successfully it works successfully; not a very profound observation. I am asking whether, in the light of the experience we have had, it is reasonable to assume that they will in fact abide by these implications. The evidence seems to me to suggest that only the most ardent optimist can take an affirmative position on this point. For he has not only to explain, or explain away, the significance of Continental and American experience during the war. He has also to show that the unity of the state can be maintained when men differ finally about the foundations upon which it is to rest.

Distinguished observers do, indeed, make the attempt; and it is worth while to examine their case with some closeness. "If for propaganda purposes," Professor Gregory writes,[1] "the Western intellectuals choose to identify Fascism with capitalism in decay, let it at least be recognized that there is not the slightest warrant for their doing so." He takes this position on three grounds. The essence, first, of Fascism is authoritarian; "the essence of the capitalistic system is freedom of enterprise and the right of the individual to economic self-expression." "The twenty-five points of the National Socialist Programme," in the second place, "and the creed of the Russian Communist have much more in common than either has with the philosophy of the capitalist state." And, thirdly, "if capitalism is breaking down, one would look for evidence of its break-down in Great Britain and the United States, rather than in the Balkans, South America, or Italy, for the very simple reason that in these areas a fully fledged capitalistic system never existed, and the same thing is, of course, still more true in the case of Russia." The problem of German Fascism Professor Gregory explains by saying that "the German social and economic structure has been exposed to peculiar strains, but that those strains have nothing to do with the inherent defects of capitalism at all." Professor Gregory

[1] *The Independent*, August 11, 1934, p. 28.

agrees that "there is a possibility that if a snatch Labour majority were to proceed to turn the economic institutions of the country upside down, there might be resistance; but that would prove, not that capitalism has broken down, but, on the contrary, that a large number of people still believed in it." "The rise of Fascism," Professor Gregory concludes, "is no proof of the break-down of the capitalist system; it is only proof that in certain countries the post-war situation was regarded as unsatisfactory, and, in certain cases, at least—for instance, Germany—making all allowances for self-deception, non-economic factors played as large a part as economic ones."

Let us take this argument point by point. It is, of course, true that Fascism is authoritarian in its essence, as it is true that capitalism is built on "freedom of enterprise and the right of the individual to economic self-expression." But what we have to examine is the purpose for which Fascist authority is used. When we find that it destroys the free trade unions, protects the private ownership of capital, and reduces wages and labour standards in the interests of profit-making, it is surely not illogical to argue that those individuals for whose "right to economic self-expression" Fascism is concerned are not members of the working-class. Fascist authority is used, in short, to protect the system of class-relations which capitalism requires; and "Western intellectuals" regard it as an expression of capitalism in decline on the simple ground that without the use of such authority for its support, these class-relations could not be maintained.

It is, again, true that the resemblances between the programmes of Fascism and communism are, in verbal terms, interestingly close; had the Fascist programme been anti-socialist and anti-trade union in announcement it would not have ventured to ask for working-class support. But we have not to judge Fascism by its intentions; what matters is its actual practices. I do not suppose Professor Gregory imagines that the Italian generals who backed Mussolini,[1] and the German industrialists like Hugenberg and Thyssen who backed Hitler, did so on the basis of an expectation that they would translate the communist elements of their programmes into practice. It is, of course, true that there has been Fascist interference with "freedom of enterprise"; but the character of that interference, both in Italy and Germany, has been interference of capitalists in the interests of capitalist recovery. Professor Gregory is entitled to judge that it is interference which has proceeded upon the wrong lines; but when he examines the incidence of that interference upon the economic institutions and position of the working-classes he is not entitled to infer that it is a serious or sincere attempt to realize the formal programme of Fascism.

Nor does it help us to ask us to judge capitalism in maturity, as in England and the United States, rather than relatively undeveloped capitalism, as in the Balkans or South America. For the test of an economic system is everywhere the same: it is the test of its capacity to exploit to the full all the potentialities of its productive power. Judged by that test, it is surely not illegitimate to speak of a "break-down" of capitalism both in England and the United States. In the former, two million unemployed; devastated economic areas like South Wales and the North East Coast; the staple export

[1] On Mussolini's relations with the Italian army cf. Salvemini, *Fascist Dictatorship in Italy* (1927), pp. 60–162; on those of Hitler with big business in Germany see E. A. Mowrer, *Germany Puts the Clock Back* (1933), pp. 117–8, 122, 127–8, 131, 146–7; and E. Henri, *Hitler over Europe* (1934), *passim.*

trades, like cotton and coal, iron and steel and shipping, announcing that they verge on bankruptcy; other industries going hat in hand to the government in quest of subsidies to keep them alive; a situation like this, with a government in office which proclaims its faith in the necessity of private enterprise, may fairly be described quite soberly as a break-down. And anyone who reads the description of the American position furnished by President Roosevelt shortly after his assumption of office [1] will be driven merely to the choice of an analogous synonym if he is to be denied the right to the use of "break-down" to describe it.

Professor Gregory admits that a Labour majority of a "snatched" character might meet with resistance if it were "to proceed to turn the economic institutions of the country upside down"; but he would regard such resistance not as proof of a break-down, but "on the contrary" of a faith in capitalism held by a large number of people.

It is not easy to know exactly what Professor Gregory means by a "snatch Labour majority." Most electoral victories appear to be "snatched" victories to the defeated party. In the post-war period, that was the view taken of the 1918 election by the opponents of Mr. Lloyd George; it was the view taken by the Labour Party of the Conservative victories of 1924 and 1931. Is it a "snatched" victory when the electorate gives a majority to a party whose essential programme has been for nearly a score of years a matter of eager public debate? Or is it the size of the party's majority which determines the character of its triumph? If Professor Gregory means the latter, it is, I think, pretty obvious that no party

[1] F. D. Roosevelt, *On Our Way* (1934), pp. 3–35. For a similar picture cf. E. K. Lindley, *The Roosevelt Revolution* (1933), Chaps. I–III.

would conceive itself entitled to "turn the economic institutions upside down"—Professor Gregory's genial periphrasis for a socialist policy—unless it was assured of adequate support from public opinion. It is clear that the withdrawal of such support would rapidly give its measures a wholly different complexion, since urgent public opposition would make their application difficult to the point of impossibility.

But the attitude of mind is interesting which regards socialist policy in this way. The rhetoric employed suggests that to embark upon socialism is an adventure in search of chaos, and that if the Parliamentary majority which attempts this is a "snatch" one—whatever that means—resistance is intelligible. Here, clearly, Professor Gregory admits the whole burden of the case I have been making. For he assumes the possibility that, under certain not very precisely defined circumstances, men will prefer to fight rather than abide by democratic institutions. But he is wholly mistaken in thinking that, because they may prefer to fight, this proves that capitalism has not broken down. The conclusion is irrelevant to the premise. A principle, a system, an idea, is not true because a large number of people are so convinced of its truth that they are prepared to fight for it; a large number of people was prepared to fight for the monarchical idea in Russia after 1917, but that did not mean that the idea had not broken down. And so long as the introduction of a socialist policy presents itself to detached and critical minds like that of Professor Gregory as "turning the economic institutions of the country upside down," it may reasonably be doubted whether less impartial adherents of the system will approach the making of a socialist experiment with that goodwill upon which the keeping of the peace depends.

This defence, finally, urges that the roots of Fascism cannot be traced to a capitalist break-down because they are expressive of a post-war situation in certain countries in which non-economic factors were as important as the economic, and in which, also, the "peculiar strains" had, as in Germany, "nothing to do with the inherent defects of capitalism at all." Here it is important to realize exactly what Professor Gregory is doing. He erects a capitalism of concepts, the character of which depends, in each society, upon the operation of the two principles of "free enterprise" and the "right of the individual to economic self-expression." This capitalism of concepts, the pure idea of capitalism, is then differentiated from all existing capitalist societies; for wherever, in them, free enterprise or free economic self-expression are checked or hindered by legislation or custom, the resulting defects can be attributed not to capitalism in operation but to departures from it. It does not matter that this pure idea of capitalism never has existed, and that there are no political circumstances conceivable in which it would come into existence. Exactly as the idealist regards the practice of actual states as an irrelevant basis upon which to criticize the state as such, so do Professor Gregory and those who think with him similarly regard the practice of capitalist states as irrelevant to the criticism of the capitalist state of pure theory. For they have fixed the concept of the latter by criteria they will never be compelled to test by the facts. All state-intervention, on this view, whether for capitalist advantage or against it, is a departure from the norm; and its effects, therefore, cannot logically be attributed to the working of the norm.

But if we assume, as in life we are bound to do, that capitalism is what capitalists do, then we must regard the habits of those states dominated by capitalist interests as characteristic of capitalism. We must assume, therefore, that the use of the state-power by capitalists to protect their interests, when this occurs not exceptionally, but so widely as the modern tendencies to economic nationalism and interventionism reveal, is of the essence of capitalism in its modern form. For an idea is what it becomes, not what it was intended to be in its origins. A dynamic complex of developing ideas like capitalism cannot be pinned down permanently to the habits of its earliest stages, as a naturalist can pin down permanently the specimen he puts into a museum case. And if, further, the use of the state-power by capitalists assumes a Fascist complexion whenever their security is seriously in question, I do not think we can conclude otherwise than that the association is one of cause and effect. Capitalism in difficulties uses the predominant position of capitalists in any society to devote the state-power to suppressing its opponents. To secure the conditions under which it may restore profit-making, it embarks upon those experiments, wage-reductions, the destruction of trade unions, the prohibition of strikes, and so on, which it believes will assist that restoration. But when it does these things it enfolds the society within the arms of a Fascist state.

It should be emphasized that nothing in this analysis assumes that non-economic factors have not contributed to the growth of the Fascist doctrines in Germany, or elsewhere. Historical materialism is not, as Professor Gregory seems to imagine, a monistic theory of historical causation. All we need to assert is that economic difficulty has provided the foundation upon which these doctrines have grown, that without that difficulty their non-economic content would have remained interesting ideological eccentricities without the ability to use the power of the state to compel acceptance of them. There was plenty of "racialism" in Germany before the war; but only experiences as profound as the inflation could have persuaded a sober and intelligent people to take it seriously. That there is an interweaving reciprocity between all the different factors of any culture-pattern was emphasized by Marx and Engels at every stage of their analysis.[1] The claim of historical materialism is simply that the economic factor defines, in Engels's phrase, the "fundamental necessity" within the framework of which all other ideas will be selected as significant. Anti-Semitism is not a wholly economic phenomenon; but anyone who examines the comparative experience of Germany and Russia since the war will, I think, be unable, save in economic terms, to explain the different political expressions it has been given in those countries. Professor Gregory's attempt to reduce historical materialism, in short, to a simple formula in which economic causes alone suffice to explain events is only one more instance of the critic's misunderstanding of the doctrine he is anxious to refute.

V

In this background, let us set out the theory it seems to involve of the nature of the state. Let us begin by remind-

---

[1] Cf. for instance the well-known letter of Engels to Bloch, September 21, 1890.

ing ourselves of the definition with which we started. A state, it was suggested, is a society which is integrated by possessing a coercive authority legally supreme over any individual or group which is part of the society.[1] The state, therefore, is a special way of exercising power. It is special because it is supreme; and it is special, also, because it is coercive. No other authority in society can, save by delegation from the state, dispose of a similar power. Only the state, to put it brutally, has the legal right to kill and imprison its subjects, and to use its armed forces to compel them to accept its decisions. It does not, of course, normally implement its decisions in this way; generally, at least, men submit themselves to its will without the need to exercise force on its part. But that force is always latently there, to be called into play whenever there is a challenge to the authority of the state.

This state-power, as I have already pointed out, has to be exercised by men; and those who are entrusted with its exercise constitute the government of the state. Their business is to use the state-power for the purposes for which it was instituted; and these, I have argued, may be summarized by saying that the end of the state is the satisfaction, at the highest possible level, of its subjects' demands. From this it follows that the justification of state-power, the right, therefore, beyond the plane of formal law, to exercise coercive authority, is conditioned by the duty of satisfying demand. I have argued, further, that the fulfilment of the state-purpose can be accomplished only when the incidence of its actions is unbiased. Differential treatment of citizens cannot be justified unless it can be shown that such differentiation secures equally the good of those against whom it works not

[1] *Supra*, p. 8.

less than of those who, on a prima facie view, seem to be benefited by it.

For reasons I have already put forward in the first chapter of this book, these seem to be the assumptions with which we have to start. These define a conception of the state which can then be tested against historic experience. For by finding how states actually do work, we get an insight into their nature which clarifies the assumptions upon which we build. If we can discover the conditions which necessarily bias the operations of the state, their discovery is at least a means to their removal; it enables us, that is, to know how the state, by working in an unbiased way, can fulfil its purposes at the highest level. The criterion, in short, of our assumptions is a pragmatic one. We have to know, and thus to judge, the way in which they get applied, the results of their application, in order to know whether they fulfil their expectations of what we expect them to do.

I have been arguing in this chapter that the main index to the nature of any actual state is the system of economic class-relations which characterize it. For when we know what this system is, we shall also know the real purposes for which the state-power is used. What the state does, I have suggested, is to put coercive power at the disposal of the class which, in any given society, owns the instruments of production there. For the exploitation of those instruments is necessary to enable the society to earn its living. The more fully they are exploited the more ample the living the society can make. But the full exploitation of those instruments does not necessarily mean a just exploitation. That depends upon whether the class-relations which the system of ownership involves permit an equal response to the claims made upon the product to be distributed. And it has been the thesis of this book that the function of the state is to protect all the implications of a given sysem of class-relations at any moment of time. By doing so, it assures continuity of production, which is necessary to the maintenance of social life. But by doing so, it necessarily, also, assures those differential claims upon the result of the productive process which are implied in the system of class-relations.

I have pointed out that every society is the theatre of a conflict between economic classes for a larger material benefit, for, that is, a larger share in the results to be distributed from the productive process. Since the power to produce within any society is dependent upon peace, the state must maintain law and order to that end. But, in so doing, it is necessarily maintaining the law and order implied in the particular system of class-relations of which it is the expression. In feudal society, that is, the law and order which the state maintains is the law and order necessary to the preservation of feudal principles. In a capitalist society, the state maintains the law and order necessary to preserve capitalist principles. In a society like that of Soviet Russia, where the instruments of production are owned in common, the law and order of the Soviet state will be used to enforce the distributive consequences of such common ownership. The state, that is to say, is always at the disposal of that class in the community in which is vested the legal title to the ownership of those instruments. The law it makes will be law for their interest. The ownership it maintains will be their ownership. If the number of owners, therefore, in a state be few, the bias of the law will be towards the interest of that few. If the owners be the community as a whole, then the bias of the law will be towards the interest of the community as a whole as against, say, the particular interest of some given individual.

I have also pointed out how the system of class-relations in a given society is the main factor in shaping the general ideology of the society. Religious doctrines in a capitalist state built on free labour, for instance, will have a different complexion, will be given a different interpretation, from what they will have in a capitalist society built on slave-labour. Christianity, for example, starting, very largely, as a religion of the disinherited, preached a doctrine which was incompatible with the institution of slavery. But, very early in its history, it began to attract to its membership members of the slave-owning class. Had it insisted that they free their slaves as a condition of membership, it would have effected an economic revolution incompatible with the relations within the system of production then existing. That would have made it the enemy of all whose interest it was to maintain the institution of slavery; and it could not afford to incur their enmity since, behind them, was all the coercive power of the Roman state. It therefore explained that the duty of slaves was obedience to their masters; and it justified that departure from its original attitude by arguing, first, that slavery is a mere external badge irrelevant to that salvation secured by membership of the state, and, second, that it was the duty of all slave-owners to treat their slaves kindly. By these adjustments, it made its adoption by the empire as the official religion a feasible adventure. As, moreover, it became itself a powerful organization with large properties whose value depended upon their exploitation by slaves, its original dislike of the institution fell more and more into the background.

We may say, then, that the power of the state is coincident with the power of private property, in any society where the essential instruments of production are in private hands. Wherever we encounter a society of this type, we always find that the exercise of the state-power is ultimately in those hands. They decide what is to be the law. They settle, therefore, the ends to which the use of the state-power is to be devoted. And since their conception of those ends will be determined by their position in the scheme of class-relationships, they will seek for the maximum material benefit they can obtain from this scheme; this will be the basis upon which they build their idea of good; and they will shape the law of the state to secure their title to that benefit. But, since other economic classes will be doing the same, it follows that whatever conception of good is backed by the supreme coercive power of the society, that is, by the state, will predominate in the society. There is, therefore, inherent in any society built upon a class-structure of this kind a necessary struggle for the possession of the state-power. For those who possess it are able to impose their conception of good upon the others.

I have pointed out that this conception of good is not a static thing. With the growth of knowledge, there are both a change in the methods of production and an increase in our capacity to produce. Class-relationships must adjust themselves to that change and that increase. For they set what men conceive themselves entitled to expect from the system of production; and they will regard the sum of their expectations at any given period as the equivalent of justice. Clearly, moreover, men in the same general position in a scheme of class-relations will tend to have the same general expectations. They will, therefore, have a solidarity of interest, a similar notion of what constitutes justice. The wider the disparity of position they occupy in the scheme of class-relations, the wider will be the difference in their notions of justice. And since these notions are always struggling against each other for survival, the degree of their difference sets the measure in which the state can maintain unity between its citizens. When the difference is too profound for compromise between opposing views to be possible, the unity of the state is broken. To break the unity of the state, of course, means the interruption of peace, the suspension of the orderly processes of law. A breach of unity threatens the life of the society by interrupting the process of production. When this occurs, the unity of the state has to be re-established; and this is achieved either by re-affirming the purposes of the state (if those are successful in the struggle who previously operated its power), or by re-defining those purposes (if their opponents are victorious).

The unity of the state can be broken only by the antagonisms of the class-struggle. All other oppositions, religious, national, racial, which result in open conflict may change the personnel of the government, but they will never break the fundamental unity of the state in the sense of involving a re-definition of class-relations. South American states remain much the same despite the bewildering succession of revolutionary changes in their governments. The victory of Hitler in Germany was a change of government and not a change in the state; it was not a revolution in the same essential sense as the French Revolution of 1789, or the Russian Revolution of November 1917. For, with the victory of Hitler, the same class-relations persisted after his capture of the state as before it; essentially, that is, he did not in practice alter the definition of the purposes of the state.

Both the French and the Russian Revolutions did precisely this work of re-definition. The French Revolution, broadly speaking, affirmed the right of property-owners to a share in the results of the productive process indifferently to the question of whether they were or not of aristocratic birth; the Russian Revolution, again broadly speaking, affirmed the right of working-class citizens to a share in the results of the productive process indifferently to the question of whether they were or not the owners of the instruments of production. The French Revolution attained its end by using the power of the state to abolish the privileges of the aristocracy; a new legal equilibrium was organized in which ownership as such was the basis of rights. The Russian Revolution attained its end by using the power of the state to abolish private ownership in the means of production; it transferred the title to the rights of ownership from the individual to the association of citizens organized as a state. The French Revolution, therefore, used the state-power to defend a conception of good interpreted in the interest of those who owned the instruments of production. The Russian Revolution used the state-power to defend a conception of good in a similar interest; but, in its case, whether the methods of defence were wise or unwise, that interest was co-extensive with the total membership of the state.

It is, no doubt, true that the state always claims to be a neutral arbitrator seeking the good of the whole society impartially; its effort to resolve the antagonisms inherent in a system of production will always, at least nominally, be made to that end. But if the analysis here made is correct, the claim of neutrality can never be valid when one economic class owns the instruments of production. For since ownership determines the use to which political power will be devoted, its possession by the few must always mean its use for a few. Their view of good, of justice, of right, will colour all the operations of the state. By maintaining private ownership in the hands of the few, the state necessarily excludes others from access to its fruits. The state is a legal instrument for making the claims of private owners to the resources of production predominant over other claims from those who do not own. On this view, the state can never be neutral as between its citizens in matters which relate to material welfare so long as the instruments of production are not held in common on behalf of the society.

One further point we may reiterate. Class-antagonisms, that is, differences between economic classes as to the way in which the social product shall be distributed, issue into social conflict whenever the class-relations which a state maintains prevent that exploitation of the productive forces which is deemed possible by the class excluded from the full benefits of ownership from being realized. There may be revolutions in the personnel of government upon other terms; it is upon these terms only that there will be a revolution in the state. We should not, therefore, expect a revolution in any state where the class excluded from the full benefits of ownership is receiving a continuous addition to its material well-being. We should expect it only when the material well-being it expects is, over a period, denied at the level it deems possible of realization, and when it connects that denial with the system of class-relations which the state maintains. Any class which becomes conscious of that connexion will, from the moment of that consciousness, move towards the capture of the state. For, thereby, it may hope so to re-define the system as to realize the material well-being to which it believes itself entitled. By capturing the state, in other words, a class hopes to make its view of justice prevail.

This view was compressed by the *Communist Manifesto* into a famous sentence. "The executive of the modern state," wrote Marx and Engels, "is simply a committee for managing the common affairs of the bourgeoisie." It is important to note the implications of that insistence. The state may be viewed from two angles. On the one hand, it appears as a small body of men issuing orders, behind which there is the supreme coercive power, to the rest of the community; on the other, it appears, much as the idealists conceived it, as an influence which permeates every nook and cranny of society and shapes all institutions and persons to its ends. The two aspects are only sides of a single process. The state as a committee of men issuing orders is concerned, at bottom, with ordering the relations upon which the mode of production depends; and the state as this widely permeating influence defines the relevance of all behaviour, institutional and personal, to those relations. We shall therefore find the ultimate explanation of all social habits in the context of the state-process, where these habits affect the relations which grow out of the mode of production. The state will concern itself with all behaviour which touches those relations, and it will seek to control it in the interest of the class which predominates at any given time.

VI

An analysis such as this may seem to many students of politics a denial of things they have deemed fundamental in the experience of the modern state. To represent history as the deposit of the results of class-struggles, to view the state as simply the instrument of the predominant class at any given time, to insist that all law essentially takes its colour from the interest of that class, is to do profound injustice to the principles of our social arrangements. History, we are told, is the record of changes made by men in pursuit of a scheme of things better than the traditional arrangements they inherited; and the true way to regard the state is as a mechanism for the promotion of the ideal. We know that many statesmen devote all their energies to the sincere and unselfish service of the public; why assume that the result of their effort is to maintain the good of a class rather than the good of the whole community? Modern law, whatever may have been the case in earlier ages, assumes that all citizens are equal before its courts; and the incorruptibility and independence of contemporary English judges, for example, are an object of admiration to the whole world. No modern state would subordinate human rights to the interests of property; that is shown by the whole character of modern legislation. When the state concerns itself with the quality of our food, the protection of child welfare, the safeguarding of the unemployed against industrial insecurity, the provision of educational opportunity—all of them services provided at the expense of that minority, the taxpayers—it is rhetorical exaggeration to regard it as a class-instrument.

Nor is this all. The last century has seen so marked and so constant an improvement in the position of the non-possessing classes that, with increasing command over nature and a profounder social conscience, we may hope for even greater improvement in the years to come. We may note, further, the way in which the state has invaded, in the interest of the community, spheres of commercial enterprise, the railways, banking, broadcasting, for example, which were formerly regarded as legitimate spheres of private profit-making. We curb monopolies at every turn in the interest of the general consumer. We prohibit the practice of sweating in industry. Legislation like the Factory Acts, Workmen's Compensation, the limitation of the hours of labour, the prohibition of noxious materials in industrial processes, all show a concern by the state to subordinate profit-making to the public welfare. As public opinion grows more enlightened, we may expect that concern to grow; and, as it grows, the increasing tendency of state-action will be to free itself from the bias of service to any special interest in the community. The more profoundly, therefore, we analyse the functions of the modern state the more impossible we shall find it to regard its activities as no more than the expression of class-antagonisms.

The attractiveness of such a view needs no emphasis from me; but its plausibility does not conceal the defects from which it suffers. It does not explain why men's ideas of what constitutes social justice should change from period to period; why, for example, slavery should seem tolerable in one age, and intolerable in another. It fails altogether to draw attention to the fact that all the gains it emphasizes have had to be fought for grimly by those upon whom they conferred benefit. It took over sixty years of hard effort to establish in England the idea that the state should be responsible for the elementary education of its citizens; and the number of those who can take advantage of the advanced education which expert authority regards as essential to intellectual development remains pitifully small.[1] We have imposed certain limitations upon the hours of labour; but, to take only certain obvious instances, the position of shop assistants, domestic servants, and agricultural labourers remains profoundly unsatisfactory. Factory Acts and Workmen's Compensation remain a theatre of conflict between employers and employed as real, if less dramatic, as they were in the nineteenth century; the substantial difference is that we fight now not over the principle, but over the level and quality of its application.[2] We tackle the sweated industry and the slum; but there remains a wide divergence of opinion about what are sweating and slum conditions.[3] We maintain the unemployed at a certain level of subsistence by unemployment insurance and public assistance; but their own account of the life this maintenance makes possible ought to leave no observer without an acute sense of discomfort.[4]

What we call, in fact, the growth of a social conscience is simply the changed idea of established expectation which has been brought about by the class-struggle. The owners of the

---

[1] Cf. R. H. Tawney, *Equality* (1931), Chap. III, and the notes to that chapter.

[2] Cf. the discussion over the proposed revision of the hours of shop assistants. Parl. Papers (1930–1), Vol. IX, Rep. 148.

[3] As was revealed in 1934 in the discussion over railway wages and the criticism of Sir Hilton Young's proposals for clearing the slums. Cf. the correspondence in *The Times* (London) for October, 1934.

[4] H. L. Beales and R. S. Lambert, *Memoirs of the Unemployed* (1934); E. Bakke, *The Unemployed Man* (1934).

instruments of production are compelled, by the pressure of that struggle, to give way at certain points, even, on occasion, at critical points; but they surrender the outworks, they do not yield the central citadel. The effective measure of the title to material benefit in society remains what it was in the origins of the capitalist system—the possession of wealth. Conceptions of justice have still to operate within the framework of possibility set by that fundamental postulate. When we are told that we cannot afford the cost of raising the school-leaving age to fifteen at the same time as we begin a new competition in armaments; [1] when the restoration of the economy cuts of 1931 has to be balanced against the demands of the super-taxpayer; when the housing subsidies can be suspended simultaneously with the making of large grants to shipping, sugar-beet, and the fat-stock farmers (all without the exaction of any limits to the industrial condition of the labour employed therein); it is surely obvious that the conflict of values is no less profound than in any previous age. What has changed is the purposes about which it concentrates. The conflict is still there.

Its decision, moreover, still depends upon the power of economic classes to influence the action of the state. And while the latter is dominated by the class which exploits the instruments of production in terms of the profit-making motive, it is difficult to see how any other consideration than this motive implies can determine the things our social conscience is likely to approve. A period of economic expansion will, no doubt, extend the boundaries of the social conscience; but the history of the post-war period shows decisively that

[1] Lord Irwin in the House of Lords. *Hansard* (House of Lords), Vol. XCIII, pp. 495–6.

its boundaries contract with the contraction of profit. So long, that is, as the legal relations of a society are intended to protect the implications of its class-structure, the necessities of that structure set the limits within which the boundaries of our social conscience can extend. Their flexibility is, as I have sought to show, well emphasized by the experience of Germany and Italy; and the only way to alter the limits within which they move is by altering the class-structure which defines them.

It will be helpful, at this point, to examine the idea of equality before the law as the supreme instance of the way in which the claim of a principle to universality is narrowed in its application by the need to subordinate its working to the fundamental postulates of the society where, formally, it is applied as a universal. We do not need to argue that all law is a product of the class-struggle. It is clear enough that a good deal of law, in commercial matters, for instance, and, even more, in procedure, represents principles quite remote from it. But it is equally clear, I think, that the idea of the class-struggle permeates legal notions at every point of pivotal importance. The law of sedition is unintelligible except as an effort to protect the *status quo* from the threat of invasion. It is a safeguard, we say, of law and order; but the law and order it safeguards are what maintain a particular system of class-relations from the threat of challenge. The attitude of our courts in trade-union cases is, again, unintelligible except as the expression of a mental climate which has never freed itself from the belief that trade unions are organizations threatening the equilibrium of a society built upon the principle that the means of production must remain in private hands. The use of the injunction in labour disputes by the

American courts[1] is as a weapon in class-warfare. The attitude of the Supreme Court of the United States to social legislation was largely built, as its great member, Mr. Justice Holmes, had occasion to remind it,[2] upon the half-conscious assumption that the Fourteenth Amendment had written Mr. Herbert Spencer's *Social Statics* into the fabric of the Constitution. The House of Lords—which does not overrule its own decisions—has laid down in *Roberts v. Hopwood*[3] principles of statutory interpretation which suggest that a local authority, entitled by statute to pay "such wages as it thinks fit," must use its discretionary power "reasonably"; and "reasonably" is then explained—or explained away—as meaning wages not more than ten percent above the level prevailing in the district for the class of work concerned. Judge Parry has shown how the early interpretations of the Workmen's Compensation Act would have rendered its whole intention nugatory because they were built upon a judicial dislike, intelligible enough in a capitalist society, of collectivist legislation. Anyone who reflects upon the treason trials of the Napoleonic period,[4] or the atmosphere which has surrounded the "free speech" cases in the United States in the last fifteen or twenty years,[5] will not find it difficult to insist that the judiciary cannot transcend the class-structure of the society in which it works.

Nor must we forget the fact that wealth is a decisive factor in the power to take advantage of the opportunities the law affords its citizens to protect their rights. The ability to

[1] F. Frankfurter and N. Greene, *The Labor Injunction* (1930).
[2] *Adair v. U. S.* (1908) 208 U. S. 161.
[3] (1925) A. C. 578.
[4] Cockburn, *An Examination of the Trials for Sedition in Scotland.*
[5] Chafee, *Freedom of Speech* (1920).

undertake an action in the courts, even with the provision made for legal aid to the poor, remains a grim financial question, and, on the civil side of the law, with its massive hierarchy of appeals, the advantage is solidly with the rich. Broadly, there is equality before the law only when the price of admission to its opportunities can be equally paid; and there is no administrative equity to redress this balance. It is simply inherent in a society with the class-relations of our own. And it is those class-relations also which mean that, as a general rule, the ablest lawyers will be at the service of those only who are able to afford them. The successful lawyer—the class from which, in the Anglo-American system, the members of the judiciary are mostly drawn—spends his life in ministering to the dominating class of our society. It is wholly natural, therefore, that he should come, as a general rule, to share its outlook, that his intellectual influence, therefore, should largely be exercised on its behalf. It is a sound instinct that has persuaded the working-classes to look upon the legal profession as one of the protective ramparts of conservatism.[1]

I am not, it must be noted, in any way or in any degree challenging the goodwill of the lawyer or the legal system. I am merely saying that, once the postulates of the society in which they function imply inequality, the main burden of their influence should be towards maintaining it. And when, as with ourselves, so large a part of law is rooted in precedent, it is natural for the lawyer's mind to dwell upon continuity with the past rather than departure from it. Judge-made law is rarely innovating law unless, as with the work of Chief Justice Holt and Lord Mansfield, it deals with a situation in which the guiding precedents are few or non-existent;

[1] Cf. my *Democracy in Crisis* (1933), pp. 128 f.

and where the lawyer, as with Mr. Chief Justice Marshall, or Lord Abinger in *Priestley v. Fowler*,[1] confronts an experiment in which the rights of property are in serious hazard, the emphasis of his work will always tend to be towards supporting them rather than attacking them. That is surely why most great movements for legal reform have either come from outside the profession altogether, or from members of it who, like Bentham, have had a very peripheral connexion with it. The business of a legal system is to make the postulates of a society work. It would be remarkable indeed if it could be so worked as to secure their fundamental transformation.

Liberal-minded thinkers are often moved to traverse this position by two considerations. The typical modern state, they argue, especially when it is a democratic state, is a *Rechtstaat*; it is built upon the rule of law. And that this rule of law may bind, not merely the ordinary citizen, but also the very government which operates the state-power, its judiciary is separate from, and independent of, the executive in order that the law may, both as to doctrine and as to persons, be impartially applied.

But the idea of a *Rechtstaat* is a purely conceptual notion; it is a category of essence and not of reality. It makes the rulers of a state bound by the law they make; but it still leaves them free, through the use of the appropriate organs, to make the law. The Hitlerite state, equally with that of Great Britain or France or Czechoslovakia, is a *Rechtstaat* in the sense that dictatorial power has been transferred to the *Führer* by the legal order. The British government is bound by a mass of legal rules like the Habeas Corpus Act and the principles governing its right to take property laid down in

[1] (1837) 3 M. & W. 1.

the *de Keyser's Hotel* case;[1] but it has the power, under a statute like the Emergency Powers Act,[2] to suspend all these rules when it thinks fit. It can be guilty, as in *ex parte O'Brien*,[3] of grave illegalities, and decide that it shall not bear the penalty for their commission by an Act of Indemnity. The idea of *Rechtstaat* is always qualified by the fact that the state is able, through its sovereignty, to change the substance of the law. Formally, the idea of legal absolutism is inherent in the nature of sovereignty; and, in a crisis, the needs of the established expectations of the *Rechtstaat* will always give way to the view taken by its rulers of the needs revealed by the crisis. No one, certainly of those who made the Weimar Constitution in 1919, expected Article 48 to be used as the foundation upon which to build the Hitlerite state.

We need not, either, deny the value of the separation of judicial from executive power—which I believe to be very great—to realize that its importance in this realm is definitely limited. For, in the first place, the doctrines which the judges must normally apply are given to them by the legislation they interpret; and this expresses, in a capitalist society, the fundamental purposes of that sociey. The judges, secondly, are nominated by the executive power; and the greater their authority in the state, the greater care will the executive take to see that it nominates men to judicial position upon whose general attitude, broadly speaking, it can rely. Anyone can verify this conclusion for himself by analysing the history of nominations to the Supreme Court of the United States; the attitude of the proposed appointee to political and eco-

---

[1] See the special report *The Case of Requisition*, ed. L. Scott (1920).
[2] Text in Keir and Lawson, *Cases in Constitutional Law* (1929), pp. 365–7.
[3] (1923) A. C. 603.

nomic questions has always been a pivotal consideration in his choice.[1] And the fact that the lawyer is usually a member of the property-owning class tends to make him, in any case, sympathetic towards the general outlook of that class [2]; the difficulty the British Labour Party has confronted in this realm is well known. And where, as on the Continent of Europe, the doctrine of the "free discretion" of judges has found institutional expression, it has, significantly, been a profoundly conservative influence in statutory interpretation.[3]

To appreciate fully the significance of this limited value in the separation of judiciary and executive, it is worth while to dwell for a moment upon the operation of the American Supreme Court. For in no other country has economic development been so largely shaped by judicial decision. Anyone who examines the first fifty years of the court's history will find the clue to its attitude in that line of decisions of which *Fletcher v. Peck* [4] and the *Dartmouth College* case [5] are the most notable, where the purpose of the judges was to protect the vested interests of property from invasion by state legislatures which were being driven by the economic difficulties of their constituents to inflation, the reduction of debts, and the cancellation of property rights. This epoch of judicial nationalism, so remarkably inaugurated by Marshall, was obviously an expression of Federalist effort to secure the conditions under which commerce could flourish without inter-

---

[1] On this the *locus classicus* is the Senate inquiry into the appointment of Mr. Justice Brandeis in 1916; and see G. Myers, *History of the American Supreme Court* (1912), which must, however, be used with caution.

[2] Cf. Mr. Winston Churchill in 26 *Hansard Debates* (fifth series, 1911), 1022, and Geldart, *The Present Law of Trade Unions* (1914), p. 44, for the attitude of the British courts in trade union cases.

[3] Cf. F. Neumann, *Die politische und soziale Bedeutung der arbeitsgerichtlichen Rechtsprechung* (1929).

[4] (1810) 6 Crouch 37.

[5] (1819) 4 Wheaton 518.

ference from those who had suffered through the poverty resulting from the Revolutionary War. This explains the court's view both of the Commerce Clause, as in *Gibbons v. Ogden*,[1] and the "obligation of contract" clause in the Constitution.

These first fifty years summarize a period in the history of the United States in which the pattern of a modern industrial society is only beginning to emerge. The work necessary for that stage was well accomplished by Marshall and his immediate successors. From 1830 until the Civil War the court hardly needed to do more than apply the canons of constitutionalism it had already laid down. Its attitude, indeed, to the land and monetary experiments of the West showed that it associated the vested interests of property with something very akin to the idea of fundamental law.[2] The *Dred Scott* decision made it clear that the issue between industrial and agrarian capitalism had still to be decided.[3] But once that issue was clearly posed, as it was after the *San Mateo* case,[4] it is clear, above all in the work of Mr. Justice Field, that the driving motivation of the court was to protect the needs of expanding industry even if its decisions were, as Mr. Choate put it in *Pollock v. Farmers' Loan and Trust Co.*,[5] "to incense a mighty army of sixty million citizens." By 1880 the Supreme Court had become the passionate exponent of economic *laissez-faire*.

It remained this for a quarter of a century. During this

---

[1] (1824) 9. Wheaton 1.

[2] Cf. C. G. Haines, *The American Doctrine of Judicial Supremacy* (1932), pp. 400 f.

[3] (1856) 19. Howard 383.

[4] *County of San Mateo v. Southern Pacific Railroad* (1885). 116 U. S. 138.

[5] (1895) 158 U. S. 601.

period its dominating purpose was simply to prevent interference with business enterprise by government regulation, whether state or federal. It evolved conceptions of liberty of contract, of due process of law, of the police power, of reasonableness, all of which operated to protect business men in the unhampered pursuit of profit. *Smyth v. Ames,*[1] the *Employers' Liability* cases,[2] *Lochner v. New York,*[3] *Pollock v. Farmers' Loan and Trust Co.,*[4] are all decisions which illustrate that selection of the postulates upon which the judge proceeds to build his conclusions in relation to the dominant economic pattern of the time. For all their attempt to be law rather than politics, they illustrate the inevitability that constitutional law must be subordinated in a capitalist society to the needs of capitalism.

And it is interesting to note that the last thirty years of the court's history have not changed the fundamental emphasis of its work. The doubts and hesitations of the American people about the operations of giant capitalism, the attempt at regulation, the movement, as in the application of the Sherman Law, to limit the size of trusts, even, as with Mr. Justice Holmes,[5] the scepticism of the wisdom of judicial control of legislation, have been reflected in the decisions of the court. It has bent before great emergencies like the war and the great depression more slowly indeed, and more tentatively, than Congress; but it has bent before them. The emergence of an active communist movement excited it more soberly,

[1] (1898) 169 U. S. 466.
[2] (1908) 207 U. S. 463.
[3] (1905) 198 U. S. 45.
[4] *Ut supra.*
[5] Cf. my *Studies in Law and Politics* (1932), pp. 146 f.

but not less profoundly, than it excited business enterprise.[1] It showed the characteristic inability of the capitalist to realize that a pacifist could be a good patriot.[2] It admitted, though doubtfully,[3] the constitutionality of the Roosevelt legislation. Anyone who examines the work of the court in the last thirty years generally, and the last fifteen years in particular, will, I think, be tempted to one broad conclusion. He will feel that the growing volume of protest in America against the unrestricted capitalism of the period from 1865 to 1900—a capitalism itself reflected in the decisions of the court—have now penetrated to the mind of the Bench. But it has not yet learned how to weave the needs of capitalism, on the one hand, and the needs of social regulation, on the other, into an harmonious body of constitutional criteria. Only two of the judges in this period have approached that task with a considered philosophy. Mr. Justice Holmes approached it on the principle that what a legislature wants it must have unless its desires expressly deny the plain intent of the Constitution [4]; and Mr. Justice Brandeis approached it on the principle that a capitalist structure can be evolved the units of which are small enough in size to permit of their effective regulation in the public interest.[5] But it has yet to be shown that either philosophy can solve the grave contradictions in which American capitalism has become involved.

I have not attempted this analysis of the attitude of the

---

[1] *Whitney v. California* (1927) 274 U. S. 357.

[2] *U. S. v. Schwimmer* (1928) 279 U. S. 644.

[3] Though much of this is still subject to challenge in the present (1934–5) year of the court.

[4] *Noble State Bank v. Haskell* (1911) 219 U. S. 104.

[5] Cf. Frankfurter (ed.), *Mr. Justice Brandeis* (1933), esp. the admirable essay of Mr. Max Lerner.

Supreme Court because there is anything different therein from that which has moved the courts of other countries. On the contrary, I have attempted it because the special functions of the Supreme Court compel it to make explicit assumptions which, elsewhere, are more usually set out in actual legislation. And what is plain in the history of the court is the outstanding fact that the texture of its law is never remote from the texture of life. Each is shaped by the same pressures; and the forms of these are given by the ultimate economic background of the society. Law, that is to say, is never impartial in the sense of being above the battle, or indifferent to the results which may emerge. The courts, on the contrary, are a fundamental instrument in that battle. They shape the contours of the society, more interstitially, perhaps, because less directly, than either the legislature or the executive; but they are bound to the same purpose. They give effect to the result of the conflicting class-antagonisms which pervade the atmosphere in which they have to work.

VII

Ultimately, therefore, the denial of the argument upon which this book is based must be built upon the ability to show that the present phase of class-relations is no hindrance to the full use of its productive power by society. If it is demonstrable that capitalism can always find a practicable way out of its crises, that a depression like that by which the world has been afflicted since 1929 is merely a halt on the road to recovery, rather than a symptom of a fatal disease, then, clearly, it becomes possible, with recovery, to transcend the immediate contradictions of the system by moving to a new productive equilibrium in which the demands of the working-classes for material benefit can be satisfied at a new high level. Where this can be effected it is unlikely, as I have argued, that there will be an effort by the working-class to re-define the class-relations of the society. Revolution only comes when a class in its position is convinced that, within the existing class-relations, the new high level, though potentially there, is in fact unattainable.

The attempt to prove that recovery is possible takes various forms. One school of thought attempts to show that the depression is the result of our failure to act in terms of what the postulates of capitalism require; and we are told that we can secure the conditions of a recovery only by returning to them. In a capitalist society, a rigorous policy of *laissez-faire* is the condition of economic well-being.

The weakness in this argument is its wholly abstract character. Its capitalism is not the capitalism of capitalists, but that of an ideal world which, in our lifetime at least, has never resembled the actual world we know. Not only are its proposals revolutionary in character—for it is difficult to see how we could abandon all the social responsibilities of the modern state without a revolution—but they all turn upon the achievement, as I have already noted,[1] of political stability. But this we cannot achieve independently of the economic condition of society; for political stability is a function of those economic factors upon which society is based. What the *laissez-faire* economists tell us is that their ideal capitalism would produce the new equilibrium we desire if the price of its realization is paid. But since (a) the price of that realization is the abandonment of something like the social legisla-

---

[1] *Supra*, Chap. I.

tion of the last thirty or forty years, and since (b) that legislation was the outcome, however unwise, of our experience of actual capitalism in operation, we may reasonably doubt whether men are prepared to pay the price.

Another school of thought is more pragmatic in its approach; and, like Sir Arthur Salter and Mr. Keynes, it finds in a much wider form of state-experiment and control the possibility of subordinating the profit-making motive to our needs. It points out, particularly, the significance of the growth of new forms of enterprise, notably the public corporation, in which the private owner of property becomes a debenture-holder, even a debenture-owner paid out after a limited period of years, without the right to participate in the control of the enterprise. By extending the field of state-regulation, in something of the temper in which Mr. Roosevelt has approached his task, it is confident that we can enter a new phase of economic well-being.[1]

At bottom this argument rests upon some interesting assumptions. It is built, first, upon the view that, amidst the economic struggle of classes, the state can be an impartial arbiter concerned only for total well-being. It infers from this view, therefore, that the economic postulates of a given society do not push the state in the direction called for by those postulates. It infers, further, the power of law to override the capitalist desire for profit, by dividing it into categories of "good" or "bad," "excessive" or "legitimate," according to its source and extent, the category itself being determined by the judgment of the impartial state. It realizes

[1] Cf. Sir Arthur Salter, *Recovery* (1932), for one of the best expressions of this attitude.

the impossibility of a return to the habits of the *laissez-faire* period; but it assumes the possibility of a *via media* between capitalism and socialism directed by the state in the interest of the whole community, but without any change in the essential structure of class-relations.

I have already given reasons why this view seems to me incompatible with the facts we have to face. Its assumption of an impartial state which can rise above the class-antagonisms its power has somehow to settle has no roots in reality. Given the character of our society there may be states willing to go further than others in the price they will pay for social peace; of more than this we have no evidence. "Good" and "bad" in economics cannot be made effective categories of the kind assumed; they mean, in their economic context, "leading to profit" or "not leading to profit." Anyone who considers the history of capitalism, not least in its imperialist phase, will find it difficult to believe that its inherent drive to profit will suddenly accept ethical limitations from which the whole of its past has been singularly free. For it is, I think, a fatal weakness in this demand for ethical limitations that it views them as standing apart from the economic process instead of being born of its operation. The ethically valid is always pretty co-extensive with the economically possible. The history of British exploitation of Africa is surely sufficient proof of that. We have set up admirable principles of trusteeship through which to safeguard the interests of the native races there; but immediately gold is discovered on the native reserves, we can exhaust the resources of human reason to discover grounds upon which to invade those reserves. We can even persuade ourselves to believe that the native ought to accept our view that it is for his benefit that we are above all concerned.[1] Can men who, between 1930 and 1933, are capable of changing the whole emphasis of land policy in Kenya really be trusted to use the state as an impartial instrument?

But these men are sincere; they are seeking to do their best; they genuinely will the good of the whole community. Of course they are and do; this book will have been written wholly in vain if it suggests that I cast any doubt upon the motives of statesmen. My argument is the very different one that ideas of good are never absolute, but relative always to a given economic environment. And I have urged that, in this environment, the function each class performs in the economic system will, broadly, shape its ideas of good. To argue this is to deny the possibility of an impartial state; for it is to insist that, once the claims on material well-being are different, the class which owns the instruments of production will be able, unquestionably with the conviction of beneficent purpose, to use the power of the state to make its ideas prevail. But such a use of that power will not produce the same conviction in those members of the society who do not own the instruments of production.

The argument of this second school of thought, moreover, does not really meet the essential charge which is implied in the theory here put forward. My case has been that, whenever the class-relations of a given society make it impossible to distribute the results of the productive process, men whose expectations of material benefit are continuously disappointed will seek to change those class-relations; and I have suggested that, unless the possessing class voluntarily

---

[1] Sir Philip Cunliffe-Lister, December 20, 1932, *Hansard* (fifth series), Vol. 273, p. 912.

abdicates—the rarest event in history—the resultant position involves a social revolution. I have not suggested that the revolution will necessarily be successful; I have suggested only that such an attempt is inescapable.

I believe that we have reached a phase in the history of capitalism when this contradiction between class-structure and potential productivity is insoluble in terms of the present social order. I do not accept, therefore, such a diagnosis as President Roosevelt makes when he declares that our present difficulties are due to the unethical practices of some business men, and acts upon the presumption that the removal of those practices will restore the health of the body economic.[1] I do not, either, believe, as Mr. Keynes believes,[2] that there is an inherent tendency in all large-scale public enterprise to develop an ethical practice in which private interest is subordinated to an abstract and objective social good.

The roots of our difficulties surely lie deeper than is suggested by these hypotheses. "There must be something fundamentally wrong with our economic system," Mr. Lloyd George has said,[3] "because abundance produces scarcity." That is the pivotal fact from which we have to start. There has been an immense increase of our productive capacity; the Director of the International Labour Office, to take only a single instance, tells us that "if 200 out of the 1357 boot and shoe factories in the country (the United States) worked full time, they could satisfy the whole existing demand, and the remaining 1157 establishments could be closed down. Simi-

---

[1] Cf. *On Our Way* (1934), pp. 250 f.
[2] *Essays in Persuasion* (1932), p. 314.
[3] Speech at Cambridge, *The Manchester Guardian*, April 17, 1933.

larly, 1487 out of the 6057 bituminous coal mines could produce all the coal that was needed."[1] That situation can be paralleled in every country and for most industrial processes. It leaves us with immense populations for whom no employment can be found. It compels us to subsidize out of taxation whole industries to limit their productivity. It drives us feverishly to search for markets at all costs abroad, even, as with Japan in Manchuria, to risk war with half the world for that end; and to protect the domestic market from invasion it drives us to an economic nationalism which, in the years from 1929 to 1932, was responsible for a decrease in production in capitalist countries of over thirty-seven percent.[2] And this is not a temporary phenomenon due to the kind of depression we have known in the past. It has lasted, so far, for fourteen years in Great Britain; and even in the United States, technologically the best equipped country in the world, the depression is five years old, with no sign today[3] of visible permanent improvement.

Our situation, says the League of Nations Survey,[4] is without precedent for any period over which modern statistics range; it exercises even those observers who do not doubt the adequacy of the general principles upon which our class-relationships are based. "It is still doubtful," wrote the London *Times* some years ago,[5] "whether the increased production can always be absorbed; it is a very large question whether new industries are created quickly enough to employ the displaced workers. In other words, it remains to be

[1] H. B. Butler, *International Labour Review*, March, 1931, p. 301.
[2] *World Economic Survey*, 1932–3 (League of Nations) (1933), p. 71.
[3] December 1934.
[4] *Op. cit.*, p. 82.
[5] March 8, 1930.

seen how perilously the machine has run ahead of man, and whether some readjustment of social condition may not be imperative." And this "very large question" obtrudes itself at a period when, despite our immensely increased powers of production, the share of labour, the part, that is, of wages and salaries, has fallen consistently in the post-war epoch; [1] a contradiction the significance of which it is unnecessary for me to emphasize.

That is not all. Conservative observers whose goodwill to the existing order is beyond suspicion tell us that, even if the unemployed were absorbed, the disposal of the commodities they would thus produce is not, granted the available capacity of the effective market, a feasible proposition. Of the United States, the Washington correspondent of the London *Times* tells us that "if by some magic a return could be made to the productive maximum of three years ago, there would still be no work for forty-five percent of the present twelve million unemployed" [2]; and it is argued by the same journal that the absorption of the British unemployed "would only precipitate a new crisis." [3] Professor Robbins tells us, with all the authority that belongs to a convinced adherent of orthodox thought, that a reduction in the hours of labour is, despite the new level of individual output, no remedy unless the worker is prepared to accept a further reduction of wages.[4] Migration is no longer a remedy, for the effective reason that no country is any longer willing to risk the burden of an addition to the number of its unemployed. The gravity of the

---

[1] Cf. for the U. S. A., Paul Douglas, *Real Wages in the United States* (1933), and, for Great Britain, Colin Clark, *The National Income*, 1924–31 (1933).

[2] November 2, 1932.

[3] *Times Trades Supplement*, July 23, 1932.

[4] *Op. cit.*, pp. 126 f.

situation was put bluntly to the House of Commons by Mr. Ramsay MacDonald when he warned it that even the return of prosperity might leave Great Britain with the obligation to maintain "great bodies of men and women, perhaps amounting even to a couple of millions, to be, to all intents and purposes, in our society, superfluous scrap." [1]

It is evident enough that the implications of this position are by their nature revolutionary. I do not think it is a serious remedy for them, to suggest, with Lord Eustace Percy, a return to the simpler life, with the right to exchange the use of political power to secure material comfort for the privilege of a quickened religious emotion.[2] I do not either believe that the eminent French statesman who would make it a function of the state to prevent the exploitation of inventions, "lest the machine devour humanity," has got to the heart of the problem [3]; the Hitlerite government has embarked upon this policy, but it does not commend itself to the enterprising manufacturer.[4] It is a fantastic notion to suggest that the science which has made possible the whole scale of modern civilization can now be asked to admit itself the enemy of humankind. If, as appears, the present scheme of class-relations makes it impossible for us effectively to utilize the instruments of production, we are left with no alternative but a change in the scheme of class-relations. And it is not a change that we can effect piecemeal, by reason of the closely knit texture of our industrial society. We have to satisfy the established expectations of millions of men and women who

---

[1] *Hansard* (fifth series), Vol. 273, pp. 33–4, November 22, 1932.

[2] Government in Transition (1934), last chapter.

[3] M. Joseph Caillaux in *Times*, March 2, 1934, and cf. *ibid.*, March 10 (leading article).

[4] *Economist*, February 24, 1934.

compare their position as "industrial scrap" with the productive possibilities of our machines. We have to do so remembering the significance of Mr. Keynes's famous remark that men will not always starve quietly.

There is another remark of Mr. Keynes which is immensely significant also in this context. He has pointed out that the very nature of capitalist society requires it to be immensely more successful than any alternative if it is to maintain its hold upon the allegiance of men.[1] It is precisely this doubt of the foundations that has come into our horizon. Capitalism in expansion could maintain that hold because its success enabled it to be tolerant, to confer political emancipation, to offer to citizens a standard of life which seemed to keep pace with its own development. Capitalism in crisis can do none of these things. More than this: as doubt of its foundations grows, it is compelled to exact by violence what previously it could win by consent. As its own security is jeopardized, it has increasingly to rely upon the power of the state to impose a code of behaviour which, half a century ago, seemed to most citizens coincident with the order of nature. But, over a period, as I have argued, any system built upon repression by force must be able to transform itself into a regime of consent if it desires to be secure; for security is always the condition precedent to economic well-being.

The only way in which the capitalism of crisis could discover this security would be by inventing a new ideology which persuaded men to be satisfied with the material standards of its epoch of decay. But new ideologies are not invented out of whole cloth. They rise and fall, as I have sought to show, with the rise and fall of new systems of class-

[1] *Essays in Persuasion* (1931), p. 307.

relations. And if it be said that Fascism is such a new ideology, the answer is, I think, the sufficient one that, so far from this being the case, Fascism, when closely examined, proves to be nothing more than an ill-assorted rag-bag in which all kinds of remnants from the most diverse philosophies seek, as best they may, to find a place.

This is clear from the proclamations of the leaders themselves. The letter of Mussolini is well known in which he demanded from Bianchi a programme for the movement as the very condition of its survival; [1] and the miscellaneous borrowings from Hegel and Sorel, Bergson and Machiavelli, have given it no doctrinal standing. In 1921, Fascism stood for republicanism, international disarmament, the confiscation of church property and of excessive war-profits; it wanted the land for the peasants, and the transfer of industrial control to syndicates of workers and technicians; it proposed to abolish the Stock Exchange, and to dissolve the banks and limited liabilities companies.[2] It was hostile to the churches [3]; it was bound, wrote Mussolini himself, "to do away with these temples that are doomed to destruction." [4] It was unequivocal in its insistence that practice must go step by step with this theory. It is hardly necessary to point out that it is now in no sense republican, that it has done nothing for disarmament, that it has left the land and industrial property untouched, that it has not only concluded a concordat with the Roman Church which gives the latter control over marriage and a large part of the educational field, but that it now, in Musso-

---

[1] Letter of August 27, 1921; reprinted in *Messaggi e Proclami* (1929), p. 39. Cf. *Political and Social Doctrine of Fascism* (1934), p. 10.

[2] Carlo Avarna di Qualtieri, *Il Fascismo*, p. 17.

[3] Cf. Salvemini, *op. cit.*

[4] *Popolo d'Italia*, April 3, 1921.

lini's own phrase,[1] regards religion "as one of the deepest manifestations of the spirit of man, thus it is not only respected, but defended and protected." Stripped of all its rhetorical trappings Italian Fascism appears quite simply as an insistence upon compulsory obedience to a state whose purpose is to protect existing class-relations.

Nor is the German position different. There, again, we have a mass of ill-digested doctrine. There is racialism, there are highly original theories of what Christianity means, there are new conceptions of the meaning of the *Rechtstaat*.[2] There is the famous programme of Feder, adopted in 1920, and declared unalterable in 1926.[3] Unearned income was to be abolished; the "slavery" of interest was to be broken; all war-profits were to be confiscated; all trusts were to be nationalized; all large concerns were to be based upon the principle of profit-sharing; land required for communal purposes was to be confiscated without compensation. But even before Hitler attained office, it was privately explained that the programme was put forward only "for reasons of diplomacy"; "we must talk the language of the embittered socialist workmen," a capitalist subscriber was told,[4] ". . . or else they wouldn't feel at home with us." "The German," wrote Hitler in his autobiography,[5] "has not the slightest notion how a people must be misled if the adherence of the masses is sought." Once the Nazis were in power all pretence of a reality in their programme was dropped. As in Italy,

---

[1] *Political and Social Doctrine of Fascism* (1934), p. 25.

[2] Cf. O. Koellreuter and Carl Schmitt's writings since the advent of Hitler to power.

[3] Published in an English translation in 1934.

[4] E. A. Mowrer, *Germany Puts the Clock Back* (1933), p. 150.

[5] *Ibid.*, p. 257. Mr. Mowrer points out the interesting fact that these words have been omitted from the twelfth edition (1932) of Hitler's book.

there was endless rhetoric about the new purposes of the state in the Third Reich; but, apart from its attack upon the Jews, the Hitlerite government seems never even to have contemplated an interference with the existing class-relations of society.

On analysis, in short, the corporate state appears as simply a piece of unedifying mythology. When the needs of rhetorical demagogy have been satisfied, it always appears that the fundamental basis of capitalism—the private ownership of the means of production—is to remain undisturbed. There is a change in the form of the state, a substitution of naked dictatorship for parliamentary democracy; but that is all. There may be an insistence, in one of the myriad variations upon Mussolini's "conception of the state as an absolute," that the individual must be subordinated to the social welfare of the whole. But when we examine the inner content of all these high-sounding phrases, they become no more than a garment which serves to conceal the ideological poverty of the new dispensation. Fascism is no more free than any other system from the need to demonstrate that it makes possible a fuller exploitation of the potentialities of the productive system than alternative ways of operating the state-power. And, so far in its history, it has not produced the demonstration for the simple reason that, its rhetoric apart, it is merely an old image with a new face. Since it is built on the maintenance of private ownership of the means of production, it "implicates," in William James's phrase, the present structure of class-relations; and its use of the state-power to regulate those relations, while more forcible and dramatic than that of a parliamentary democracy, cannot, upon the assumptions it makes, find new purposes to which to devote it. The nature of a state is not changed by the adoption of a new terminology; nor does the achievement of old ends by new methods change the character of those ends.

Not, indeed, that the methods are new. The use of force to repress opposition to government is as old a technique as anything in the history of the world. It was the method of the Eastern despot, of the Greek tyrant, of the Roman emperor whose legions were obedient to his will, of the petty princelings who dominated the mediæval Italian city and the small German province. What, perhaps, is new in the situation is the avowed purpose of the new rulers to destroy what Mussolini has called the "stinking corpse" of liberty, and thus to make an end of what, at least from the time of Hellas, has been the noblest motive to action man has so far known. What is, perhaps, new also is the ability of foreign observers to discover in the experience of Fascism a creative synthesis worthy to inaugurate a new epoch in human affairs. What, I think, is new also, at least since the sixteenth century, is the insistence that the reason of men must be uncritically subordinated to faith in a leader whose purpose and practice it is not open to them to examine. It had become, previous to this age, the common assumption of Western civilization that consultation with the common man, his freedom, therefore, to report upon the meaning of his experience, was the one sure road to wise social action; and it was accordingly inferred that ability to satisfy the expectations of that experience was the test of the adequacy of states. In the new dispensation we are offered, there is a denial both that the experience is valid and that the test can be applied. We are invited to return to an age of faith whose orthodoxy has behind it not the sanction of a theology which claims to be founded on the Divine Will [1] but the sanction of violence which knows no limits to its cruelties. It is, I think, legitimate to doubt whether the conditions such an age of faith requires possess the character which can maintain an enduring social order.

VIII

We are now in a position to attempt some positive conclusions. If the analysis here made is correct, it follows that the essence of the state is its power to employ coercion in order to enforce the will of that group or groups which control the government; for it is by the government that the authority of the state is brought into operation. The will of the government is, in its turn, finally determined by the character of the class-relations in society. If these give a different and unequal interest to different classes in the results of the productive process, then the power of the state will always be used to protect the interest of the class which owns the instruments of production. The character of that ownership will determine the rules to be made under which the continuity of production is assured. It will determine, also, the end for which law and order are preserved when these are threatened. It will shape, by its ultimate impact upon society, the behaviour of all institutions which are affected by the preservation of law and order. It will therefore devise a system of ideas by which to convince citizens that the achievement of the purposes it serves are coincident with the good of the society. So long as it

[1] Though Hitler has claimed to be, and has been acclaimed as being, an instrument of the Divine Will.

is a successful economic method, it will be able to win acceptance for its system of ideas. When it begins to fail, its system of ideas and, therefore, its conception of goodwill appear less attractive; and if it is unable to persuade men of its power to become successful again, a power which is a function of its ability to exploit the potentialities of its productive methods, then those whom the system of ownership excludes from the possession of economic power will seek to change the system.

To do so, I have argued, they must utilize the supreme coercive power of the state. They must use it to re-define the system of ownership, which means re-defining the class-relations of the society. That means a change in the ultimate purposes of law which, in the context of property, is always concerned with conferring legal right upon some method of distributing what is produced by the economic process. Behind the title implicit in any given system the state puts all the force at its command. It makes the barren title of law actual by satisfying its demands. The character of each state is therefore determined by the kind of title that it satisfies. This pervades and colours all the relationships in society.

This view is in no way weakened by the changes Western civilization particularly has witnessed during the course of the last seventy years. We have seen the negative state become the positive state, or, to put it in a different way, we have seen the police-state of the nineteenth century become the social-service-state of the twentieth. I have argued that the vital principle in this evolution is the fact that it has been a function of the struggle between economic classes for the possession of the state-power. The change is the price that a capitalist society has had to pay for the retention of the private ownership of the means of production. On the evidence, it has been willing to pay the price so long as it could do so consistently with satisfying the claims of those who owned those instruments. When a contradiction developed between the profits of capitalism and the cost of social service, the assumptions of the latter were necessarily attacked because their increasing realization would render capitalism bankrupt.

But the social-service-state had, as it evolved, given birth to ideas for which men were prepared to fight. Just as capitalism, in its hey-day, produced political democracy as the ultimate answer to the system it overthrew, so the social-service-state gave birth to the idea of social democracy as the answer to a negative or police-state which seemed to make wealth the only effective title to consideration. By the latter part of the nineteenth century that peculiar synthesis we call capitalist democracy had become the accepted ideal of most citizens in Western civilization. It had established political equality. It implied the right of its members to use their political power to improve their material situation. They did so, broadly speaking, by using the taxing-power of the state to confer amenities upon themselves which they could not afford from the wages they received. They came to regard themselves as entitled to expect these amenities from the state; more, as the productive capacity of the economic system expanded, they came to regard themselves as entitled to receive those amenities at a constantly higher level.

The system of capitalist democracy worked well, as I have explained, so long as it was in its period of expansion. But, granted its assumptions, it needed always the capacity to sell its goods in a profitable market. Once it was unable to do this, the fund from which taxes could be drawn, the amenities, therefore, which could be distributed, were bound to shrink unless the capitalist was prepared to forgo his title to profit. But since this title was the assumption upon which capitalist democracy was founded; since, to put it another way, the predominating conception of good in that society was built upon the validity of the title; either there had to be a diminution in the amenities, or there had to be a change in the assumptions of the society. And since, over wide areas of Western civilization, men had become accustomed to identify political democracy, with all its implications, as the ideal form of the state, large numbers were found willing to demand its continuance. Capitalist society had either to surrender to them or to use the power of the state to suppress political democracy. By the latter it was able to maintain the title of the capitalist to profit without the need to satisfy the demands of an electorate for a continually advancing standard of life. When, that is to say, the contradiction between the economic oligarchy of capitalism and its democratic political foundation was revealed, where the adventure was possible, the contradiction was resolved by suppressing the democratic foundation.

Our grasp of the significance of this evolution is not a new thing in political philosophy. It was seen clearly by Aristotle [1]; it was seen by Harrington when he made the foundation of his political system the maxim that economic power precedes and determines the character of political power [2]; it was the basis of Madison's insight into politics which made him say that "the only durable source of faction is property." [3] Alexander Hamilton was not mistaken when he insisted upon

---

[1] *Politics*, Bk. V, 1: 14.
[2] *Oceana* and the *Prerogative of Popular Government.*
[3] *The Federalist*, No. 10.

the incompatibility between democracy and the predominance of a commercial class [1]; and, when Macaulay warned the House of Commons that universal suffrage would destroy the security of private property, he was speaking the language of sober moderation. Even the idea of class-warfare as rooted in the economics of capitalism has a long and honourable intellectual pedigree from Sismondi [2] and Saint-Simon [3] downwards; the real change lies in the twofold fact that with Marx and Engels the idea became a movement, and that, with the decline of capitalism, the movement became an army prepared to do battle for its principles. Our sense of dismay at its onset is in part the product of our long habituation to experience of capitalism in expansion, and—a new and sinister fact—in part to our realization that the use of the weapons science has placed at the disposal of violence may by their destructive power injure the very fabric of our civilization.

I am not at the moment concerned with this prospect; though I shall deal, in the last chapter of this book, with some of the inferences it seems to me to involve. Here it is sufficient to point out that the problem of capitalist democracy can—save in the dubious event of economic recovery—only be solved either by the supersession of capitalism or by the suppression of democracy. The first means an economic, the second a political, revolution. The first means the communal, instead of the private, ownership of the means of production; and inherent in that transformation, a change first in the class-relationships and, thereby, in all other relations in so-

---

[1] Cf. Parrington's brilliant discussion. *Main Currents in American Thought* (1927), Vol. I, pp. 292 f.

[2] *Nouveaux principes d'économie politiques* (1819).

[3] *Lettres d'un habitant de Genève* (1802); and cf. Bazard in *Doctrine Saint-Simonienne* (1829), 6me Séance (ed. Halévy, 1924), p. 235.

ciety. It would mean a revolution in our way of living comparable in profundity to the changes of the sixteenth century, or to those induced by the break-down of the aristocracy at the end of the eighteenth. The suppression of democracy would involve no such fundamental change in class-relations. But it would, on the other hand, deny to a large part of mankind the enjoyment of those goods which we have long come to consider the main justification for the capitalist way of life. It is clear that a heavy price would have to be paid for that denial, and it is clear also that the resultant state would operate in terms of the force at its disposal rather than the free obedience it could secure.

What, however, is here important is the theory of the state to which these inferences lead. Let us put them first in a negative way. The state, we argue, is not above classes. It does not transcend particular interests and lead to the expression of the total good of society. It is not a way of moving towards the fulfilment of the desires of its citizens. It does not seek to realize the rights they must claim in order to maintain the full dignity of their capacity as moral beings. It does not maintain law and order simply as the atmosphere vital to the maximum satisfaction of demand. It does not legitimate the force it employs by devoting that force to the service of a community regarded as a body of men and women with an equal claim to what of common good imperfect human beings may hope to achieve.

What, then, on this view, is the state? It is supreme coercive power used to protect the consequences inherent in the postulates of any given society. That power is exercised by the government in the name of the state since, of course, the latter can act only through persons. If the postulates of the state are capitalist, it must logically follow that the state will protect the consequences that a capitalist system requires. This does not mean that the state will protect a theoretical conception of capitalism worked out in the thinker's laboratory. It merely means that the state will protect ideas of social good which capitalists put forward as necessary inferences in a society in which theirs is the dominating interest to be satisfied; in a capitalist society, therefore, the power of the state will be co-extensive with capitalist ideas of social good. There may be dissent from those ideas, there may even be tolerance for that dissent; but the only way in which the dissent can become the major principles of social action is by the transformation of the capitalist basis of the society. And since that basis is maintained by the state, if necessary by the use of armed force, it follows that the state must be captured by dissent if it wishes to transform the basis of society.

It is this fact which makes it so significant in the modern state that its armed forces should be responsible to the government alone. For once their loyalty to the government can be assumed, it is largely, though not wholly, in a position to enforce upon the general body of citizens any decision it may choose to make. The facts that, under modern conditions, the general population is both unarmed and normally without the means to arm itself on the scale that the state can do, place dissent from the decisions of the state always upon the defensive; that is why all modern revolutions depend for their success upon the attitude of the army. That is why, also, it is so significant that, in the capitalist state, positions of authority in the army always belong, in overwhelming proportions, to members of the capitalist class; the ideological outlook of those members is, normally, a guarantee of their loyalty to the government they serve. The same is true, of course, of a communist state; it is notable that the Russian Commissar for War can congratulate his party on the increasing proportion of Communists in high command in the Soviet army.[1] And, similarly in Germany, it was not accidental that a struggle should have developed within the ranks of the Hitlerites as to whether the army should be a separate power from that of their party-membership or fused with it.[2] The separation of coercive authority in society from the mass of the population is essential to the maintenance of law and order there, once an unequal interest in the results of the property-system has to be secured.

This is the truth in the Marxian argument that in a classless society the state, as we know it, will "wither away." For the state as we know it has always had the function not of preserving law and order as absolute goods seen in the same broad way by all members of the state; the function of the state has always been to preserve that law and that order which are implicit in the purposes of a particular class-society. And since the character of a given class-society is always set by the interests of those who own the instruments of production, it follows that the law and order maintained serve, at every critical point, those interests and those interests only. If, then, the instruments of production were owned by society in common, it follows that the state-power would protect the interests of the whole society and not the interests only of a class in it. Under those circumstances the habits of the state, as we have known them, would clearly undergo a

[1] Cf. the address of Voroshilov to the 17th Congress of the Russian Communist Party.

[2] This, of course, was the crux of the struggle which ended with the execution of Röhm and his colleagues on June 30, 1934.

profound transformation. A common organ of government would still be necessary. But the postulates on which it would proceed would not involve the elevation of supreme coercive power to maintaining the economic interests of the property-owning class. Whatever oppositions still existed in the society, this, with all its implications, would have been removed.

And it is worth while to note what is involved in its removal. Let us take, as an example, freedom of speech. Most people, at least in democratic countries, agree that its preservation is desirable; and most people, also, agree that there are limits to its operation. As a rule, those limits are set by punishing any utterance which contains a threat to the preservation of law and order. The offender, we usually say, is not punished for the end his argument sought to serve; he is punished because the way in which his argument was framed might have led, or did in fact lead, to a breach of the public peace. But, in a capitalist society, what we mean by the "public peace" is, substantially, the system of legal conditions by which the postulates of capitalism are kept working. Any examination of the cases before the courts in which free speech is involved show that the vast majority of the offenders are critics of capitalism in whose utterance the prosecutor detects the presence of a threat to law and order. And any examination of the canons of interpretation by which the law is applied reveals at least a contingent width of ambit of which Professor Dicey, speaking of Great Britain, has rightly said that, rigorously enforced, it would make political discussion impossible.[1]

Nor is this all. The penalties of the law are one thing. But

[1] *Law of the Constitution* (ed. of 1915), p. 240.

the penalties of public opinion, if more indirect, are equally real. Once the right to employment is dependent upon the will of the owner of property, it is in his power to make occupation a function of orthodoxy in whatever sense he may choose to give to that term. A man who openly expresses anti-capitalist views would, emphasizes a great journal of public opinion,[1] "find it extremely difficult to make his way in business, would be debarred from most types of public employment, and would find himself handicapped even in the professions. The wealthy men who have careers, honours, and employments in their gift frown upon such heretics and ostracize them. If this is broadly true, of the highly educated few, it is much more obviously true of the mass of average men. When we consider the clerical class, still largely unorganized, we are aware of thousands who hardly dare to harbour 'dangerous thoughts,' much less to express them, lest they incur the displeasure of employers, customers, or clients. Insofar as the manual workers have emancipated themselves from this continuous pressure, it is because they work in masses with a strong trade union behind them. But they find, as we have seen in a number of recent cases, that the law does not necessarily protect them in the exercise of the elementary rights of free speech and public meeting. Moreover, the coercion implicit in poverty and unemployment often seems to them to make talk of equal rights a mockery. . . . And as soon as we leave the great industrial areas we discover that in very many areas even the right to vote freely is not a reality. Apart from the fact that property owns nine-tenths or more of the popular press, and has the advantage in all the

[1] *The New Statesman*, August 18, 1934.

more customary kinds of propaganda, opinion is threatened and democracy thwarted by the patronage and the economic power that the employing class possesses."

The proof of this is available in every phase of social life. Academic freedom in the United States has, as is well known, been constantly invaded by pressure from business men who have secured the dismissal of professors guilty of "radical" opinions.[1] There is hardly an autobiography of a trade-union leader which does not recount the history of his difficulties in retaining his employment once he became active in promoting the organization of his fellow-workers; the supreme instance of the Tolpuddle martyrs is only a minor incident in a terrible record. We have irrefutable testimony to the methods by which employers keep careful watch upon the growth of "undesirable" opinion among their workers, and the special connotation they attach to the idea of undesirability.[2] Upon the perversion of truth in the news, a technique now highly expert in character, there already exists a considerable literature; and the art of propaganda in the twentieth century has reached dimensions which threaten to rival the gains of popular education in the nineteenth.[3]

When, therefore, we say that the defence of liberty is a principle beyond all other principles, we must be careful to give our concept a precise meaning. Effective liberty cannot exist in any society where there is not merely a class interested in preventing its expression, but also both with the power to do so and, in the last analysis, the capacity to use the authority of the state for this end. The chance to think

---

[1] Cf. the *Bulletin* of the American Association of University Professors which gives a full account of these cases.

[2] R. W. Dunn and S. Howard, *The Labor Spy* (1924).

[3] H. D. Lasswell, *Propaganda Technique in the World War* (1927).

freely has always been a function of economic independence; and a society which associates economic independence with the ownership of property is, in fact, limiting freedom of thought, for all save a small minority of its members, to the owners of property. So long as a workman can be dismissed, not because he is inefficient, but because his economic or political opinions arouse distrust in his employer, their relations impose constraint upon the former which are likely to be fatal to his freedom. That is why freedom of opinion under capitalism has always seemed less real to the working-classes than it has to the employer or to the intellectual. The implications of intellectual freedom to each are so different that the interpretation they will give to its operation sometimes seem to proceed from different worlds.

But capitalism, writes Professor Gregory, is built on "the right of the individual to economic self-expression." [1] It is difficult, under the actual conditions we know, to take such a view seriously. The "right to economic self-expression" of a worker in a Pennsylvania steel town is not high.[2] Granted the level of modern wage-standards, the insecurity of industrial tenure, the degree to which, without unemployment insurance, the worker is incapable of picking and choosing between the jobs open to him, the limitations of his educational training, the barriers, of constantly increasing height in the post-war period, to his migration, it is surely pardonable for him to feel a doubt whether "economic self-expression" exactly describes the situation in which he finds himself. And if it be said that these are invasions of the "pure idea" of

---

[1] *The Independent*, August 11, 1934.

[2] Cf. the *Report* of the Interchurch World Movement of North America on the steel strike of 1919.

capitalism, the answer is the obvious one that they are all invasions protected by laws which the capitalist has himself had the major share in making. The "right to economic self-expression" becomes real exactly at the point where no penalties hinge upon its exercise. But in a capitalist society it is surrounded by these at every point for all who do not enjoy the privileges associated with the ownership of property.

Any state, therefore, in which the instruments of property are in private hands is, by that fact, biased in its incidence. It may state the rights it confers in universal terms; it confines their effective enjoyment to the owners of property. Its claim to obedience, in the light of this, apart from the actual power of enforcement—a power wholly devoid of moral foundation—is clearly a function of its ability to persuade its members that their lot is better under such a regime than it would be under some alternative. That ability, I have argued, will always depend upon the capacity of the state to satisfy the demands that it encounters. Where it is organized as a dictatorship, the area of demand of which it will have to take account will be narrower than where it is organized as a democracy. But, so long as it is an organzed society, there is no test save this of its adequacy.

No state, therefore, is ever entitled to the allegiance of its members upon its own terms. It is not what it represents itself as doing, or seeking to do, but what judgment they make of that effort which forms the basis of the obligations in which they are politically involved. Each of us, so to say, makes his own right and his own wrong in politics; they grow out of the experience in which we find ourselves immersed. We induce from that experience a level of demand we deem reasonable; we expect the state to realize that level of demand. Where it fails to do so, we seek, if we can, to make ourselves heard. If our complaints receive attention, the chances are that we shall be content thereby with the proof thus afforded of the state's goodwill. But if our complaints are ignored or suppressed, they will begin to assume the form of a considered doctrine. In a democracy, as in Great Britain, a party will arise in their support. In a dictatorship, as in Russia, the bolder spirits among those who complain will form a conspiracy for the remedy of grievance. But both party and conspiracy will aim at the same end. They will seek to alter the legal principles which deny them satisfaction for principles that secure it; and each will discover, as it goes about its task, that the alteration of legal principle means, once it touches the foundations of social structure, the conquest of the state itself.

I have argued that an attempt to touch the foundations of the social structure is an adventure of a special kind. For to do so is to attack the basis which mainly determines the nature of all social institutions and ideas. In a dictatorship, clearly, the conquest of the state must be a revolutionary adventure; the nature of the regime leaves no alternative to a citizen who dissents from its purposes. It is, therefore, clear that, under such a regime, the political obligation of a dissident member remains on the plane of formal law only. Allegiance is an attitude of the mind; and only naked coercion can bind men to purposes which their minds deny. Any state, therefore, which desires to put its claims upon a basis more profound than the formal has to win obedience by consent, and not exact it by coercion. This it can do only by making its purposes satisfy the demands of the vast majority of its citizens. By remaining a dictatorship it is denying to itself the only means by which it can make its title to allegiance valid on the moral plane—its ability to build itself in the free consent of men.

Is the situation different in a democracy? My own view is that the difference is, under certain conditions, a substantial one. Where the members of a state enjoy fundamental political rights in a degree real enough to make effectively possible the transformation of dissent into orthodoxy, I believe that it is the duty of the citizen to exhaust the means placed at his disposal by the constitution of the state before resorting to revolution. I admit that the nature of capitalist democracy weights the scales unduly against him. I admit, also, that this is a counsel of prudent expediency rather than of ultimate moral right. But I believe that the gains which are inherent in the technique of constitutionalism are profounder, even though they are more slow, than those which are implicit in the revolutionary alternative.

This, however, is to enter into the strategy of politics rather than into its philosophy. Here, for my purposes, it is sufficient to note two things. First, that the question of whether the enjoyment of fundamental political rights is in fact real enough to make peaceful change of social foundations possible is a matter in which the opinion of those who dissent from, is at least as valid as that of those who accept, the implications of a given society. We may judge them mistaken or unwise in deciding upon the revolutionary alternative; we cannot judge them morally wrong save as we can prove moral wrongness to have been inherent in their purposes or their methods. The Irishmen who rebelled against Great Britain in 1916 were, I think, unwise in the sense that their adventure had no prospect of actual success; but I do not think a moral condemnation of their decision could make a serious pretence of validity. They broke the law; but the whole history of Anglo-Irish relations had come to deny for them the attribution of moral obligation to the law. When men are driven to that attitude by the experience of what they believe to be wrong there will always be sufficient reality in their grievance to make a simple moral condemnation of them quite incapable of being justified.

The second thing I have to note is, in my judgment, not less fundamental. Because changes in the class-structure of society have rarely been made without revolutionary means, those who draw the inference that our experience is not likely to be different from that of the past, that, therefore, the expectation of revolution is legitimate, and preparation for it the part of prudence, have a case that has not been answered by the proponents of peaceful change. It is the fact that the owners of property rarely yield save where they must; that most reforms come too late to satisfy the grievances with which they are intended to deal. It is the fact, also, that the owners of property are rarely tolerant of criticism as soon as the security of their position moves into the zone of danger. The proof they ought to offer of their goodwill is the ability to be tolerant even when, as Mr. Justice Holmes has finely phrased it,[1] they find themselves in the presence of ideas fraught with death. They do not offer that proof. On the contrary, the more proximate the challenge, the more they demand of the state the full exercise of its repressive function. That has been notably the case in all countries during the present epoch of economic crisis. To draw from it the inference that capitalist democracy is no more capable of peaceful

[1] *Abrams v. U. S.* (1919) 250, U. S. 616.

transformation than other forms of the state is wholly reasonable. If states are only tolerant because they feel secure, insecurity is bound to lead to those adjustments of constitutional expectation in which peaceful change becomes improbable.

And it is not only the question of tolerance that is involved. A democratic constitution is always a living thing which depends as much upon the spirit in which it is applied as upon the words on which it rests, perhaps even more so. To strain it in the interests of the *status quo* is to hazard the loyalty of those who are told that they may put their confidence in the spirit in which it is operated. The political unity of a people is so largely a function of habits, conventions, unwritten understandings, of constitutional procedure that the biased exploitation of these is, at critical moments, a blow as nearly fatal as any that can be struck. Yet the evidence suggests a willingness on the part of every propertied class to attempt this exploitation which bodes ill for the preservation of peace. That was the capital error of the Stuarts; it lay at the root of the unwillingness of the bourgeoisie to accept the bona fides of Louis XVI; it wrecked the faith of the Russian people in the constitutional experiments of Nicholas II. In our own more recent history, there are similar instances in which an exploitation of this kind has brought us near to crisis. The attitude of the House of Lords to the Reform Bill of 1832; its rejection of the Budget of 1909; the deliberate attempt of the Conservative leaders, over the events in Ulster in 1913–1914, to tamper with the loyalty of the army; the mysterious circumstances which surround the birth of the National government in 1931; the abandonment, in 1932, and for narrow party purposes, of what had been regarded, at least from the time of the younger Pitt's famous letter to Lord Thurlow,[1] as the fundamental doctrine of collective cabinet responsibility [2]; all these are events which strain the faith of men in the power to maintain peace in a period of profound change. The Federalists were guilty of the same tactic in their use of the Alien and Sedition laws in 1798,[3] and again in John Adams's last-minute exploitation of the Presidential power over judicial nomination in 1801.[4] The use of Article 48 of the Weimar Constitution in the last years of the German republic was an outrage upon constitutional decency.

Those, in short, who work a constitution evolve certain rules for its operation by which they expect their opponents to abide. The rules are respected so long as the class which is in power is broadly identical with those who evolved them; but there is a grave tendency, whenever a new class is about to assume political authority, for those who have been accustomed to office to think themselves entitled to change the rules for their own benefit. Sometimes they strain well-defined interpretations; sometimes they revive obsolete formulæ which they justify on the ground of national emergency; sometimes, with the brutal frankness of Hitler when, in August 1934, he assumed the Presidency of the Reich, they abandon them altogether. That attitude is fatal to the goodwill upon which so delicate a mechanism as a constitution necessarily depends. We tend to forget how difficult and slow was the evolution of the majority-principle in the history of government, how complicated are the conditions of its suc-

---

[1] Todd, *Parliamentary Government in England* (1869), Vol. II, p. 328.
[2] Cf. my *Crisis and the Constitution* (1932), pp. 59–64.
[3] For a full treatment of this subject cf. A. J. Beveridge, *Life of John Marshall* (1916), Vols. II and III.
[4] *Ibid.*, II, pp. 559 f.

cessful functioning. A class which threatens, let alone attempts, constitutional sabotage when the verdict of democracy goes against it invites that suspension of the democratic process which is fatal to most of the spiritual gains of civilized life.

III

THE STATE AND THE INTERNATIONAL COMMUNITY

I

NO state can live a life to itself alone. It is a member of a community of states, each of which has, from the standpoint of theory, the same kind of rights and duties. Each of them is involved in a network of international relationships, for the control of which rules have to be formulated. No theory of the state can pretend to completeness which does not account for the facts involved in the existence of this international community.

A theory of the state, that is to say, must be, from one angle, a philosophy of international law. It must explain why states should regard themselves as bound by the rules of international intercourse. It must build itself upon postulates which satisfactorily fit the kind of world to which we belong. It must be wide enough, in its foundations, to weigh the significance of the immense changes we have witnessed in the relations of states since Grotius, some three hundred years ago, first formulated a scientific approach to the problems of international law. No foundations for such a philosophy can be adequate unless they provide for the rules of international intercourse the assurance of that continuity of application which enables the state, within its own community, to make its law the measure of the behaviour of all other associations with which it has contact.

In the history of the theory of international law the concept of the state as sovereign has, inevitably, a central place. For, clearly, since the state is a sovereign organization, it can be bound by no will save its own; and the problem of making rules for an international community the members of which can, logically, be bound only as they agree to be bound is a grave one. The essence of the internal relationships of the state is its right, as sovereign, to impose its will upon all who live within its territorial ambit. But, outside that sphere, the logic of its nature compels us to assume that the only way to bind a state against its will (as when another state makes demands upon it to which it is unwilling to yield) is by war; and the ultimate arbiter of international relations is, as a consequence of the theory of sovereignty, victory in the field.

We meet this idea of sovereignty in international law in two ways. On the one hand it is a logical concept the validity of which is purely formal; from this angle we obtain the positive theory of international law which assumes that all the rules of the law of nations are derived exclusively either from international custom or from treaties, since these alone represent the wills of states. Here, with unquestionable validity, it is inferred from the nature of sovereignty that the will of the state is necessarily the sole source of law. If we assumed otherwise, then the will of the state would be bound by rules to which it had not consented; and it would then cease, by definition, to be a sovereign organization.

On the other hand, the idea of sovereignty in international law is a philosophic one. Here, its effect is to justify the positivist theory by arguing that the state has an absolute moral value beyond which we cannot go; that, therefore, the validity of international law must necessarily consist in its furtherance of that value. And, since the only judge of this furtherance must be the state (since, otherwise, it would cease to be itself the embodiment of absolute moral value), it follows that the state, in judging whether it should or should not accept as binding a proposed rule of international law, need have regard to its own interests only. In doing so, by reason of its assumed nature, it realizes the highest purposes at which it can aim. For in securing its own self-interest it is securing, also, the interest of that absolute moral value which it embodies.

Those who built the classic structure of international law have not, indeed, shrunk from these conclusions. Assuming, with Hegel, that the state is that "objective spirit" through which alone "the individual can reach his objectivity, his truth, and his morality,"[1] they have inferred, quite rightly, that the rule of law ends at the frontiers of the state. The rights of other states "are not realized," says Hegel,[2] "in a general rule which is so constituted as to have power over them, but their rights are realized only through their particular wills." The state stands above the rule; international law is nothing but external municipal law. Its force is derived simply from

---

[1] *The Philosophy of Right* (Eng. trans., 1821), Sec. 258.

[2] *Op. cit.*, Sec. 333.

the will of the state or states which are prepared to enforce it; it is therefore impossible to conceive of an international order, of which states are constituent parts, so long as they retain their sovereignty. "The state," wrote Lasson in a well-known passage,[1] "cannot . . . ever be subjected to a legal order, or, speaking generally, to any other will but its own . . . it is an unlimited will of selfishness." That is why Kaufmann can insist that no general rule of law binding states is conceivable save the rule that might is right; from which it follows that victory in war is the highest ideal the state can know.[2] For victory in war means self-preservation, and this, by definition, secures the triumph of absolute moral value.

The acceptance of this attitude has been widespread; it is well known, for example, that it determined the outlook of English idealist theory in politics. When Bosanquet could write of the state that "it has no determined function in a larger community, but it is itself the supreme community. . . . Moral relations presuppose an organized life; but such a life is only within the state, not in relations between states and other communities," he was, in fact, insisting that beyond the state-boundary there is necessarily anarchy, save insofar as states can agree or determine the issues between them by war. It was this belief in sovereignty which underlay the whole conception of the League of Nations in 1919. It is this belief, also, that makes it so difficult to reach agreement in the field of disarmament. For once we grant that war is the ultimate arbiter of international destiny, it follows quite logically that each state can agree only to such limitation as is, in its own judgment, compatible with its highest self-interest;

[1] *Prinzip und Zukunft des Völkerrechts* (1871), p. 22.
[2] *Das Wesen des Völkerrechts* (1911), pp. 146, 151.

and since it is the only ultimate guardian of that self-interest, the limitation it can accept will be only that which leaves it the full assurance of victory in the field. And if, as with some famous men, we regard peace as merely another way of waging war, since the use of force is always contingently in the background, the same difficulty permeates every aspect of international relationships, whether it be tariffs or migration, the working of the gold-standard, or the hours of labour, in which agreement between states is the prelude to necessary action.

The positivist doctrine, indeed, involves itself in grave logical difficulties as soon as it faces the facts of international life. It is not only that its own adherents insist that states are bound by international law whether they will or no,[1] a theory incompatible with the idea of sovereignty. It is not only, also, that, in order to explain that international law is binding, the positivist has to accept the postulate of an international legal order in which each state has, whatever its size and power, its due and equal place; a doctrine which imposes duties upon the state which are there independently of its will.[2] There is the difficulty of reconciling this view, unless we use the crutch of fiction, with the practice of international tribunals.[3] There is the further difficulty, save with the use of a similar crutch, of reconciling it with the statute of the Permanent Court of International Justice.[4] There is the growing recognition that it is impossible any longer to regard states as the only subjects

[1] e. g., L. Oppenheim. *International Law*, Vol. I (1920), p. 116.

[2] This was the point finally made in Kelsen's classic monograph, *Der Begriff der Souveränität* (1920).

[3] Cf. Dr. Lauterpacht's brilliant book, *Private Law Sources and Analogies in International Law* (1927), esp. pp. 60 f.

[4] *Ibid.*, p. 67.

of international law [1]; and this is, in itself, fatal to the positivist outlook. There is the body of inconvenient problems created by the existence of international servitudes and of non-sovereign states.[2] Positivism, which enjoyed its midsummer of bright credit during the War of 1914, now seems to have fallen upon evil days. For its postulates are not merely irreconcilable with the facts; they also contradict the whole tendency of the evolution of international relations in our time. We are being rapidly driven to the point where, once we assume the sovereignty of the state, we have to infer the impossibility of those international institutions which the facts themselves are compelling us to establish.

It is significant that this evolution is compelling legal philosophers to build the postulates of international law upon foundations of a quite different kind. The tendency now is to start not with the state, but with the international community, the *civitas maxima*, in which the state is reduced to the level of a province. The rules of the international community are then regarded as supreme; and they have logical primacy over the rules of municipal law.[3] Upon this basis, wherever municipal law and international law conflict, it is the former which must give way; and a state which breaks a rule of international law is, on this footing, in the same position as an individual who breaks a rule of the municipal law of his state. A failure, then, to bring the offender to book is not a failure of the law as such. It arises from the imperfectly organized sanctions of international law in the world-

---

[1] Strupp, *Éléments de droit international* (1927), pp. 22 f.

[2] Verdross, *Die Verfassung der Völkerrechtsgemeinschaft* (1926), esp., pp. 189 f.

[3] Cf. my *Studies in Law and Politics* (1932), p. 267, and the works there cited.

community as it has so far evolved. Hence the effort to close the gaps in the Covenant of the League, as in the Geneva Protocol of 1924. Hence, also, the development of instruments like the Pact of Paris by which the individual state renounces its sovereign right to employ force for the realization of its will. Hence, also, the evolution of the idea of the collective security of states against the aggression of a single state. Hence, finally, the slow growth of a doctrine of world-loyalty which, as in the formal proposals of the Labour Party,[1] would make it legal for the individual to resist the will of his state to war save where this was waged with the authority of the League of Nations.

I have myself no sort of doubt that this approach to the philosophy of international law is the only one that corresponds to the needs of our epoch, for the facts of the last generation have shown, tragically enough, to all who have eyes to see that the sovereign state and civilization have irreconcilable interests. But if the older theories of international law, whether of positivists like Kaufmann, or of idealists like Hegel, have their eyes fixed too firmly upon the objective historic conditions of the past, it is, I think, legitimate to argue that the exponents of the newer views tend unduly to write brilliant essays in the optative mood. For if we sign Optional Clauses, or Pacts of Paris, we sign them, invariably, with significant reservations,[2] and these, in all matters of fundamental importance, still leave each signatory state making a reservation the judge in its own cause. Some future British Government may induce Parliament to pass, as it is wholly

---

[1] *Labour and Peace* (1934).

[2] See Dr. H. Lauterpacht's remarkable analysis, *Economica* (1930), pp. 138–72.

desirable that it should pass, a Peace Act; but since no Parliament can bind its successor, its repeal is always a legal possibility, perhaps even more. All attempts to revise the Covenant of the League so as to make its sanctions automatic have so far broken down, very largely through the action of those member-states most insistent upon their loyalty to the Covenant. There is no sign of any abrogation of the doctrine of unanimity in the near future. All states loudly insist that a serious scheme for collective security is impossible without disarmament; but, if the Disarmament Conference of 1932 has shown anything, it has shown that we do not yet live in a world in which the prospects of serious disarmament are real. The League of Nations solemnly condemned Japanese aggression against China in Manchuria; but the result of its condemnation was as great (or as small) as if its resolution had been passed by a synod of Christian clergymen. We may bow the sovereign state out of the front door of our international edifice; but there are still sufficient entrances at the back through which it can creep to its old pre-eminence.

The pivot of the whole problem, it is generally agreed, is the need to make it impossible for any state to use war as an instrument of its policy. We may agree that few states definitely desire to use that instrument. We may construct instruments to minimize the prospect of its use. We may prove that, under modern conditions, war simply does not pay; that it is an instrument as economically disastrous to the victors as to the vanquished.[1] We may feel convinced that the end of war, certainly in the defeated states, and perhaps also in the victorious, leads to social revolution in matters of

---

[1] As in the famous thesis of Sir Norman Angell. Cf. his *Great Illusion* (1933).

internal constitution. We may watch the steady growth of individual belief that it is morally wrong to wage war, that it is therefore an obligation upon the individual citizen to refuse to serve the state when it embarks upon it.[1] We may even note the view of eminent scientists that, as servants of humanity, it is their duty to refrain from such experiments as will assist the state to secure more powerful weapons for war.[2] Even if we grant all this, the conditions of an effective international community are absent from the situation we occupy.

And it is to the implications of these conditions that all discussion of the issue must go back. It is widely recognized that the sovereign state is incompatible with the establishment of an effective world-order; yet every serious move which looks to the erosion of its sovereignty is checkmated at some pivotal point. The state, as guardian of the highest national interests, finds it essential, where these are concerned, to remain judge in its own cause. It will, of course, insist that the motives for this attitude are wholly unselfish, and it is an error of judgment to doubt their sincerity. When an eminent British Admiral insists that a strong British navy is the best guarantee of world-peace,[3] I am confident that he is wholly genuine in thinking so. But he does not inquire into what that peace is for. He assumes, quite unconsciously, that the power of Great Britain to impose its will on the rest of the world is definitely for the good of the world. So, also, I do not doubt at all that those statesmen who argue that Great Britain is in India

---

[1] As urged with great vigour by Lord Ponsonby. Cf. his *Now Is the Time* (1926).

[2] Cf. a remarkable letter signed by Dr. Joseph Needham and others in the *News Chronicle*, May 29, 1934.

[3] *The Times*, August 11, 1934.

solely for the benefit of India are utterly sincere. But it is still important that Americans and Japanese do not take quite the same view of the functions of the British navy as Lord Beatty, and that our statesmen, particularly in more recent times, have not been able to secure Indian assent to their conception of British responsibilities in India. And this does not apply to Great Britain alone. It is true, for example, of the relations between the United States and Nicaragua, of Holland with Java, of the attitude of General Göring to German military aviation. Where interests to be promoted are regarded differently, the concept of sovereignty becomes merely a legal title to enforce one view of what those interests involve.

We have therefore to approach the sovereignty of the state from the basis of the view we have already set out of the state's essential nature. It exists to maintain some given system of class-relations; and in the international, as in the internal, sphere it is bound, by its own inherent logic, to promote the interests involved in that given system. Those "highest national interests" that the state therefore secures must always be set in the context of its own economic constitution. For it is this which ultimately shapes the ends of the state; what it demands the state will do. If what it demands is something that war alone can secure, no doubt the state will exhaust all the resources of diplomacy before it employs that terrible expedient; but, when they are exhausted, it will make war. It will do so, no doubt, for the sake of "national honour," or its "civilizing mission," or to "make the world safe for democracy," or some other verbally noble end; and no one who examines the psychology of peoples engaged in war but must admit how much of sincerity there is in these protestations. But when each of them is soberly examined in concrete terms, they always appear as the attempt to achieve some tangible economic good for the class which dominates the belligerent state at the time of making war. It is always this tangible economic good which is the basis upon which the ideological superstructure is erected.

I do not think this conclusion is vitiated by the fact that the occasion for war is rarely an obviously economic one. Nor do I think that it is weakened by the further fact that, not seldom, the economic welfare of the dominating class is, externally regarded, linked with that of those over whom it rules. The fact that the War of 1914 was precipitated by a bomb at Serajevo does not conceal the fact that it was, in essence, a struggle between competing imperialisms. The fact that America's entrance into that war in 1917 was, formally, a protest against unlimited submarine warfare by Germany is in nowise at variance with the far more important fact that her financial commitments to Great Britain and France had by that time become so heavy that she could not afford to see them lose. Great Britain's presence in India is, effectively, a function of her trading interests there; and these are, as recent economic history has shown, vitally related to the interest of those workers who are employed by reason of our Indian trade. But they are no more vitally related than, say, our export trade to the United States upon which, also, the interests of large numbers of British workers depend. Yet we do not infer that the protection of our interests in the United States involves its occupation by us.

The view, therefore, that I take is in essence a simple one, even though its expression in a complex world is intricate. It is the view that the state in a capitalist society needs to remain sovereign in order to protect the interests of capitalism. In the last resort, these interests have to be protected by war, which is the supreme expression of sovereignty in international relations. So long, therefore, as the effective purpose of the state, internally regarded, is to protect the principles of capitalism, so long, in its external aspect, will it require to retain the use of war as an instrument of national policy. If sovereignty and an effective world-order are incompatible ways of life, then, also, capitalism and a world-order are incompatible; for war is rooted in the capitalist system in our experience of its necessary functioning.

II

This is, of course, stoutly denied by the protagonists of capitalism; and it is well to examine, at the outset, the burden of the argument they make. "There is not a tittle of evidence to show," writes Professor Gregory,[1] "that capitalism necessarily leads to war—it was not the era of capitalist supremacy in the nineteenth century which is richest in armed conflict, and, in any case, were there no wars before the middle of the eighteenth century?" Or we are asked to remember that the strongest opponents of war in the nineteenth century were exactly those statesmen who, like Cobden and Bright, were most concerned to develop the full assumptions of capitalist democracy. Its whole theory is based upon the effort to make state-intervention minimal in character. To attribute to it a causal relationship with war—the supreme expression of state-intervention—is to deny its fundamental premises. "Free Trade," wrote Cobden in 1842, "by perfect-

[1] *Loc. cit.*, p. 28.

ing the intercourse, and securing the dependence of countries one upon another, must inevitably snatch the power from the *governments* to plunge their people into wars." [1] And free trade is the vital postulate of capitalist theory.

But we have to analyse not the pure theory of a conceptual capitalism, but the habits of the capitalists we know. It is obvious that a capitalist society in which, alike, the capitalist refrains from asking the state for assistance, and the state refrains from assisting the capitalist, the operations of the economic system will not result in war. If the capitalism we know had been a capitalism of this kind, thinkers of Professor Gregory's school would be entitled to say that war is not necessarily inherent in capitalism at all. But the capitalism of which they speak has never existed outside of economic literature; it is a creature of their conceptual imagination. The capitalism we know has at every stage of its history sought the protection of the state for its operations. It has demanded, and secured, tariffs, subsidies, quotas, the influence of the Foreign Office for its trading-agents abroad, the use of the state's prestige (a pseudonym for the right to call upon its armed forces) to protect the claims it has thought fit to make in foreign countries. The history of Egypt since the British occupation, the history of Africa in the last two generations, of China, of Mexico, of the Central American states, are quite unintelligible except upon the basis of a capitalism which has been able to put the force of the state behind its enterprises. We may regard it as unfortunate that the state has made these interventions. We may say that the trader would have been far wiser if he had trusted to the use of his power to give or withhold trade independently of aid from the

[1] Morley, *Life of Richard Cobden.* (Eversley Edition). I, 248.

state. But the fact remains that if he had done so, the capitalism we know, while it might have made a better world, would have been a different capitalism. After all, it is with the actual, and not the hypothetical, that we have to deal in constructing our assumptions.

Nor does the argument that, since there were wars in plenty before capitalism, therefore capitalism cannot be the cause of war, really take us very far. By capitalism in this context is meant only the assumptions of *laissez-faire* political economy in Great Britain in its classical period. The argument then proceeds in a vicious circle. It starts by defining a capitalist society as one characterized by freedom of enterprise. It means by that freedom operations of commerce in which the state does not interfere. When, therefore, it counters interference from the state it simply shrugs its shoulders and says that whatever of evil has resulted cannot be due to capitalism. Clearly, if we define capitalism in this way, the conclusion is logically incontrovertible for the simple reason that it is already implicit in the premises.

But this capitalism, as I have insisted, never existed except as a body of partially realized tendencies for a few years in the nineteenth century. The capitalism we actually know has a character of a wholly different kind. It is the capitalism which has expressed its nature in the American tariff, in the expansion, by military and semi-military adventure, of commerce in Africa, the capitalism of heavy subsidies to German agriculture, the capitalism which, as in Haiti and Nicaragua and Santo Domingo, has made and unmade governments in terms of their attitude to its operations. No one is entitled to disregard the innumerable events of this kind in order to save a theory which contradicts their most decisive implications. There were, no doubt, many wars before the nineteenth century, in which non-economic motives, dynastic, religious, political, were of great significance. But, even in those wars, a careful scrutiny of their purpose always leaves the economic context a relevant one. The drive to war is never divorced from the search by the state after economic power. The search may be indirect, as when a state seeks for a strategic frontier; or it may be mixed, as in the French desire to recover Alsace-Lorraine, where sentiment born of historic tradition and the interest of French heavy industry were united in perhaps fairly equal proportions. But the explanation of war is never adequate where it fails to find an economic perspective to its occurrence.

The position today, indeed, has become far more serious than in the past by reason of two things. The first is the association of the idea of statehood with national feeling; the second is the immense improvement of the state's administrative technique. The first enables the state to put behind its policy all the sentiment, passionate, exclusive, only partly rational, which nationalism arouses. The second enables the state to organize the nation for war upon a scale, and with an intensity, unknown even to a supreme administrator like Napoleon. So that when the state-policy is dominated by the will of the capitalist to make profit—which is the *raison d'être* of his being—the forces he thereby calls into play are colossal compared with anything we have known in the past. Until the War of 1914, Great Britain had never placed in battle an army of more than one hundred thousand men; in that war, she mobilized for military purposes one-third of her manhood. The intensity of the impact of modern warfare upon the state-life of our time is qualitatively different from what it has been in any previous epoch of modern history. We shall not again in our civilization have classic novels like those of Jane Austen, in which hero and heroine can do their stately minuet unconscious of the need to reflect upon the impact of war upon their environment.

We have, therefore, to look upon capitalism as it is, and not as it would be if tendencies once seeking for expression had fully realized themselves. The capitalism we know is a system in which the instruments of production are privately owned, and in which the effective motive to production is the profit made possible by such ownership. This system implies, as I have sought to show, a special system of class-relations, and the essence of its habits lies in the fact that the power of the state is used to maintain the implications of these class-relations. The whole effort of the state, therefore, is directed to securing the owner's right to profit. Given the postulates of the system, it could not, as I have argued, be otherwise. Whatever interferes with the making of profit the power of the state will be used to repress, if it can be repressed; for there is always a struggle in society between the classes which own, and the classes which do not own, the instruments of production for a larger share in the product of the industrial process. In a capitalist society, the internal function of the state is to safeguard those ultimate principles of law which assure to the owner of property a predominant share in that production. And, again as I have argued, from this fundamental fact, all social activities take their shape and complexion.

Now the argument of the school of thought which denies any inherent connexion between capitalism and war is, broadly, built upon a refusal to accept this view of the state.

If supply and demand operated without friction in an open market where all capitalists knew all the wants of their customers, and all labour was completely mobile, state-intervention would be unnecessary; social relations would be built on contract and not on force. But since there is neither this knowledge nor this mobility, what we are given, and what we have got to explain, are the operations of a society in which they do not exist, in which, therefore, the intervention of the state is required by the capitalists themselves, and utilized to promote their interests. This they can do because their ownership of the means of production gives them the power to determine the direction in which that intervention shall go. I have already analysed its consequences; and my point about their relation to the capitalism of Professor Gregory's school of thought can be made quite simply by saying that, in its view, these consequences are merely the result of the abuse of an ideal. It saves its hypothesis by insisting that theory can deal with the pure instance only. It is, no doubt, regrettable that we do not encounter this pure instance in the actual society we know.

Now what the state is in its internal, that, also, in my view, it is in its external relations. Exactly as it uses its force to protect the interest of the capitalist at home, so it uses force to protect his interest abroad. The value to it of its sovereignty in the international field is precisely that, in extreme cases, it can bring force into play against any rival which seeks to interfere with the expression of its will. If it surrendered that sovereignty, it would be subject to rules; and, so long as it observed them, it would not be able to make the might at its disposal the measure of the right it may seek to enforce. A world of non-sovereign states is one compatible with all the ideas of international organization which are ultimately implied in a system like that of the League of Nations. But these ultimate implications are not compatible with the class-relations which capitalism requires since they bring into the light of day the basic contradictions into which our society has fallen.

For the basis from which we have to start is the accumulation, in states of a developed economic character, of more capital than can find the opportunity of favourable domestic employment. It emigrates because it cannot find the security or the rate of profit which foreign investment offers; and, when it emigrates, it looks to the state to protect it from risk as best it can. The reason why accumulation takes place more rapidly than the power of domestic absorption lies in the maladjustment of production and distribution. The consuming power of the public is not equal, by reason of the class-relations of our society, to its productive power. The wants of consumers in the modern wage-system are not "effective" wants in the technical sense of that term. The emigration of capital arises because the incidence of wealth in any given community is too unequal to enable its capital to be employed profitably at home. Had distribution been more equal, it is obvious that the demands of the wage-earners, being then "effective," would have resulted in a greater demand for the domestic employment of capital. In the absence of greater equality, its owners accumulate far greater resources than they can spend even in terms of the luxurious display characteristic of an acquisitive society. They therefore look abroad for the chance to place their capital profitably. They are not seriously concerned with the purposes to which it is devoted. It may be for armaments; it may be for the sterile pleasures of an Oriental autocrat; it may be, as with the famous French loans to Tsarist Russia, to prop up the decaying foundations of an ugly despotism. So long as there is the prospect of profit, the investor does not inquire too closely into the objectives to which he lends his support.

The root fact, in short, of that rapid accumulation of capital in advanced countries which results in the need for its export is the existence there of a markedly unequal society. Were the wage-level higher, it is obvious that the demand for commodities would create a greater demand for the domestic employment of capital; houses for the working-class might be built instead of an extra battleship for a bankrupt state. The situation, in fact, of a working-class whose income-limit is set by the very margins of subsistence means necessarily a search by capital for quantitative rather than qualitative expansion since the latter does not involve the creation of equivalent purchasing-power for the commodities produced. And wherever capitalist expansion is quantitative rather than qualitative in character, the risks it runs involve the technique of conquest, whether direct, as in India, or indirect, as in South America, for the protection of the investments made. For the risks run are, as a rule, so high, the concessions to be secured so valuable, the rates of interest charged so formidable, that only the contingent pressure of military power can guarantee their security.

There is another reason, also, why the domestic position makes the export of capital both profitable and attractive. The existence, in the less advanced states, of great reserves of ill-paid native labour makes possible a lucrative return on the capital employed largely inadmissible under the more sternly regulated conditions of Western civilization. Long hours of labour, poor wages, little necessity to pay attention to the modern demands of sanitation and safety, the absence of any well-organized trade unions, even, at the worst, a condition of contract-labour which is hardly distinguishable from slavery, these offer prospects of profit of which the investor is naturally inclined to take full advantage. In this respect, all the phenomena of sweated labour present themselves for exploitation; and the history of industry in Egypt and India, in the factories of China and the plantations of Africa, show that they are utilized to the full. And the danger that the profit may not be secured is always obviated by the fact that behind the effort of private enterprise there are diplomacy and military power to see that the trader's ingenuity does not lack its reward.

It is worth noting, moreover, that economic imperialism offers other prospects by no means negligible in character. The requirements of trade involve a well-settled territory; and this necessitates a civil and military administration. So there have grown up the civil services of India, Egypt, and our African dominions, to take only the most notable examples, in which a large number of the sons of the middle and upper classes have found the opportunity of dignified and financially adequate careers. This development has had a number of important effects. On the one hand, it has bred a real hostility to self-government for the territories involved; for every nationalist movement among the subject-peoples necessarily attacks the foundations of a system which enables a number of young men year by year to find employment of a kind not otherwise easily open to them. On the other hand, it has involved the necessity, in these territories, of adequate military occupation, itself involving further employment; for public opinion at home, naturally enough, demands proper safeguards for the security of its sons against rebellion or revolution. No one need doubt that much of this service is both necessary and valuable. But no one need doubt, either, that it creates a vested interest against progress in self-government of which the power, notably in India, has been remarkable indeed.

One further characteristic of this economic imperialism makes an important impact upon first principles. So long as competition for markets was largely confined to the Western industrial nations, it was competition between peoples of not dissimilar industrial standards of life. With the entrance of the Far East into the field, new factors have entered into the situation. The factory standards of Japan, for instance, have enabled it to beat the Lancashire cotton manufacturer out of many of his historic markets; and the intense nationalism of India, and soon, it may be, of China, involve the growth there of protective tariffs devised to secure a predominant share of their own markets for their own nationals. The result of the first development is either grave unemployment in the industries of the defeated competitor; or the intervention of the state to mitigate by legislation the force of an unequal competition. The reaction of this latter alternative upon the disadvantaged state is to force it to take measures in its own defence. That is the result, also, of the development of protective tariffs. The economic autarchy it encourages dries up the stream of international trade just at a time when its continuous increase is fundamental to the full employment of capital which, through scientific progress, has so enormously enhanced its productive capacity. The whole economic machine then gets out of gear; and depressions like that of 1929, with its grave disturbance of the whole social equilibrium, are the necessary outcome. And it is a commonplace which now hardly needs discussion that, in the conflict of interests produced by this situation, it is certainly difficult, and perhaps impossible, to avoid an ultimate catastrophe.

The inference from these theses is clear. The profits made possible by foreign investment developed that imperialism especially characteristic of the last third of the nineteenth century. To protect and reinforce the gains so acquired, each state which embarked upon these adventures was driven into an increase of its armaments to safeguard its interests from invasion. But from the increase of armaments came those mutual fears and suspicions which, in their turn, led to the complicated alliances and counter-alliances of the first years of the twentieth century; nation-states stood in the posture of gladiators to one another. The colony, the protectorate, the sphere of influence, the sphere, even, of legitimate aspiration, all illustrate different phases of the development. All involve the politics of prestige, and the politics of prestige involve a system in which the armed forces of the state become the ultimate measure of its authority. Realistically scrutinized, the politics of prestige are nothing more than the power of the capitalist in any given state to call upon it to defend profits he either has acquired or hopes to acquire. The British occupation of Egypt was undertaken to secure the interests of British bondholders. The South African War was simply a sordid struggle for the domination of the gold-mines.

No imperialist power has been exempt from these influences. The French control of Morocco was an effort to protect the investments of French capitalists. The Russo-Japanese War was, at bottom, the outcome of an endeavour by a corrupt government to defend the immense timber concessions in Manchuria of a little band of dubious courtiers. Nicaragua, Santo Domingo, Haiti, have all been reduced to the position of American provinces in the interests of American capitalists. The savage cruelties of the Congo, the struggle between British and American financiers for the control of Mexican oil, the fight between Germany and the Entente for the domination of the Near East in the pre-war period, the Japanese strangulation of Korea and its recent creation of the puppet-state of Manchukuo, all these are variations upon an identical theme. Men have sought and, as they think, found a particularly profitable source of investment; they have been able to mobilize their governments to protect their interests, in the end, the government becomes so identified with the investor that a threat to his profit is equated with an attack upon the national honour. In these circumstances, the armed forces of the state are, in fact, the weapon he employs to guarantee the enjoyment of his privilege.

It is clear that a state which lived in this atmosphere was bound, in the logic of the system, to regard war as the supreme expression of its sovereign power. Its statesmen might not desire it; but the forces which drove them permitted them no alternative. For not to make war was, given the postulates of the system, to risk the profit-making which was the essence of capitalism. Not to make war was to nullify the whole purpose of the state's sovereignty. And the association of national feeling with capitalist adventure had, by 1914, become so strong that even socialist leaders who were pledged to resist war abandoned their hostility to it and distinguished between the special circumstances of that particular crisis and all previous wars. By its end, they had realized that their interpretation was a mistaken one; but by that time it was too late to repair the consequences of their error.

The thesis I am here concerned to defend is that the sovereignty of the state cannot be abandoned so long as its power is at the disposal of the owners of capital. That is why the League of Nations has failed before so many of its major problems. It failed before the menace of Japanese imperialism; it failed before the menace of armaments; it failed before the menace of economic nationalism. If it be said that the failure was rather that of its members—the unanimous condemnation of Japan in March 1933 being a notable achievement—that does not affect my argument; for the source of the failure lay in its conception as a league of sovereign states. To have the prospect of success, it would be necessary for the League to prevent war from being regarded as a possible instrument of state-policy. For that prevention, the erosion of the idea of sovereignty is essential. For until it is eroded, any serious cohesion on the international plane cannot be realized. It is only when that is done that the League can seriously devote its energies to dealing with the causes of war. Every step it takes to that end, so long as the state remains sovereign, is narrowed by the inherent consequences of sovereignty. An international police-force, the abandonment of the submarine, the abolition of military aircraft, the use of the economic boycott against an aggressor, all affect the national interest of some state; and it employs its sovereignty to prevent agreement upon any of these issues. And since the basis of the League requires unanimous agreement in all save procedural questions, each state's sovereign right to safeguard what it conceives to be its interest means that, upon the major issues, nothing is done at all. And, meanwhile, the growing crisis of capitalism produces an atmosphere ever more exacerbated, with the result that states which are aware of the disastrous consequences of war nevertheless find themselves driven to prepare for its coming as an event they are powerless to control.

My argument, therefore, is the simple one that the postulates of the imperialist phase of capitalist development necessarily involve war; and that an effective international order is, *a priori*, incompatible with it. That international order must fit the categories of a unified economic world, and this has completely outgrown the limitations which the sovereign state, as a political category, puts upon it. An international order, to be effective, must control things like currency, tariffs, labour standards, migration, access to raw materials, the penetration of backward areas, and so forth. But to control these things, it must be able to override the existing vested interests which use the sovereignty of the state for their protection. It cannot override them, as the world is at present organized; for they arise inherently from the class-relations of a capitalist society. The forces which protect them are exactly the same as the forces which protect the power of the capitalist inside the national society to which he belongs. Exactly as the sovereign state protects, in the internal sphere, a system of legal rights intended to safeguard his supremacy, so, externally, its authority, by the sheer logic of his relationships with it, must be used to impose that supremacy, so far as may be, upon others. It is only as these class-relations are transformed that state-antagonisms become capable of any fundamental reconciliation. Upon the existing basis, the utmost goodwill in international relations can only postpone, without being able to avoid, the ultimately inevitable conflict.

III

Several things in the post-war epoch unite, I think, to confirm the accuracy of this interpretation. It is significant that the semi-Fascist or wholly Fascist states, Japan, Germany, Italy, are all in search of colonial gains; and it is not less important that they are all frankly militarist in temper. Each of them is confronted by serious internal discontent which an autocratic government suppresses in the interest of the capitalists it represents; and each pursues a spirited foreign policy in the effort, thereby, to divert attention from domestic grievance. Everyone knows that, in the long run, policies like those to which Japan and Hitler and Mussolini are driven by their internal position inevitably mean war; everyone, similarly, watches the safeguards in alliances and armaments which they involve in the other Powers. Their policies put a strain upon the peace-system it is impossible to dissipate while class-relations remain what they are. But each of these policies is the logical outcome of a capitalism so driven by its distresses that it must, somehow, secure a field of expansion if it is to save itself from disaster. And, as the world is now organized, it has no means to expand except at the cost of some other state which, in its turn, cannot surrender the territories it occupies, lest, by so doing, it multiplies the economic problems it confronts itself.

Not less revealing has been the growth of economic nationalism in Great Britain in the post-war years. A faint revival of a protectionist movement in England can be seen as early as the eighties of last century,[1] and the Conservative Party has been more or less committed to protectionist ideas since Mr. Chamberlain's campaign of 1903. But the electorate has steadily condemned tariff reform at every election since 1906; and as recently as 1923, when Mr. Baldwin specifically dissolved Parliament upon this issue, he was overwhelmingly defeated. Not only was this the case. Even in the panic election of 1931, which returned the largest Conservative majority of modern times, the electorate was assured by the leading members of the National government that they were not being asked for a mandate for protection [2]; it is pretty certain that the Liberal Party would not have gone into a coalition government on those terms. Yet within a few months of its formation the free-trade system had disappeared, and steps had been taken, at the Ottawa Conference of 1932, to develop those closer economic relations with the Empire which successive governments had refused to attempt for over a generation.

The evolution is remarkable enough to need some consideration. Great Britain was the first nation to benefit from the Industrial Revolution; and, under free trade, she had become the primary manufacturing nation of the world. She depended upon her exports; and to limit these by cutting down imports seemed to her manufacturers of cotton and wool, of iron and steel and coal, a policy of suicide. But as other nations transformed their economy from an agrarian to an industrial character, they began, as notably in the

[1] Winston Churchill, *Life of Lord Randolph Churchill* (1906), Vol. I, pp. 290 f.

[2] Cf. the documents on this assembled by Lord Snowden, *Autobiography* (1934), Vol. II, pp. 991–5.

United States, to protect their domestic markets in the interest of the home producer; and, though Great Britain remained predominant until the war, she began to feel keenly the competition of other peoples. The war gravely intensified this position. Not only did it revolutionize the wonted channels of trade; its peculiar problems gave birth to a nationalism which rapidly expressed itself in the economic sphere. Great Britain then found herself in a position where a revenue from a tariff offered solid advantages to the taxpayer. The loss of exports made the authority of the exporter far less profound than it had been in the previous generation; while the concern of the domestic producer to protect himself from competition made it possible, in the presence of heavy unemployment, to revive the old balance-of-trade argument in a way which made men as unwilling to realize its patent fallacies as they had been in the mercantilist epoch. No new argument on behalf of a tariff was introduced; business men simply accepted the position that circumstances had so changed as to make free trade an outworn dogma void any longer of meaning. The result, of course, was gravely to jeopardize the economic position of those countries, like Belgium and Denmark, whose well-being had largely depended upon their access to British markets. But the change was made with hardly a ripple upon the surface of domestic politics; and it revealed the degree to which the nation, whose economic technique above all rendered it indispensable for her to maintain an international outlook, was driven to sacrifice her historic specialization to that ideal of autarchy whose implication is the depth to which our power to produce is in contradiction with our power to distribute. And that contradiction, once more, is the necessary outcome of the system of class-relations in which capitalist society is involved.

A third notable feature of our epoch is at once the agreement of economists upon the measures which would give a new lease of life to the capitalist system, and the impossibility, in the framework of existing class-relations, of giving practical effect to their recommendations. It is a matter of general agreement that we need to put the control of all public foreign loans in the hands of the League; only in this way can we avert at once dubious expenditure by the debtor nations and the undesirable pressures that go therewith. We need the reduction of tariffs and similar devices of restriction. We need a concerted world monetary system. We need an improvement in the technique of domestic investment and, particularly, ways of preventing those speculative manias which are induced by the present methods of the stock exchanges. We need, also, a drastic reorganization of industrial methods. We have to co-ordinate, by international agreement, the volume of production of basic raw materials; and to prevent both the dumping of commodities produced by sweated labour and that policy of subsidies to industry which, like the beet-sugar industry in Great Britain, live only, as they live unnecessarily, by artificial stimulus of this kind. We can, in short, lay down the outlines of an international economic policy which, granted the maintenance of peace, might offer to capitalism a sufficient degree of recovery to make possible an increasing standard of life.[1]

---

[1] See Sir Arthur Salter's *Recovery* (1932) for a programme of this kind. His conclusions are substantially identical with the programme of the economists put forward at the Preparatory Economic Conference at Geneva in 1927.

But it is clear from our experience since 1919 that such methods are not open to our competitive capitalist structure. The vested interests involved will not make the necessary sacrifices; and they count upon their power to utilize national emotions to preserve them in this outlook. It had been predicted by Sir Arthur Salter [1] that a World Conference of Governments, seeking the basis of concerted economic action, might well do more harm than good; and his prevision of 1925 was only too amply confirmed by the experience of 1933. The fact is that our system of class-relations compels us to handle the problems of an international society with a technique derived from a wholly different epoch. It is not really remarkable that the technique and the objective, being basically antithetic to each other, should fail to reach an harmonious relationship.

For the problems of an international system require the subjection of the discretion of each individual state to the common good. That subjection cannot be realized so long as discretion expresses a policy designed to preserve, and even to extend, the claims of vested interests. For if discretion may come into play, it must have the means at its disposal to give effect to its purposes; and this really means that, on any realist view, disarmament and the existing economic system are radically incompatible ideals. The enthusiast who can see that no nation really wants war, who, therefore, assumes that the path to disarmament is, or ought to be, a straight one, forgets the important fact that, while no nation wants war, the economic system of each is so organized that many of its advantages cannot, in the long run, be secured without conflict. So long as this is the case, the military and naval experts

[1] *The United States of Europe* (1934), p. 35.

in every state must demand the instruments they deem essential to securing these advantages. Nothing else can explain the long-drawn-out hypocrisies of the Disarmament Conference of 1932. What, in brief, is revealed is that, while the state is prepared to insist on its zeal for all abstract disarmament, it is not seriously prepared to relinquish any weapon which, in its considered judgment, is of special value in the struggle for power. To disarm is to trust in the power of reason to convince; and to trust in the power of reason is to surrender irresponsible discretion and the power-politics by which this is enforced. An international society which is to be effective requires this surrender. But it is a contradiction in terms of the postulates of the existing order.

A contradiction, indeed, both on the internal and on the external side. On the internal side because, since the class-structure of society denies the equal claim of men to welfare, it must search for alternative ways of satisfying the masses, and this it can do only by exploitation abroad. On the external side also; for, to protect its claim to exploit, it must maintain its title to sovereignty so as to deny, whenever its prestige is threatened, the right of reason to precedence. A capitalism is abstractly conceivable, of international scope, which surmounted the barriers of nationality. But, limited by history to alliance with the national state, it is incapable of making the necessary adjustments in its assumptions.

An international society requires economic world-planning; nothing less than this can now utilize our resources to the maximum effect. But economic world-planning means that the greater interest must prevail over the less, that, accordingly, reason is used as the master-key to the solution of our problems. But men do not give whole-hearted allegiance to reason when their interest is associated with a denial of its claims. For them, in such a context, the little platoon takes precedence over the great regiment of mankind. An organized privilege which is asked to abdicate appeals from reason to the passions which its institutions can call into play; and reason is usually impotent before their expression. Impotent because, in our given class-relations, those who prevail are the men who shape the contours of policy, and these are always the owners of the instruments of economic power. Reason cannot defend their position unless it can be shown that their special privilege is a necessary incident of the common good; and there are few economic privileges in the modern state which can seriously be defended on this ground. Their holders are therefore driven to the exploitation of ignorance, passion, and prejudice in order to maintain them; and there is no atmosphere so conducive as war to the success of this exploitation.

Men give heed to reason when they have an equal interest in the result of its operations. So soon as these threaten an institutional structure from which they derive a special advantage, they deny its title to be heard. That has been the history of all great social reforms in the past—the establishment of religious toleration, the abolition of slavery, the admission of women to the franchise, the recognition of trade unions, the electoral emancipation of the working-class. The same is true of the effort to give institutional form to the implications of the international community in which we have become involved. Its implications are a contradiction of those inherent in the class-structure of capitalism. They can work only as it enjoys peace; it can enjoy peace only so long as this is the patent interest of its members. But they will not believe that it is their patent interest if its consequences threaten some especial privilege to which they attach importance. There is then no ingenuity of which they will not be capable to defend their right to make war. They may say that their national interest or honour is at stake. They may argue that they are defending the claims of civilization against barbarism. They may insist that they are preserving the sacred obligations of historic contract. They may even deny that the war is a war at all; and it will emerge for them as a punitive expedition, or the restoration of order in the interest of the very state with which they are in conflict. We have known all these things in our time; and, so long as our society is built upon its present class-structure, there is no inherent reason why we should not know them again. But, in each case, the ingenuity, when the effect of passion has been dispersed, does not conceal the fact that it is a special economic interest which uses the state-power to safeguard or to extend its privileges.

It is in this background that all proposals built upon the idea of collective security through the League of Nations must be read. They presuppose a realizable unity of interests between states against an aggressor. They assume that each state feels so strongly the desirability of peace that it will pool its power with that of other states to preserve or to restore it. But this is an abstract approach which does not take sufficient account of what is meant by the contradiction between the economic order struggling to be born and the political order which stands in the way of its birth. The invasion of Manchuria by Japan was exactly one of those aggressive acts which should have called into play the sanctions of the collective system. None of the major states was prepared to operate even the least of these sanctions against her. Japan received moral condemnation in abundance. But she probably feels that her virtual protectorate over Manchuria, with the prospects of economic gain that it offers, is more than adequate compensation for an empty resolution of the League. The deliberate effort of Hitlerite Germany to destroy the independence of Austria has shocked the conscience of every European state; but careful efforts have been made to prevent the issue from being raised in Geneva for the simple reason that every power shrinks from the use of sanctions against German aggression. It is not easy, either, to visualize France or Italy enforcing such sanctions against their respective satellite allies; for so to employ them would destroy the purposes for which those alliances have been so carefully made. That the weapons involved are of enormous importance is clear; but it is their very importance which makes their use so doubtful within the confines of the present system. Their employment would imply an agreement upon the purposes of international organization, a will to subordinate all other objects of policy to peace, which are denied by all the inherent habits of the present social order. Could we expect, in a Russo-German war, that Poland and Rumania would apply economic sanctions against a belligerent whose power, even granted their protection by the League, might well be fatal to their own well-being? The League, we may say, would secure to them damages for any injuries they might suffer. But the experience of collecting reparations from Germany does not make that prospect a very hopeful one; and it is at least conceivable that neutrality might appear a more attractive policy to any state not immediately involved in the issues of conflict.

IV

In my view, therefore, the high road to an effective international order lies through the reconstruction of the class-relations of modern society. The more effectively this is pursued the less interest states possess in the pursuit of an imperialist policy. To develop the productive power of the community so that men share equally in its results is to prevent the perversion of its political authority to the interest of a small number of its members. Its sovereignty is then no longer a cloak for that interest. Its direction of capital investment is no longer a technique of exploitation abroad which proceeds regardless of domestic need. Its foreign relations express a commercial connexion which does not require the inherent militarism of a policy built upon the ideal of economic empire. A society of socialist states is in a position, to which no other order of life can pretend, to consider its economic problems upon a basis of genuine mutuality and goodwill. For such a society, and no other society, can plan its life in a deliberate and coherent way. It is not oppressed by those problems of prestige which are inherent in the nature of the capitalist state because they are inherent in the class-relations of capitalism. Its interest in peace is the more direct since it is not perverted from allegiance to it by the peculiar psychology of patriotism which a capitalist society is driven to invent for its own preservation. We cannot build a system of co-operation upon principles which, as they are applied, live on the exploitation of man by man.

It has been argued that the movement towards this change in class-relations cannot succeed save as the institutions of an international order are effectively organized.[1] But this is to assume that a capacity for such organization is possible within the framework of the present society. If the analysis here made is correct, it follows that the assumption is an impossible one. Capitalist peace is only, by its nature, a breathing-space between wars; for the relation between capitalism and the national state is one in which conflict is necessarily involved in the long run. Our task, therefore, if our will to peace is genuine, is to seek the transformation of capitalist society as the essential pre-requisite of an international community with the prospect of seriously functioning.

Such a transformation alone makes possible the abandonment of sovereignty in that form which strikes at the root of peace. It alone places the total interest of the international community upon a plane where it begins to have meaning. For an equal society does not need the technique of imperialism; this has been the logical outcome of the property-relations inherent in the capitalist structure. That this is the case is evident not less from the economic history of the United States, France, and Germany, than from that of the classic model of the British Empire. Imperialism comes always, to Britain as to Rome, as a means of protecting privilege from assault by making the offer of concessions to the masses an easier adventure. Once that necessity is obviated, the process of capital investment becomes genuinely conceivable upon a plane where the common well-being can receive serious consideration. So, also, with tariffs and currency and raw materials; so also with the grave psychological problems of migration. A world-order of socialist societies, by the logic of its equal interest in the result of planning, is able to ap-

[1] Prof. Zimmern in *The Political Quarterly*, October 1932.

proach their solution with a real determination that reason shall prevail.

Too much of pacifist effort is built upon the thesis that a little more will, a little more energy and determination in statesmen, would have averted the disappointments we have suffered in the post-war years. They might have mitigated them a little; I do not think they could have averted them. For the decisions of statesmen are not abstract judgments of principle; they are decisions taken in a world determined by the interplay of hard material forces. In the world in which we live an attempt to influence the behaviour of Japan by a withdrawal of ambassadors of the member-states of the League, or by the threat of economic boycott, might, at least conceivably, have resulted in war; and it is by no means certain that such a war would have had support from public opinion. The criticism that Sir John Simon, for instance, took no risks for the League omits to emphasize the fact that, had he done so, he might well have precipitated a conflict in which the League itself, and much else, would have perished. His critics may well be right in their belief that his policy was far more timid than the facts he confronted made necessary. But the timidity of which they complain was of the very essence of the psychological atmosphere created by a capitalist society. To make possible the courage which the pacifists desire they must create an atmosphere in which each state which stands by its obligations under the Covenant of the League will find itself automatically supported by its fellow-members. As things are, the interest of each state, in every dispute where sanctions may be necessary, is so different from that of the others that there is no assurance of that automatism. And, without it, we confront the position that, on the one hand, the League is uncertain of its ability to act against a recalcitrant member, and, on the other, that a member-state which loyally observes its obligations may suffer disaster for so doing.

The way of peace, therefore, is the way of economic democracy; for there is no other method of building social organization upon the basis of reason and justice. In any other form of society, it is the power of the privileged class which owns property that determines the habits of the state; and they are certain to use that power in the international field both to consolidate and to reinforce their authority. Desire then becomes the parent of principle, and reason the servant of prestige. Such a society may even will to do justice; but it cannot help equating the idea of justice with the maintenance of its own authority. It acts, as I have argued, in the field of international relations exactly as it acts towards its own citizens. Its equation of right with interest persuades it to postpone necessary external changes in the same way as it is persuaded to postpone necessary internal changes. Only a transformation of the whole property-system can alter the psychological perspective which stands in the way of an adequate international order.

Here, perhaps, it is desirable to interpolate the remark that socialism and economic imperialism are incompatible terms. For the latter cannot operate except in terms of military power; and it is the cost of this—in Great Britain five times as great as it was sixty years ago—which is the main barrier against expenditure upon social reform. More, it may be argued that, since imperial adventures take the national mind away from social reform, the vested interests, like slums and the drink traffic, which social reform must seek to attack, find the best screen for their protection in the development of imperialism; that is why brewers and slum property-owners are always enthusiasts for an expanding empire. And the poison is more subtle than this. For the more profound the imperial interests of a people, the less secure are its democratic habits likely to be. Its problems are rarely susceptible to the technique of popular control, as has been made manifest when governments of the left have sought to liberalize the operation of British policy in Kenya or in India. It becomes difficult to avoid continuity, whether in men or in ideas, from the fear that a break in tradition may cripple the prestige of the nation abroad. But the avoidance of a break in tradition has, as its result, the practical withdrawal of important public questions from popular control in the legislative assembly. This, in its turn, narrows the ground between parties, and increases the authority of the executive by freeing it from the danger of criticisms of principle. The keys of India may be, as Disraeli said, in London; but it is small comfort to an Indian nationalist to realize that, normally, there is only one occasion in the year when the House of Commons considers what doors they should unlock.

In these circumstances, two results follow. On the one hand, party government is weakened and, with its weakening, the energizing principle of representative government. Mr. J. A. Hobson has shown, in a classic book,[1] how the effort of the Liberal Party to find terms of accommodation with imperialism cut at the root of its identity as a separate creed. That made possible the fusion of the party with Conservatives, and the pursuit of common imperialist aims; from 1906 onwards there was little serious difference between the parties

[1] *Imperialism* (1904).

on matters either of colonial or of foreign policy. And the stronger the continuity, the smaller the public criticism; with the result that parliamentary control of both became little more than a polite fiction. When, later, the socialists became the second party in the state, they were driven, in their turn, either to accept continuity and thus to acquiesce in the technique of imperialism, or, by challenging it, to attack at the root the main safeguard of the domestic vested interests to which they were antagonistic. If they associated socialism with democracy in the imperial sphere, as in India, for example, they drove the vested interests to doubts of the democratic hypothesis. For the development of autocratic habits in imperial and foreign affairs, where the will of the vested interests has had its way with little challenge, has naturally had its repercussions in the domestic sphere. If economic democracy means the end of imperialism, it is natural for the imperialist to contemplate the end of democracy.

These affiliations are significant. They reveal how deep is the cleavage driven by the habits of imperialism into the national unity. For the polity it needs for its defence is one that denies equality, which is the affirmation of its own essence by the democratic system. And a society which denies equality within itself has no difficulty in denying it abroad. So to deny it is necessarily to weigh the claims of other peoples differently from one's own; and, in the long run, to weigh them unequally is to treat them with indifference. That this has been the practice of imperialism its treatment of the native races makes manifest; and it is not a large step to take from contempt for the human rights of the native to contempt for the common folk in general. It is significant, for example, that a pseudo-scientific biology which began by insisting on the superiority of the white race has continued by a general affirmation of the biological superiority of the white rich over the white poor. It uses this affirmation to attack their claim to social reforms; for the cost of these, as also their consequence, very notably in the field of education, is a threat to their own privileged position. And the more fully the pressure of imperialist forces is free from the menace of democratic control, with its drive to social reform, the more free it is to drive forward to further aggression in which it sees the prospect of profit. But the more it drives forward the less chance there is for competing imperialisms, the greater, accordingly, the chance of conflict between them. And, as conflict approaches, as we learned in the years before 1914, the more ardent are the preparations for its coming whether military, or economic, or psychological. Peace itself, in this context, becomes a troubled breathing-space in which the very men who protest their devotion to it, some of them, no doubt, in all sincerity, are driven to make preparations for inescapable war.

This may be put quite briefly in a series of affirmations. Imperialism requires militarism to protect its conquests. The conjuncture of these deflects the national attention from urgent domestic issues and spends the revenue of the state upon objects of unproductive expenditure. More, the preservation of the conquests requires continuity of policy in the spheres of imperial and foreign affairs; these cease in increasing degree to be the objects of democratic control. But this, in its turn, develops an impatience with the wants of democracy in the domestic sphere; and insistence by democracy upon its wants leads to an increasing doubt of the validity of the democratic hypothesis. When the latter begins to gain ground beyond the formal territory of politics, it is challenged; and the outcome of the challenge, where the circumstances are favourable to reaction, is autocracy in one or other of its varied forms. This autocracy, freed from the hampering limitations of democracy, is then more free to pursue its imperialist aims, and is, indeed, tempted to do so in order to draw attention away from domestic grievance. But the imperialist aims, as they grow in intensity, clash with those of some competing state; and the powers involved, as a rule with their satellites also, move irresistibly upon the path to war.

All this, it may be suggested, is illustrated not less by the history of the post-war years than by that of their forerunners. The conflict of imperialism with democracy in Italy and Germany are only the most dramatic examples of the deliberate sabotage of equality in the economic sphere to preserve the privileges of a small class. They sacrifice the claim of numbers to the demands of property; and the latter, once it has assured itself of power, begins immediately to think of the riches upon which it may lay its hands if a spirited foreign policy is only backed by a strong enough armed force. It is not accident which makes Hitlerite Germany look to Eastern Europe for territorial gains which will add to its prestige with its own people; there are solid economic advantages in that policy which may well seem to its authors to justify a gambler's throw. It is not accident, either, that makes Fascist Italy yearn for African aggrandizement; absorption of its subjects in the cultivation of a new empire will deflect their minds from the grimmer spectacle of the Lipari Islands. The price of those dreams is war; and there always comes a time when the prestige of the dreamer is so associated with their realization that his alternative lies between paying the price and being overthrown. He cannot really hesitate between such alternatives.

Nor is the history of other peoples in essence different. Even Great Britain and the United States, where the liberal tradition is most strongly rooted, find in their midst profound suspicions of democracy because, as their ability to penetrate new markets declines, the threat of democracy to economic privilege becomes ever more manifest. In each of them, the control of the state by imperialist interests poisons the international atmosphere; as is evident, for example, in Anglo-American naval rivalry, and in the difficulties of the Disarmament and World Economic Conferences. It is significant that, in both countries, the main protagonists of empire are also the most bitter opponents of socialism; it is peculiarly significant that, in Great Britain, the main attack upon democracy, especially in the economic realm, has come from men who, in the last sixty or seventy years, have been trained in imperialist habits of thought by Indian experience. An imperialist society, being built upon the implicit claim of a superior race to govern an inferior, naturally assumes that its rights are a function of its power to get its will obeyed; that is the only logic it is able to understand. But, starting from that postulate, it requires all the implications of sovereignty in order that it may make good its case. Once it parts with its discretion, it then ceases to have the right to be the judge in its own cause. At that moment, power has to run in the leading-strings of principle; which means that the whole purpose of sovereignty is void for a state which then admits a claim superior to its interest. But this is a denial of the logic of imperialism which, by its own inner impulse, equates right with power. And it is that inner impulse which the postulates of an international society exist to deny.

In a sense, this is admitted by many of those whose desire for an effective international order is beyond suspicion. The Geneva Protocol of 1924 sought to make automatic the use of sanctions against any state which violated the Covenant of the League of Nations.[1] Adopted with impressive unanimity by the Assembly of the League, it was immediately wrecked by the refusal of the British government to ratify it; to have done so would have been to part with its sovereign discretion to choose when it may act. What is the criticism passed upon the Protocol? "No one," writes Sir John Fischer Williams,[2] "would dispute the sincerity, the experience, the skill, and the good intentions of its authors, but they hardly seem to have given sufficient weight to the practical conditions in which international decisions, and particularly decisions for the application of force, have to be reached." What are those conditions? "The most," Sir John suggests,[3] "that can be done is to lay down broad principles, make them as clear as possible, and trust the good faith of the responsible statesmen who have to apply the principles when the time arrives."

The implication, surely, is clear. The "practical conditions" are that no international agreement is attainable which demands of a great state the surrender of its sovereignty. Whenever an aggressive act occurs, confidence must be placed in the "good faith" of statesmen to apply general principles

---

[1] On the Protocol of 1924 Mr. Philip Noel-Baker's *The Geneva Protocol* (1925) has the most useful discussion.

[2] *Some Aspects of the Covenant of the League of Nations* (1934), p. 216.

[3] *Ibid.*, p. 218.

by which they are morally bound. But it is surely an obvious lesson of historic experience that the "good faith" of statesmen is invariably conditioned by the circumstances in which they find themselves. "Good faith" to the statesmen who had to interpret their fairly specific obligations to Belgium in 1914 was capable of quite antithetic interpretation. The Japanese view of their obligations under the Covenant of the League and the Pact of Paris was still compatible with the rape of Manchuria. Italy did not hesitate to bombard Corfu when her prestige seemed to her to involve a demonstration of that kind. The "good faith" of statesmen has accepted a convention which prohibits the use of poison gas in warfare; but it is well known that there is no major state which is not engaged in experiments of this kind. Given the attitude of Germany to Austria, of Italy to Albania, of Japan to Russia, to take only instances where "good faith" has been demonstrated by overt acts, it does not seem excessive to suggest that reliance upon it as a sanction of international principles hardly takes us very far towards the end we have in view.

Reliance upon "good faith," in fact, is, at bottom, reliance upon reason; and it is to the power of reason in international affairs that the argument has constantly to return. We can show, it is said, that war does not pay. We can demonstrate historically that its use is fatal, on the modern scale, alike to victors and to vanquished. Not only are its horrors intense; it opens the floodgates to that revolution which, as in Russia, is fatal to the very men who embark upon it. If, therefore, we make plain enough the manifest disadvantages of war, we shall, in the long run, convince men of its futility as an instrument of national policy. But we must proceed in the conditions we are given. To go beyond them, as in the Protocol of 1924, is simply unpractical idealism which defeats its own ends. It can only discredit the great purposes it seeks to serve.

But the "conditions we are given" are conditions which, by their inherent nature, limit the power of reason to influence the minds of men. They are the class-relations of an economic society which, at every point, subordinates reason to interest. We should not have abolished slavery by trusting in the power of reason over the owners of slaves. We shall not abolish the traffic in women or noxious drugs by trusting in the power of reason to convince the traffickers that it is an immoral trade. Our class-system makes war profitable to certain persons under certain circumstances; we shall not persuade them to forgo their profit if they think they have a chance of securing their differential advantage by war. The weakness of the plea made for reason by its advocates is the final weakness that the conditions under which reason can operate effectively are absent from the system under which we live.

For it is a "reason" which has to operate in an atmosphere poisoned by the play of interests concerned to have their way with little regard to the cost. It is an atmosphere in which we cannot depend upon a supply of truthful news; in which, as Mr. Lloyd George has told us,[1] even so honourable a statesman as Lord Grey is prepared to withhold vital information from the colleagues who share responsibility with him for his policy; in which, also, our educational systems are at no point adapted to confer upon the masses that knowledge even of the larger aspects of international affairs without which reason is powerless; in which, still, the habits of diplo-

[1] *War Memoirs,* Vol. I, pp. 46 f.

matic intercourse are pervaded by ideas characteristic of the world of Machiavelli and Hobbes. We must not forget, in our emphasis upon the power of reason, that the world of international relations is still built upon Bacon's aphorism that "it is the solecism of power to think to command the end and yet not to endure the means." "I am a great lover of morality," wrote the Lord Grey of the Reform Bill to the Princess Lieven,[1] "public and private; but the intercourse of nations cannot be strictly regulated by that rule." It is a view, as Lord Acton pointed out,[2] as old as history itself. The place we give to reason in affairs will always depend upon how passionately we desire the object that reason must seek to justify.

Our world is one in which the war of classes within our given society is matched by the war of states which reflects that conflict in the outside world. We can only end this latter condition as we remove the relationships which give rise to the former. All our ideas of international right will, at bottom, be a reflection of the circumstances those relationships define. That is the significance of our slow progress towards the realization of that *civitas maxima* which is the only logical goal we can now set before ourselves. The sharper the internal war within its member-states, the more suspiciously they must regard all principles and institutions which seek to limit their sovereign authority. For it is by that sovereign authority alone that they maintain the present system of class-relations against the challenge it encounters in our time. The profounder the challenge within, the more eagerly the state looks beyond its frontiers for the means to mitigate its acer-

---

[1] *Correspondence with the Princess Lieven*, p. 234.
[2] *History of Freedom* (1909), p. 219.

bity. War is not made merely by the machinations of evil men who, had they so willed, might have chosen peace. War is the expression of an unequal society which is seeking, at all costs, to defend its privileges from invasion. We can transcend it only as we make a world in which the chief function of government is no longer the protection of that class-structure which capitalism demands.

IV

THE OUTLOOK FOR OUR GENERATION

I

REGARDED from without, every state appears as an association of citizens seeking the achievement of a common purpose; and this is especially the case when it is examined in its international capacity. We think of the sharing in a common historical tradition sanctified by dear and exclusive memories which bind its members together in a nexus as real and intimate as the link between members of the same family. We think of its social services, by which it strives to mitigate the difference in welfare between rich and poor. We think of law courts which offer an impartial justice to members of every class. We think of a legislative assembly in which not only the humblest citizen may find a place, but in which, also, even the most distinguished must win the suffrages of the community to which he belongs. We compare the functions of the state today with what they were a century, or even half a century, ago. It is easy to conclude that the change represents a definite increase in the profundity of the social conscience. It is natural to infer from that conclusion that a more profound social conscience establishes the state as an organization which seeks to realize the common good of its members.

It is an easy conclusion, but, unless the thesis of this book is a wholly mistaken one, it is also a superficial conclusion. For, on the view here set out, the unity we find in our society is not one of consent, but of coercion; and the essential feature of the state is not its search for a common welfare but its power to compel the acceptance of certain class-relationships which make that common welfare peripheral, and not central, to its aim. The true end of the state is to maintain the legal principles which secure within its confines the predominance of the owners of the instruments of production; and what of common welfare it ever establishes is always subordinate to that major end. Social legislation is not the outcome of a rational and objective willing of the common good by all members of the community alike; it is the price paid for those legal principles which secure the predominance of the owners of property. It waxes and wanes in terms of their prosperity. It is a body of concessions offered to avert a decisive challenge to the principles by which their authority is maintained.

This is, of course, unduly to simplify a situation which, particularly in its psychological aspect, is in fact immensely complicated. But it is important to put it in this stark way because it draws attention to what is pivotal in the analysis of the state. It emphasizes the control of ultimate coercive power by the owners of the instruments of production, and it insists that the concessions offered to the masses have not only in every instance to be fought for, but, also, that their limits are set by the postulates involved in the system of property-relations characteristic of the society the state has organized. If the demands of the masses contradict these postulates, there must be a change in the system of property-relations before they can be realized. Such a change, on the historical evidence we have, cannot be accomplished without a revolution.

The transition from feudal to bourgeois society was only accomplished by heavy fighting. There is no reason to suppose, unless we assume that men are now more rational than at any time in the past, that we can transform the foundations of bourgeois society without heavy fighting also; and the assumption of greater rationality is an illusion born of special historical circumstances and now fading before our eyes. The peculiar economic position of the nineteenth century led, through the impressive scientific discoveries of the age, to a sudden and immense access of productivity. From the great surplus so created, it was possible to distribute concessions upon a scale wide and profound enough to satisfy at once the owners of property and those who had nothing but their labour-power to sell. Hence arose that atmosphere of tolerance so favourable to the assumptions of the liberal creed. Where it was possible not merely to produce, but also to distribute, abundance, the ability to satisfy general expectations made conflict over the principles of proportionate distribution seem unnecessary to the major part of Western civilization. There was, no doubt, an ebb and flow in the liberal tide; but, broadly speaking, by the turn of the century it seemed as though the liberal ideal had been generally accepted by the mind of Western Europe and America.

The form in which it expressed itself was that of capitalist democracy; and those who doubted its adequacy as an instrument of permanent and peaceful beneficence were comparatively few in number; how few was remarkably demonstrated in 1914 when, despite their abstract profession of Marxist principles, the parties of the Second International were able with but little difficulty to accept the obligation to fight on its behalf. It was only when the combination of war-weariness and the Russian Revolution began to strip the mask from the tragic drama of war that men began to realize, in any numbers, how accidental was the union of capitalism with democracy. It was the outcome, not of an essential harmony of inner principle, but of that epoch in economic evolution when capitalism was in its phase of expansion. It had conferred political power upon the masses; but it was upon the saving condition that political power should not be utilized to cut at the root of capitalist postulates. It would offer social reforms so long as these did not jeopardize the essential relations of the capitalist system. When they did, as occurred in the post-war years, the contradiction between capitalism and democracy became the essential institutional feature of Western civilization.

It expressed itself, once more, in ways to which history has accustomed us in every period of critical transition. The coalescence of capitalist parties to maintain unbroken the front of capitalist interests; the intervention in Russia—parallel to the intervention in France a century and a half ago—to destroy by force a doctrinal poison which was held to threaten the basis of law and order; the summons of the moderate reformers to power, and their headlong overthrow when the price of moderate reform was realized; finally, as the contradiction became ever more stark, the brutal repudiation, as in Italy and Germany and Austria, of democracy as a danger too grave for capitalist principles to accept; there is nothing in all these developments that ought to have surprised us. Men spoke of the matchless British Constitution in 1931, as they spoke of it in 1792; and they eulogized its devotion to freedom even while, as then, they were whittling away its foundations. They accused the moderate reformers of subverting the guarantees of law and order at the very moment when they were utilizing these to protect their own interests against the possibilities of constitutional change. The process varied in degree in different countries, but the character of the process was everywhere the same. Even with a liberal President in the White House the threat to free discussion in the United States could assume panic proportions.[1]

The reason for this change in atmosphere was intelligible enough. Capitalism in distress could not afford the luxury of a liberal policy. It could afford to yield its outer breastworks to the pressure of democracy; it was outside its nature to surrender without conflict its inner citadel. To go on with social reform in a period of acute decline meant a change in the very basis of property-relations. That meant the surrender of privilege. It would transform an economic oligarchy into a society in which the ownership of the means of production no longer meant the possession of differential advantage. As always when the fundamental idea of property is threatened, its owners fell into a panic. Political democracy was seen to be the enemy; for political democracy entrusted formal constitutional authority to the masses. Dissatisfaction with its implications became a commonplace of discussion.

---

[1] See an interesting description of the threat to civil liberties in America in the *St. Louis Post-Dispatch* of August 26, 1934. I owe this reference to the kindness of Mr. Irving Dilliard.

The established expectations to which it had given birth were passionately denied. Within fifteen years from the conclusion of the war, that democracy for which millions of men had laid down their lives no longer seemed even a feasible ideal to the major part of civilization. The state, over most of the world, frankly abandoned the liberal principles it had embodied for the best part of a century and assumed once more its naked guise of protecting the rights of private property from assault.

What looms before us is a battle for the possession of the state-power. What is now clear is the vital fact that the class-relations of our society have become incompatible with the maintenance of social peace. They have brought to light the contradiction between our power to produce and our power to distribute in a way that makes the great paradox of our time—our poverty in the midst of potential plenty—intolerable to those who have to pay the price for it. Yet in the choice between peaceful transformation, and the maintenance of privilege at the cost of conflict, the owners of property now, as in an earlier day, are prepared rather to fight for their legal privileges than to give way. That attitude is shown not merely by the barbaric overthrow of democratic institutions in Fascist countries. It is shown, even more clearly, by the resistance to social reform in the United States and Great Britain, by the overt hostility of the Right to democracy in France. The state cannot, in any of these countries, make even an effective pretence at impartiality. Once the rights of property are in hazard, its essence as coercion comes ever more clearly into the foreground of its operations; and it is the masses whom it proposes to coerce.

It is sometimes said that the strain is due not to the unwillingness of capitalists to reform, but to the pace at which the reformers propose to enforce their changes. But there is no essential difference between their attitude today and that, for instance, which was encountered by Mr. Lloyd George when, a quarter of a century ago, he proposed fiscal reforms which seem to us today astounding in their moderation. The rejection of that Budget by the House of Lords was not an accidental decision. As early as 1906 Lord Balfour had told his supporters that it was their bounden duty to see that "the great Unionist Party should still control, whether in power or in opposition, the destinies of this great Empire." [1] What he meant he revealed to the House of Commons three months later, when on the third reading of the Liberal government's abortive Educational Bill of 1906 he declared that "the real discussion must be elsewhere." [2] It was an explicit claim for the right of property to rule the country whatever the will of the people, and no one who reads the utterances of eminent peers about that Budget can doubt that in their minds they felt entitled to safeguard themselves against any measure they might choose to regard as confiscatory.[3] Mr. Asquith was right when he warned the electorate that implicit in the claim of the Lords was the threat of revolution.[4]

"The Tories," wrote a commentator of the time,[5] "cannot put themselves in their adversary's place; they cannot see that, in using a weapon of which they have the exclusive use to rob their enemy of the fruits of victory, they are 'not play-

---

[1] Quoted in Asquith, *Fifty Years of the British Parliament* (1926), II, p. 44.
[2] Hansard (fourth series), Vol. 162, col. 545.
[3] See the observations of the Dukes of Rutland, Beaufort, and Somerset, as quoted by Lord Denman, *House of Lords Reports* (1909), Vol. IV, 1207–8.
[4] Asquith, *op. cit.*, II, p. 83.
[5] Mr. A. A. Baumann in the *Fortnightly Review* (1911), Vol. 96, pp. 6–7.

ing the game'; and in the eyes of the ordinary Briton, there can be no greater crime." There has been no essential change in the last twenty-five years. For the claim is still made that it is the function of the House of Lords to safeguard the country against a Labour government which should seek to translate socialist principles into terms of legislation; and all proposals made by the Conservative Party for the reform of the House of Lords have no end in view but to hinder such a government from legislating in the way that is open to its rivals.[1] But, on any reasonable interpretation, this has no meaning save the implication that the will of the electorate can operate only within limits set by an assembly whose whole character is to be found in its expression of the property-owning interest.

The attitude of the House of Lords is one of pure syndicalism. But it is important rather as an index to a wider frame of mind than for what it imports in itself. That frame of mind is displayed in the most diverse fields. It is shown in the stubborn resistance of the coal-owners not merely to the nationalization, but even to the unification, of their industry; even though changes in this direction have been recommended by every Royal Commission since the war. It is shown by the refusal of the cotton trade—underlined as fatal by Sir Josiah Stamp [2]—to consider the reconstruction of its foundations in the light of the new competitive conditions they confront; if vested interests are adamant against the advice of their friends, it is unlikely that they will lend a willing ear to the proposals

[1] See the debate on the Salisbury proposals, *House of Lords Debates*, May 8–10, 1934.

[2] Address to the Aberdeen Chamber of Commerce, *The Manchester Guardian*, September 10, 1934.

of those whom they regard as their enemies. It is shown in the resentment against the efforts of the Trades Union Congress to promote improvements in the position of the wage-earner. When this can be represented as a movement towards dictatorship,[1] it is clear that little disposition to goodwill marks the analysis of social relations in an era of social crisis. It is not, I think, unfair to say that property in Great Britain is willing to share the benefits of prosperity with the masses, but always upon the saving condition that no questions come into the foreground about its legal title to its privileges. But it is exactly those questions which economic evolution has pushed into the foreground.

Nor is the situation in substance different in the United States. The President has intervened in the industrial arena to secure the conditions of a reformed capitalism. But he finds himself thwarted by the refusal of the vested interests to co-operate in the principles of his adventure. They have no confidence in the methods he proposes; and since the recovery of the capital market is a function of their confidence, one essential condition of his success is wanting. And, on the other side, his effort to assist organized labour to secure recognition has been met by a sabotage of nation-wide intensity. The general strike of San Francisco, the textile strike of the autumn of 1934, are only major indices to a general determination of American business men to resist the pressure to reform. And this pressure, as I have noted, is accompanied by a growing hostility to democratic ideas which measures the tension of the time. Mr. Roosevelt's opponents fight under the banner of liberty; but their freedom means the perpetua-

---

[1] See Sir Thomas Inskip in the *Observer*, September 9, 1934.

tion of their right to maintain that condition in American society out of which the present crisis developed.[1]

The fact is that, in the circumstances we have reached, it is necessary to go outside the postulates of the capitalist system in order to achieve significant and lasting reform. Concessions of the older type are possible only when the margins of capitalist achievement are wide enough to permit them to be made without detriment to those postulates. We do not confront that condition. We have reached the stage of economic evolution which Marx foresaw when he predicted that the contradictions of capitalism would result in the emergence of a permanent and growing body of workers for whom no prospect of profitable employment can be found. Technological unemployment, the increasing power of finance-capital, the growth of economic imperialism, his predictions in each of these realms has been fully substantiated.[2] Within the framework of the existing legal order, we cannot control the implications of any of these tendencies. They are woven into the most intimate recesses of our social structure. Given its postulates, indeed, there is an important sense in which they may be regarded as the condition of its well-being. For any piecemeal attack upon them, as was shown by the experience of the Labour government in 1929, and is being once more demonstrated by the history of the Roosevelt experiment, disturbs that confidence upon which the efficient working of the system depends. A Fabian tactic of change assumes the co-operation in the task of attack of the very men to whom the system stands not merely as the protective arma-

---

[1] Cf. *The New Republic*, September 5, 1934, p. 89.

[2] Cf. G. D. H. Cole, *What Marx Really Meant* (1934), for an admirable discussion of Marx and the present time.

ment of their own interests, but, not less important, also as the guarantee of national well-being. And if such a strategy seeks to evade this dilemma by bribing capitalism into acquiescence, by luxurious terms of compensation for the transfer of ownership, it pays the price of being unable to increase the welfare which is the purpose it has in view.

I have explained in an earlier chapter why I do not think this co-operation is possible of attainment; stripped of their rhetoric, as I have sought to show, all the institutions of the state, all the ideology their operation imposes, point in the direction rather of conflict than of harmony. Here, as I think, it is important to note that this is not, as it is often taken to be, a moral condemnation of those who refuse to co-operate. The inability of capitalists to accept postulates different from their own is born of the situation in which they find themselves. It is no more possible for them, taken as a whole, to deny the creed they hold than it is, say, for an average Iraqui citizen to question the truths of Mohammedanism. It is not the habit of men to examine the principles to which they are accustomed except in a crisis; and the time-factor is then too short to permit of their examination in a mood of calm objectivity. We have got, somehow, to make up our minds to the fact that the debate upon the rights of property has always, in history, aroused passions more profound than those involved in the analysis of any other theme. It is wholly natural that they should, since the relations to which they give rise determine all the major contours of our social life. There are few principles we now deem obvious error which, at some stage, have not seemed to their proponents to be obvious truth. The divine right of kings, the duty of religious intolerance, the common sense of slavery, the inevitability of war, all of these have found, some of them still find, their eager defenders. It would be remarkable indeed if a principle so pivotal as the private ownership of the means of production were to be exempt from this general rule.

For we have to remember what it means to the class which benefits from the ownership in all normal circumstances. Health and security, access to culture and to those forms of labour which are not only attractive in themselves, but, as our standards go, also held in most social esteem; these are its obvious advantages. It enables a man to safeguard the position of his children. It assures him an old age free from those hazards which haunt the margins of all working-class life. It means the power to purchase service from others; the ability, through knowledge and travel, to avoid the monotonies of existence. It is to an equilibrium which means these things for men who have become habituated to their enjoyment that the transformation of our class-structure comes as a threat. To expect a voluntary surrender of their implications is to expect a conversion upon a scale more vast than the imagination can envisage. And it is not even an expectation that can claim, or seek to claim, religious sanction for its principles. On the contrary, its case is, overwhelmingly, not only built upon a rejection of the religious sanction, but encounters, for the most part, the antagonism of those ecclesiastical bodies which are, for most men, the overt expression of the religious spirit. We have only to think of the price exacted by missionary religions which, like Christianity, could promise eternal salvation to their votaries, without asking from them an essential change in the social order, to realize the great optimism involved in assuming that a possessing class, in control of the state-power, will assist in the destruction of what that state-power implies for itself. Men who are passionately attached to a way of life are rarely persuaded to abandon it without fighting on its behalf. And those, in this context, to whom the persuasion is addressed are by their very position convinced that the new world in which they are invited to participate is far less preferable than the one they already control.

II

But the transformation, it is said, has the assurance of numbers on its side. The owners of property are few; the proletarians are many. As the latter grow to a consciousness of their power, by the nature of the case they must dominate the situation. In Great Britain, for example, they may vote themselves, when they will, into political authority. They can then command exactly the same instruments—in last resort, the armed forces of the state—upon which the domination of the possessing-class depends. The state is there to be conquered by the power of numbers; and numbers are subject to persuasion by experience.

I have already discussed, to some extent, the assumptions implied in this view.[1] It is, I think, contradicted by a number of factors upon which too much stress can hardly be laid. It is important, in the first place, that there is too little assurance that numbers, even if they are persuaded, will be allowed to have their way; the evidence, especially on contemporary experience, is rather that, if the forces of the Left show a real determination to attempt the transformation of society, they will be anticipated in their reliance upon the use of the suf-

[1] *Supra*, Chap. II.

frage by the abrogation of the democratic process. In that event, of course, as today in Central Europe and Italy, only armed force can effect a social change.

But even if a socialist government, which was determined on drastic change, were enthroned in office, its difficulties would only have commenced. Anyone who considers its position will not be inclined, I suggest, to under-estimate the magnitude of the dilemma that will confront it. If it goes slowly, it will suffer from all the difficulties which confront any government which tries, upon the basis of capitalist postulates, to effect their piecemeal transformation. It tends to irritate its opponents by undermining confidence; and it fails to attract its supporters by inability to offer them the exhilarating spectacle of conviction turned into deed. If it proceeds rapidly—and the case for rapid action is overwhelmingly strong [1] —it is likely to meet with sabotage and resistance. In that event, it is dependent for its authority on the loyalty to its owners, not merely of the armed forces and the police,[2] but also of its own supporters whose security as wage-earners is directly threatened by a dislocation of this kind.

At this point, it is supremely important to realize the psychological problems involved in the class-structure of capitalist society. When the *Communist Manifesto* was published, nearly ninety years ago, it was natural for Marx and Engels to emphasize the historic antithesis between bourgeoisie and proletariat, and to treat the *petite bourgeoisie* as a factor of minor importance which would be forced to choose between

---

[1] See it interestingly put in Mr. G. R. Mitcheson's *The First Workers' Government* (1934), which gives a good idea of the magnitude of the changes envisaged by a British socialist on the left wing for a five-year period.

[2] On the problems involved in this loyalty, cf. my *Democracy in Crisis* (1933), especially pp. 105–10.

the two great contending parties. Recent economic development, which has made for an increasing complexity of social structure, makes the issue more difficult for us than it seemed to them. Marx, on the evidence, was profoundly right in his insistence that the proletariat alone was an advancing class capable of claims which, if successful, would destroy the class-relations of capitalist society. He was right, further, in his insistence that the *petite bourgeoisie* was destined to a dependence which unfitted it by its nature for independent revolutionary action.

But the real question is not answered by an analysis which stops there. Our position is not simply one in which a small number of capitalists confront a vastly larger number of proletarians increasingly miserable and driven to revolution by the sense of an intolerable burden. There has been nothing like the sharp antithesis of class-consciousness he imagined outside of Russia. Class-boundaries are confused and not precise. The economic development of capitalism has effected an *embourgeoisement* of large sections of the working-class, the psychological effects of which are important. The bank-clerk, the shop assistant, the civil servant, the minor technician, the office-worker, those engaged in personal services of all kinds, these, to take only the more notable examples, seem little susceptible to the influence of trade-union organization, and, still less, to the evolution of a proletarian consciousness. So far from being natural material for socialist propaganda, they have proved, on the contrary, the most favourable soil for Fascist ideas. And they appear to be joined, in an epoch of great distress, as in Germany after the war, by those large numbers of unemployed workmen to whom the future seems to offer no reasonable hope.

We have, that is to say, to confront a situation in which the difficulties of capitalism in distress, so far from uniting the working-class, divide it, and thus enable the capitalist to maintain his hold on the state by rendering possible the kind of Fascist alliance which can overthrow democratic institutions. That was the position in Central Europe and Italy. Fascism was successful there by being able to unite the *grande* and *petite bourgeoisie*, on the one hand, and to divide the working-class on the other. Being possessed of the state, it controlled the army; and it illustrated once more the pivotal truth that an unarmed section of the workers is powerless before forces such as these. It is, I think, true that the alliance between *grande* and *petite bourgeoisie* is never destined to be lasting; their pictures of the end to which the authoritarian state must be devoted are not ultimately reconcilable. Giant capitalism of the modern type clearly requires a concentration of management which makes it impossible, as Germany and Italy are showing, to satisfy the claims of their partners in victory. And it is, I think, further true, as Veblen has shown in convincing detail,[1] that the interests of finance-capital develop both economic and psychological habits which make its union with the technicians extraordinarily difficult to maintain over a period. For finance-capital, unless it can command a constantly expanding market—and this is denied it by the conditions of economic imperialism—must build upon scarcity rather than plenty as the basis of its policy. This offends the mind of the technician; and it is, of course, alien from the interests of the *petite bourgeoisie*. It means industrial crisis and unemployment in exactly the same way as in capitalist

[1] *The Engineers and the Price System* (1921); *Absentee Ownership and Business Enterprise in Modern Times* (1923).

democracy; and these, in the long run, will break the alliance which enables capitalism to defeat the working-class in the first instance.

I do not think this analysis is vitiated by the experience of Russia. For, in the first place, capitalism there was of recent growth, was largely alien in the sources of its strength, was weak in the numbers upon which it could depend to form the kind of defensive alliance of which I have spoken.[1] Russian capitalism, moreover, was overthrown in quite special circumstances. Unsuccessful war and brutal ill-treatment had made the army the spear-head of revolutionary discontent. The machinery of government had completely broken down. The peasantry was prepared to support any government which promised it peace and the land. Neither Miliukov nor Kerensky could rally behind them forces with even the chance of victory. And the circumstances in which the Revolution of February was made brought about a condition possible only in the aftermath of unsuccessful war: it left an armed proletariat confronting a bourgeoisie which could call no comparable defence force to its support. When to all this was added the supreme strategic insight of Lenin, the scene was staged for events to which the European or American position offers, at present, no possible comparison.

From this certain principles seem to me clearly to follow. In any country where the *petite bourgeoisie* is strong, its psychological affiliations are likely, in the first place, to be with capitalism rather than with the working-class. Unless the latter can win over the technicians, the black-coated proletariat,

---

[1] Cf. Trotsky, *History of the Russian Revolution* (1932), especially Vol. I and Appendix 1 to that volume for a superb picture and analysis of the Russian scene.

the administrators, and a strong section of the professional classes, its effort to conquer the state by constitutional means is unlikely to be successful; and its militancy in making demands upon a state which retains democratic institutions is likely only to precipitate their abolition. More: it seems to me clear that an unconstitutional conquest of the state by the workers, through insurrection, for instance, or by the use of such a weapon as the general strike, is bound to fail so long as the army remains loyal to the state in being, and the normal machinery of government remains in effective operation. Such an attempt, once more, would only result in the abrogation of democratic, and their replacement by Fascist, institutions. And the consequence of this would be the kind of iron despotism which Mussolini and Hitler have established in their respective states, until the economic contradictions of Fascism push the *petite bourgeoisie* to the side of the working-class.

That it will so push them, I do not doubt; for a reason that has been implicit in the whole argument of this book. It is, simply, that the development of the potential productiveness of society demands the suppression of the small manufacturer and trader. His victory in a Fascist society is bound to be a Pyrrhic one. He is destined to become the mere dependent on large-scale capital if the means of economic expansion are to be found. But this is to say that he will be driven to attack his ally if he wishes to survive, and his only chance of success in that attack is in alliance with that very proletariat whom, previously, he had helped to defeat. And an alliance with the proletariat, in these conditions, is feasible only by the offer of that change in the class-relationships of society which he formerly struggled to avert. In those circumstances, under effective leadership, there is the prospect of proletarian victory. For the ability in this position of any government to depend upon its armed forces perpetually to suppress the expression of civilian discontent is, I think, not likely to be operative over any considerable period. The atmosphere of disturbance becomes profound enough, as in 1848, to weaken the control of the government over the state-power. Disaffection can be organized upon a serious scale; doubts and uncertainties begin to invade the minds of those who deemed their economic interest to lie on the side of capitalism. No class which, in this fashion, loses its self-confidence can hope to retain power unless its opponents are guilty of unpardonable errors of strategy.

There is one further situation with which, in this context, it is necessary to deal. Our discussion has assumed an internal struggle for power unrelated to foreign conflict. But if the diagnosis of the capitalist state which I have made is correct, we cannot rule out foreign conflict from our consideration. On the contrary, as I have sought to show, the inherent nature of capitalism in its imperialist phase makes foreign war a logical part of its procedure.[1] What is likely to be its effect? We can, I think, say with some confidence that defeat presents a favourable opportunity for revolution under modern conditions. It was defeat which made possible the Russian Revolution. By destroying the morale of the army, it not only prevented it from remaining a reliable instrument in the hands of the state; it also made it supremely open to the influence of those discussions which, in the end, sent it over to the side of the Bolsheviks. It was through its effective disorganization that the workers were able to arm themselves;

[1] *Supra*, Chap. III.

and the evidence is overwhelming that this was the pivotal condition of revolutionary success. The break-down of discipline in the armed forces was fatal to the attempt alike of Miliukov and Kerensky to form a stable government. Upon that basis, neither the ministry of Prince Lvov nor that of Kerensky was able to issue orders which ever had the prospect of being obeyed. The military break-down not only coincided with, it was also effectively responsible for, the inability of civil authority to recover the right of command. In that situation power was bound to fall into the hands of the one party which built its strategy on a program corresponding to the half-articulate demands of the masses. What is surprising in the victory of the Bolsheviks is, in the circumstances, not that it occurred, but that Lenin should have had to battle so fiercely with his colleagues of the central committee for the right to make the final attack.[1]

But properly to grasp the significance of the Russian experience, it is necessary to set it in the perspective of the German Revolution of 1918–9. In both cases, military defeat preceded political catastrophe. In the Russian case, however, the Bolsheviks followed up their seizure of power by breaking the legal principles of the state they had overthrown. They made themselves the masters of its institutions by adapting them to their requirements. They dismissed the personnel in whom they had no confidence. They suppressed all counter-revolutionary organizations. They had learned Marx's essential lesson that one can never play with revolution. Their iron supremacy would probably have never suf-

[1] Cf. Lenin, *Collected Works* (Eng. trans.), Vol. XXI, *Toward the Seizure of Power,* Bk. II, pp. 57–145, especially the letters on pp. 133 and 144, and cf. the documents printed at pp. 326 f. of that volume.

fered serious attack if those who opposed them had not been financed and armed by the Allied Powers. And it is notable that they did not compromise with dissent until they judged internal consolidation sufficiently complete for them to be able to regard the new equilibrium as reasonably secure.

The German situation developed upon different lines. The break-down of the imperial regime put the power of the state into the hands of a Social Democratic Party which was quite unprepared to deal with it. It had no unity of purpose. Instead of leading the masses, it had to be driven by them; and, even while it appeared to follow them, it was making secret agreements with those very forces of the older system with whom its own logic ought to have made compromise impossible. It left the great industrial magnates in control of economic power. It left the civil and penal codes of the imperialist epoch in being; more, it left in office the old judiciary, with all its conservative traditions, to interpret them.[1] It built up an army officered by the men most alien in habit from the new principles it was anxious to impose. It so respected the theory of civil service neutrality that, even here, its changes were trifling. The church, in Germany a stronghold of reaction, was left untouched; in a few years it was even to receive new revenues and new rights. Refusing to confiscate the property of its opponents, it left them with the means, of which they took full advantage, to endow the counter-revolution. Attempts upon the new regime, like the Kapp Putsch, or the Hitler-Ludendorff attempt of 1923, were punished with extraordinary lightness. It allowed its chief of

[1] For the results of this interpretation see the remarkable book of F. N. Neumann, *Die politische und soziale Bedeutung der arbeitsgerichtlichen Rechtsprechung* (1929).

police, Noske, to play the part of a German Cavaignac on the very threshhold of its advent to power, and thus to break in pieces that very unity of the working-class upon which alone a democratic republic could depend. The Weimar republic, in brief, was so anxious for the goodwill of those enemies whom it could not hope to conciliate that it forgot the necessity of depending upon its friends. Economic distress and foreign demand no doubt intensified its inability to maintain itself; but the ease with which it was overthrown was essentially a measure of its own authors' lack of confidence in the work to which, in 1918, they put their hands.

The comparative experience of Russia and Germany—borne out fifteen years later by the somewhat different lesson of Spain—seems to establish clearly the fact that unsuccessful war is no guarantee of successful revolution. It is not enough for the makers of the revolution to capture the state; they have the additional obligation of transforming it to the purposes they wish it to serve. Ebert and his colleagues, in 1918, made only a preliminary gesture of revolution, and then withdrew from completing it by reason of their horror at the price it would entail. The system they created was, formally, a complete political democracy. But its weakness was the vital one that they had left untouched the central question of economic power. The essential class-relations of pre-war Germany were left unaltered; and that at a time when, for reasons I have already put forward,[1] formal political democracy, in union with a profound capitalist crisis, was unable to create a stable equilibrium. In the logic of post-war German evolution, the new system had either rapidly to consolidate itself

[1] *Supra*, Chap. III.

by destroying its enemies, or to be destroyed by them. Instead, it sought to placate them by asking for the forms of freedom while refusing to demand the substance in which those forms are driven to seek expression. The result was inscribed in the original compromise of Weimar. The German democracy was not defeated by Hitler in 1933; it was destroyed by its makers fifteen years before. The interval was only the relentless working-out of the principles upon which the edifice was originally founded.

The conclusion seems clear that the logic of a revolution excludes the possibility of compromise, if it is to be a successful revolution. The state-power is not the kind of authority that can dwell in the twilight world of forms. Being all or nothing by definition, it must be institutionally accommodated, both in principle of form, and in personnel, to the new objectives it has to serve. Anything else means confusion; and in the kind of dual power which thus emerges—as in Russia between March and November 1917—what may happen depends not upon reason but upon the strategic insight of the forces in conflict. The Russian Revolution made that accommodation; and, however painfully, a new state was born able thereby to consolidate its power. In Germany that was not the case. Political power was transferred to the masses, while economic power remained in the hands of those who had formerly possessed it. In an epoch of prosperity, this might have been a feasible division of power. From its riches, enough concessions of material welfare might have been available to satisfy the aspirations of the workers. But it was, in fact, an epoch of depression deepened by the bitterness of defeat. A division of power was unthinkable under those circumstances.

The attempt to maintain it only resulted in the passage of supremacy to the men who, unlike the socialists in 1918, were prepared to pay whatever might be the price of their victory. The only result—an inevitable result—of the Weimar compromise was to postpone the battle which Ebert and his colleagues then refused to join to a later period of history.

If this analysis be correct, it follows quite simply that, while history presents men with their opportunities, it leaves them also to take advantage of them. The Russian Revolution is an example of the full use of favourable circumstances by men who had steeled themselves to the task of grasping their opportunity when it occurred; the German Revolution is the history of a missed opportunity. For while the Social Democrats willed the creation of a socialist state, when the state-power fell into their hands they were not prepared to adapt it to socialist purposes. They left the main instruments of political authority in the hands of their opponents; effectively, the counter-revolution in Germany was in being from the day when the old regime was overthrown. And there was never present in the Weimar republic the frame of mind which consolidates political foundations. In its anxiety to win the assent of its enemies to the new forms it had established, it evaded the need to take account of their unbroken hostility to the ends those forms necessarily involved. After, at least, Versailles, nothing was wanting to the German counter-revolution except the opportunity of success. When this came, it proved far easier than its most optimistic protagonists could have hoped. But what it really proved was less the resistant power of capitalism to attack, than the fact that history takes its revenge upon those who do not use the opportunity with which she presents them.

III

It is not easy to over-emphasize the importance of the favourable moment in any effort to overthrow the state-power. "History," wrote Lenin to the Bolshevik Party on the eve of the November rising,[1] "history will not forgive delay by revolutionists who could be victorious today (and will surely be victorious today), while they risk losing much tomorrow, they risk losing all." The balance of forces in a state is always a dynamic matter; and a successful assault upon it is a function always of a situation where the psychology of the masses is, in its half-coherent way, already conscious of the need to break the class-relations which are incompatible with the demands they are making. The genius of Lenin as a revolutionary leader lay, supremely, in his insight into that psychology. He saw more deeply than any other figure in the events of the Revolution not only how complete was the break-down of capitalist authority, but how intensely antagonism to it had pervaded the minds of worker and peasant throughout Russia. But he saw also how impossible it is in a revolutionary epoch to leave undetermined the seat of authority. A society can live only by the re-establishment of its productive process; very rapidly, it needs to reconstitute the principles of law and order. The situation in Russia, in 1917, had reached a point when the plain alternative was between the seizure of power by the Bolsheviks and some kind of military dictatorship. And the latter would have involved exactly the rebuilding of the class-relations of capitalism

---

[1] Letter of November 6, 1917, *Collected Works* (Eng. trans.), Vol. XXI, *Toward the Seizure of Power*, Bk. II, pp. 144–5.

which Bolshevism sought as a doctrine to prevent. Had he failed to persuade his party to make the attempt of November 7, the triumph of the bourgeoisie in Russia would have been inevitable.

Whether that would have been for the benefit of Russia is not here my concern; the purpose of this book is not to justify but to analyse. And once we realize that the balance of forces in a society is always dynamic, the light thrown for us upon the conquest of state-power is of vital significance. It is particularly important in the case of the older capitalist societies like Great Britain and the United States. For there it is clear that only the pressure of great events enables the working-class to realize its own unity of interest, on the one hand, and the incompatibility of its purposes with the class-structure of capitalism on the other. In the absence of a catastrophic fall in such well-being as these systems achieve, its decline is too unevenly distributed to provoke the atmosphere of revolution. They do not involve a common assault on all working-class standards of life. The attack is rather of a fragmentary character; and this has the effect at least as much of persuading those not in immediate jeopardy to hold on to what they have as to drive them into the announcement of solidarity with their fellows. There is not a universal extremism such as the pressure of great experience, like that of Russia in 1917, produces. The sense of outrage is sporadic and not general in character.

And the fact that it is sporadic must be linked up with other psychological factors of importance. The worker-owner in England, the United States, and France has nothing like the sharp proletarian consciousness of the Russian worker before 1917. How should he have it who so often possessed a house or a savings-bank account, a motor car or a modest insurance policy? How should he who so largely has shared in a standard of living rising generally until quite recently, conferring upon him, as compared with Russia, the sense of something to lose if the productive mechanism be violently disrupted? And in Anglo-Saxon countries, and, very notably, in Scandinavia, the proletariat is still deeply influenced by the tradition of democratic success. He has seen the ambit of state-function widen by the pressure he has put upon it. His tendency is to assume his power to continue that pressure. Revolution, for him, is a violation, not a continuation, of the methods in which he places reliance by reason of his own historic past. The Russian communist, for example, who is astonished at the conservatism of the British worker judges his outlook by Russian standards instead of British standards; he ignores the category of time in his assessment of the impact of experience.

That is, I think, particularly the case in countries so comparatively rich as the United States and Great Britain. In the first, the illusion of an infinitely mobile society, the tradition of the worker with the millionaire's baton in his knapsack, the legend of infinite wealth to be exploited, still dominate the multitude. That has, so far, prevented any effective trade unionism in the United States. It has also made socialism, to the American Federation of Labor, very largely seem an exotic growth unsuited to the specially favourable conditions the working-class there has enjoyed. How profoundly rooted in American soil is the historic psychology of the *petite bourgeoisie* has been revealed remarkably by the great depression. It is clear enough that only immense catastrophe in America could cause any rapid erosion of that outlook. More, it is further clear that its operation there makes the tendency of American development much more likely to be towards the safeguarding of the existing class-structure by a Fascist growth than by a striking swing-over to a revolutionary position.

In a lesser degree this is true of Great Britain also. The faith in constitutionalism among the working-class is profound; and trade unions whose habits have been framed by so long a record of the economic success of capitalism not unnaturally cling to a belief in the possibilities of profiting from the pressure they can exert upon it. They are unwilling to jeopardize their own safety by what appears to them, especially in the light of German and Italian events, a gamble with revolution. The whole ethos of the British attitude is set by the realization that the electoral defeat of Conservatism now means the victory of Labour. This, to most, means not only the prospect of peaceful transformation. It means also the right, if a Labour government is unconstitutionally challenged, to utilize the state-power for its defence.

Now it is the inescapable necessity of any revolutionary strategy that hopes for success to be able to count upon the support of the masses. This support is absent in both England and America. It is not absent, as the proponents of revolution are inclined to argue,[1] because of the cowardice of non-revolutionary socialists, on the one hand, and the superior demagogy of their capitalist opponents on the other. It is absent because the historic experience of these countries has not produced the conditions, and, therefore, the psychology,

[1] See R. Palme Dutt, *Fascism and Social Revolution* (1934), where the rise of Fascism is brilliantly traced, but where the inability critically to account for the divisions of the working-class in historical terms is equally remarkable.

which successful revolution requires. Defeat in war might have that effect; or it might be produced by a catastrophic decline in the standard of living which continued long enough to persuade the masses that hope of recovery was futile; or, in England, it might be produced by a juggling with the Constitution which broke the workers' faith in constitutionalism. The essential point is, I think, the simple one that the slow erosion of capitalism is not dramatic enough to have either an intense or wide effect in a short space of time. From this angle, clearly, the obvious technique of anyone who desires to change the existing class-structure of society in these countries lies in the fullest possible exploration of the constitutional opportunities they offer.

For any other policy confronts a fatal dilemma. The working-class is not, by its economic position there, united enough to be able to seize power alone; and, even if it were united, it could not seize power unless it were armed. And, in the modern state, it cannot arm itself except with the benevolent assistance of the state-power; this by definition is not available. On the other hand, it is surely common sense to insist that, if a constitutional victory is bound to prove illusory, the simplest way to demonstrate the illusion is to make the electoral victory of the working-class as speedy as possible. The tactic of the revolutionist, in British conditions, ought, on these terms, to be a united front with the reformist as the surest way of proving the futility of reform.

Here, perhaps, it is worth while to analyse briefly why the revolutionist's effort to secure that united front has proved so disastrous a failure in the post-war years. It is, of course, easy to understand why it was not seriously attempted until Fascism became a widespread menace. It was the assumption of the Third International that world-revolution was imminent after the war; and a union of its forces with those of reformist socialism no doubt seemed a mere prolongation of the death-agony of a rapidly decaying system. Exhilaration at the ease of the Russian success produced, I believe, an excessive optimism about the prospect of its imminent extension to a wider historical theatre.

But, once it began to be apparent that capitalism had achieved a new, if delusive, stability, the postulates upon which the revolutionary strategy was built appear to have been gravely defective. They were based upon the famous theory that social democracy was social Fascism; and it is important to realize the implications of this view. It was put, perhaps, in its sharpest form by Karl Radek at the seventeenth Congress of the Russian Communist Party. "There is no struggle," he said, "for the cause of the working-class apart from the struggle of the Bolshevist Party under the banner of Lenin and the leadership of Stalin. Whoever attempts to oppose the general line of the Party of Lenin automatically places himself on the other side of the barricade." Why is this? Because, said Stalin, "social democracy is objectively the moderate wing of Fascism. There exists no reason for supposing that the fighting organization of the bourgeoisie can achieve decisive success in their struggles or in their leadership of the country without the active support of social democracy. . . . These organizations do not contradict one another but complete each other. They are not antipodes, but twins."

The futility of this outlook is clear. For Fascism, as its experience has shown, can triumph only by destroying the institutions of social democracy—its trade unions, its political party, its co-operative movement. All, therefore, that can be said against the social democratic theory is that its zeal for legality weakens the chance of using those whom it influences for revolutionary purposes; that, through this weakening, the resistance of the masses to Fascism is rendered abortive. But the strength of social democratic parties lies in their control of those masses who are not yet prepared to follow a revolutionary leadership. The communist regards it as his fundamental task to win them over to his side. That is why he preaches the doctrine of the united front. But as he explains that he preaches it in order to capture the very organizations from whom he invites co-operation, naturally enough, the invitation is rejected. The doctrine of the united front proves unable to wean the masses from a reliance, however mistaken, upon their social democratic leaders. Rightly or wrongly, the workers refuse to assist in the disruption of their own institutions.

The clearest case of the inadequacy of this outlook is surely seen in the experience of Germany. For there the Communist Party used the theory that social democracy is social Fascism as the ground which justified it in breaking the unity of the German working-class. It sought, on the lines of this strategy, a united front from below. It attacked the leadership of the social democrats root and branch. But when it needed union with it, in the last days of the Weimar regime, the bitterness it had created was fatal to united action in time to organize any serious resistance to Hitler. The theory led to disaster because the assumption that the social democrats were really a part of the Fascist apparatus was false; the inference drawn therefrom, accordingly, that Brüning, Schleicher, Papen, and Hitler could all equally be regarded as Fascist, the social democrats being so because they did not openly revolt with the Communists against them, was false also. And the failure to realize this was the more remarkable when it is remembered that the last years of the Weimar regime presented conditions peculiarly favourable for united working-class action. When, after Hitler had already come to power, the Communist International recommended its constituent bodies to approach the leadership of the Social Democratic Parties with a view to joint action against Fascism, the central point of its offensive had been lost. It was ready then "to refrain from making attacks on social democratic organizations." But in fourteen years of previous denunciation it had gone far to destroy that confidence in joint action which alone might have rendered successful an assault upon the state-power.

Another implication of this error is important. The vital difference—and it cannot be exaggerated—between capitalist democracy and the Fascist state lies in the fact that, under the former, the protective working-class institutions are not destroyed. Where, therefore, they work upon a common front against the effort to attack their purposes, their overthrow is a far more difficult matter. But where they are not merely divided, but, as in pre-Hitler Germany, almost as hostile to one another as they are to their common foe, their defeat is well-nigh inevitable in all normal circumstances. For their disunity not only operates to minimize the strength of which they themselves dispose. It also has the additional result of deflecting away from both large numbers of working-men who are persuaded by their controversy that neither deserves their faith, and these, if they do not learn, as scores of thousands of German working-men learned, to accept the attractive slogans of Fascism, become apathetic to politics and, thereby, if only indirectly, strengthen the prospects of Fascism. When, therefore, Fascism makes its assault upon capitalist democracy, it is found impossible to improvise that power of resistance which can alone repulse it. The theory of social Fascism, in any society where the active working-class is seriously divided, ensures its defeat before the battle is joined.

The only justification for such a view would lie in the theory that a Fascist state is a necessary experience through which the working-class must pass in order to form a united front against its opponents; it must be taught by Fascism, that is, the need for revolutionary action. But this is an error comparable in character to that of which Lenin accused the Mensheviks. They insisted that Russia must pass through a capitalist phase, in the form of a bourgeois, though democratic republic, as the necessary prelude to a socialist society. They did not perceive that the objective conditions were present which made possible a movement directly from the March to the November Revolution. The problem is one of the strategic disposition of forces. A united working-class in Germany might have been defeated in March 1933. But at least it would have been in a position to fight; and, in the struggle, skilful leadership might have altered the disposition of forces in such a way as to destroy the prospect of Hitler's success. And, *mutatis mutandis*, this is true of any capitalist democracy in which the working-class forces do not paralyse themselves beforehand by division. But nothing is as likely to sow that division as the acceptance, by any considerable part of the working-class, of the theory of social Fascism. It emphasizes the belief of social democrats in a legalism maintained even when the belief in it has been rendered barren by the action of its opponents. It reinforces the faith of the communist in revolutionary methods by the very intensity with which belief in constitutionalism is preached by the social democrats. The division between them becomes ever more sharp; and the price paid for its sharpness is the ease of a Fascist victory.

That this is an accurate analysis is, I think, demonstrated by the policy of Lenin during the Russian Revolution at the time when Kornilov attempted to seize power. Lenin himself, it will be remembered, was in hiding; Trotsky and other leaders of the Bolshevik Party were in prison. More than this. For Lenin, Kerensky, against whom Kornilov was in revolt, stood as the personification of that bourgeois regime for whose overthrow he was passionately concerned. But Lenin did not hesitate to urge upon his party that it was their duty to assist Kerensky with all their power. He realized that the differences between them were essential to the future of the Bolsheviks themselves. He was not prepared to support the Kerensky government; but he understood at once that its overthrow by Kornilov gravely weakened the chance of a proletarian victory. He realized that the latter only became possible if Kornilov was destroyed.[1] For a Kornilov victory would have meant the end even of the March revolution. It would have altered completely the whole incidence of the relations which were developing. It would have enabled the Russian bourgeoisie to re-establish their authority.

The same situation is presented by capitalist democracy. So long as its institutions remain, the working-classes, if they are united, are in a position to take the initiative; once they

---

[1] Lenin, *Collected Works* (Eng. trans.), Vol. XXI, *Toward the Seizure of Power*, Bk. I. p. 137. Letter of September 12, 1917.

are overthrown, as in Italy and Germany, the power to take the offensive remains in the hands of their opponents. To divide the working-classes, therefore, is to confuse them. To fight social democracy in the way in which the communists have done is at once to weaken the confidence of the workers in socialism without, as events have shown, being able to transfer their allegiance to communism. Had the communists remained an integral part of the socialist front, the common danger which both wings of the working-class movement confronted would have impelled common action against the foe. As it was, each was fighting on two fronts, uncertain which of its opponents was the most deserving of hatred. The only way to unity lay in the abandonment of the theory of social Fascism. That would have left social democracy and communism alike free to battle jointly against their common enemy, while, at the same time, it would have left the communists in a position to win over the masses, at the crisis, to a policy of action. But the method they adopted paralysed the possibility of action long before it was necessary; the theory of social democracy to which they held had destroyed that confidence which is the necessary basis of co-operation. When, on March 17, 1933, the Communist International recommended its affiliated parties to propose joint action to the social democrats against Fascism it was fourteen years too late.

The implication is, I think, an obvious one. The success of the Russian Revolution can only be repeated in the conditions of the Russian Revolution. When these are absent, the working-classes can attain power only by remaining coherent and united, whatever may be the differences within their party-organizations. For their strength is in their massed power; and, as soon as they lose this strength, they enable their opponents to defeat them by profiting from their divisions. It is conceivable that the calling of a general strike against von Papen in 1932 would, had it been pursued with determination, have led to his overthrow and, with it, the erosion of Hitlerism. But the appeal for a general strike emanated from the communists; and, though it was the unquestionably right policy to pursue, it was denounced by the social democratic leaders essentially because they had no faith in the men from whom it came. And though the rank and file of the social democrats were probably prepared for action of this character, the fact that the call for it came from the communists was sufficient to persuade them to accept their leaders' view against it. How could they think otherwise when the communist leaders themselves had elaborately explained that there existed "fundamental and irreconcilable differences" between the leadership of the two parties, that they struggled "against social democratic politics, against the Social Democratic Party, and against its representatives" [1]?

The dilemma is a vital one. Unless the organization of a state has broken down, the working-classes can achieve power only by maintaining the integrity of their own institutions. But this they cannot do if there is the kind of division in their own ranks which communism has provoked since the Revolution. The only way, therefore, to secure unity of working-class action is to defend those institutions at all costs, and to use the pressure of events to direct them towards a satisfactory policy. Any other method than this is exactly that "playing with revolution" against which Marx warned the working-class in measured words. The very nature of capitalist democ-

[1] *Rote Fahne*, July 5, 1932.

racy means, in a period of crisis, a balance so unstable that it can easily be overthrown. And nothing is so likely to upset it as uncertainty of direction on the part of the working-class. Once this occurs, like any army, it loses confidence in itself. It misses the psychological moment for action. Its power is impaired at the very moment when it has most need of that power. And since the whole essence of the state is the use of force to prevent the realization of its objectives, the paralysis of its will by division results in its destruction in the field. The Austrian example shows how small is the chance of success for the workers in arms in the absence of an anarchy like that of 1917. But, in Austria, the working-class was at least united. When, as in Germany, internal conflict has destroyed self-confidence, the battle is lost before the forces have joined issue with one another.

IV

There is evidence and to spare in the historic record that the capture of a state is invariably a difficult adventure. It requires for its success a unity in the attacking forces which neither persons nor principles can break. That was the history of the Cromwellian Revolution: once his supporters had failed to agree among themselves, the way was prepared for the return of Charles II. That was the history, also, of the Revolution in France. Napoleon inherited its possibilities because, once the regime of aristocratic privilege had been overthrown, the men who made it had no objectives in common. In our own time, the conditions of fundamental change are present; but we seem likely to fail to utilize them, less because there is disagreement upon objectives than because there is disunity about the methods whereby the objectives can be maintained.

The conditions, I suggest, are present which make for fundamental change. There is the vital economic fact that, under the class-relations of our present society, the potentialities of production cannot be fully utilized; in the past, at any rate, this has always denoted the coming of fundamental change. Our literature has moved into that temper where established values are critically examined which, as at the Reformation, and with the Romantic movement, has been the invariable precursor of crisis. Our governing classes have lost confidence in themselves. The habits of tolerance, which are the mark of a system which feels secure, no longer win the favour which was widespread a generation ago. Faith in the power of reason to settle controversies with justice no longer awakens the same response as in the nineteenth century; ideas hasten to clothe themselves in arms for fear lest their own virtue be too unsubstantial to prevail. The forces which deny have proved stronger than the forces which affirm. We had faith in the power of science; and it has been shown that science is a social danger unless it can be harnessed to common purposes upon which men in their various societies are agreed. Religion was a unifying force; but the discoveries of science, on the one hand, and its own subordination to the interests of privilege upon the other, have proved fatal to its claim upon the allegiance of men. We believed that an acquisitive society might win such riches that a principle of satisfactory division could be found. We have discovered only that in an acquisitive society no principle of division can be maintained which the masses will accept as just. We sought, within its terms, to buy off the demands of justice by a policy of concessions to the multitude; but we have found that the logic of our system limits abruptly and severely this effort to postpone the fundamental issue.

That issue may be stated in quite simple terms. An unequal society, which is built upon the privilege of the few, can only maintain its authority either by consent or by force. It can win that consent only as it is able to offer those who are excluded from privilege the continuous hope of bettering their position. It must provide them, that is, with the grounds for believing that they can attain both security and hope. When a regime of privilege is expanding, that is a possible adventure. The implications of the regime are not challenged because its achievements appear as its self-evident justification to the great mass of its citizens.

But as soon as it passes into an epoch where, through crisis, neither hope nor security can be proffered, it is inevitable that grave difficulties should be encountered. Men forget its achievements because they are angry at their suspension. They begin to examine the foundations. They ask for rational justification of rules and ideas which are habitual rather than either rational or just. Grievances are multiplied and vociferous; the men who feel them clamour for the continuance of the concessions which, in the past, could be granted without undue hesitation or effort. But to grant them in an epoch of crisis is to call for the voluntary surrender of privileges from those in whom their habitual possession has bred a veritable religion of ownership. What once seemed reasonable now begins to seem destructive. What once appeared as an issue to be debated now appears as a threat to law and order. Those who dominate the life of the regime deny its power to grant the claims that are made. They regard the reformers as revolutionaries; they insist that the revolutionaries are the enemies of society. They mobilize the coercive power of the state to annihilate dissent. Fear begins to pervade the ranks of those who live by ownership; and, when the minds of men are pervaded by fear, it is the voice of the extremist only to which men give attention. The privileged then begin to rally about those who promise by drastic action to restore the traditional power of the state. Extreme provokes extreme; and in the clash of mighty opposites the prospect of rational compromise is lost.

That, as I think, is the situation we confront at the present time. For something over three centuries we have been building a state affected to the purposes of an acquisitive society. Those purposes have permeated every aspect of its institutions. They have involved a system of class-relations to the preservation of which its religions, its laws, its armed forces, its civil service, its legislative apparatus, its educational institutions, have all alike been devoted. But within the ambit of those class-relations it has become no longer possible to satisfy the aspirations of those in the community who live only by the sale of their labour. When the process of expansion characterized the acquisitive society, it was possible to buy them off with concessions. Today, the grant of these upon any scale which is deemed adequate by the proposed recipients itself strikes at the root of the power by which privilege maintains itself. To safeguard what it deems its rights from invasion, it is driven to attack the foundations of the institutional system through which the concessions could in the past be made. It is caught in the dilemma of being required either to go forward to an egalitarian commonwealth or backward to a social order in which the mass of men is no longer entitled, as in the theory of political democracy, to affirm its own essence.

In that dilemma the owners of property invoke the power of the state to protect themselves from invasion. Why should they not who have been taught by the argument of three hundred years that they are entitled to do so? They hewed their way to authority through war and revolution in the past; they had no doubt of the moral rightness then of their cause. The challenge, as they see it, is a threat of the average man, the failures, the incompetent, the half-alive, the routineers, to those who have won their place in the sun by ability and energy and effort. They have the law on their side. They have all the majestic claims of prescription with its persuasion to men to recognize in the habits of the past the rules of an eternal order. They can appeal to that fear of the unknown and the untried which has never failed to affect the allegiance of the timid and the inert. They have the sense of command which comes from long habituation to its exercise. They know that any system of authority to which men have become accustomed creates intimate and deep affections from which they cannot easily be separated. They see the apathy of the multitude and conclude from it that the discontent they encounter is largely the work of wicked and envious men who can be destroyed by drastic attack at the appropriate moment. They do not believe that their day is done. The crisis, for them, is always a temporary one that a bold front can bestride like a colossus. The system in itself, they tell themselves, is healthy enough; it is only this or that temporary excrescence which needs to be removed.

So Louis XVI told himself in the last days of the *ancien régime;* so Nicholas II was convinced in the final dissolution of the Tsarist tyranny. But both were mistaken because they failed to realize that the system whose principle they embodied stood in the way of the fundamental change that had become inevitable. The agitator does not influence the multitude unless the grievances for which he demands redress are grievances they profoundly feel; and grievances do not express themselves in terms of violence unless they are the outcome of popular suffering. To avoid grievance there must be a policy of unremitting reform. But this there cannot be if its cost and extent is incompatible with the nature of the system under which it is demanded. We could not win the reforms necessary for the free commercial system of the nineteenth century from the feudal state because the implications of the one were incompatible with the requirements of the other. On the evidence, we seem unlikely to secure from a capitalist society the acceptance of the principles which the establishment of socialism involves. For this is to ask from capitalists acquiescence in their own erosion; and in Western civilization, at least, no class has yet been willing to surrender those privileges it has organized the state to maintain.

Why should it do so when, again as the evidence shows, it believes profoundly in their justice? Hitler and Mussolini, the great masters of the American financial empire, the industrial rulers of Great Britain, are all sincerely convinced that their abdication would be fatal to the well-being of the societies they control. They have little respect for majority rule, they know too well how easily it can be manufactured. They are not prepared to abide by the results of reason; or, rather, they insist upon their power to define the premises within which reason must argue, and they take care so to define them that the power of the state can be invoked to prevent inquiry into their legitimacy. They play a game, in short, in which they start with the immense advantage on their side of being able to lay down the rules by which it must be conducted. And they take care so to define the rules that the men who question them are by that fact expelled from the game.

That is what is meant by their possession of the state-power. It enables them to use force to determine what the result of the contest shall be if their advantage is challenged. If it is a strike, like the textile strike in the United States in the autumn of 1934, then its effective conduct is prevented by the arrest of local leaders so that all contact between unions and their members is lost.[1] If it is protest against war, then the law makes it a crime to utter words giving aid and comfort to the enemy; and under this formula there seems no limit to the possible range of penalty.[2] And not only do they use the state-power to define the terms upon which they permit the contest to be staged. Largely, they own the press; and the power of control over news has an influence it is difficult to exaggerate. Largely, also, and especially in times of crisis, the new weapon of broadcasting is in their hands. And by their possession of the schools [3] they are able to prepare the mind of the new generations to accept the principles they desire, naturally enough, to impose.

In these circumstances there is little danger of an effective challenge to their authority save under two conditions. It is possible in the aftermath of unsuccessful war, when de-

---

[1] *The New Republic*, October 3, 1934, p. 197.

[2] Cf. Walter Nelles, *Espionage Act Cases* (1921), for evidence of American experience in this regard.

[3] On which, for American experience, see an article by Mr. H. K. Beale in *Harpers Magazine* for October 1934.

feat and disillusion have undermined the normal respect for the state. It is possible, also, when long experience of what is held by a considerable minority to be tyranny violates expectations so deep-seated that the state cannot rely upon the traditional loyalty of the instruments upon which it depends. Apart from these situations, a government which is determined to maintain the state-power whatever the cost is almost certain, unless it be guilty of criminal strategic error, to be able to do so. And this is the more true in our own day than at any time in the last three hundred years for two reasons. It is the more true, in the first place, because the highly disciplined forces of the modern state are at an immense advantage in any struggle with a half-organized mass; and it is the more true, in the second place, because the necessary weapons of successful revolution, the aeroplane, poison gas, heavy artillery, massed machine-guns, are practically inaccessible, in the necessary volume, to men who desire to capture the state. The experience of Austria and of Spain makes it decisively clear that no revolution can have the hope of success unless the armed forces are on its side or decisively neutral in the circumstances in which it takes place.

For these reasons, it seems to me legitimate to conclude that a class which controls the power of the state will not surrender it if surrender involves the abdication of its privileges. It will reform when it must if reform does not mean the destruction of what it regards as essential. But it will reform only when it believes that concessions can be made without essential sacrifice. On any other terms, a ruling class will fight; and history goes to show that it will invariably fight with a profound belief that right is on its side. If, particularly, the conflict emerges in that special form of society we call capitalist democracy, I believe that the holders of economic power will seek to suppress the democratic system if this, in its operation, interferes with the foundations of capitalism. And, except in the special circumstances to which I have referred, I believe that they will be successful in their effort at its suppression.

The implication is the clear one that the alternative to government by consent is naked dictatorship. There is little inherent reason that I can see why it should not endure for a considerable period. I see no ground for supposing that men who have been willing to lose political freedom will be able, or easily willing, under modern conditions, to organize themselves for its conquest. In the long run, doubtless, dictatorships destroy themselves by their inability to satisfy the population over which they rule; but it is in the long run only that this occurs. It is, indeed, true that, in our own time, the economic circumstances of an autocratic state which seeks, like Germany or Italy, to perpetuate the class-structure of capitalism provokes the kind of militant foreign policy, which, again in the long run, means war. But the outcome of war where, being unsuccessful, the dictatorship is overthrown is certainly not democracy, and not necessarily a proletarian dictatorship.

It is not the first because the disorganization which results from the overthrow of an autocratic regime is rarely one that can be transcended by the methods of democracy. Russia, Spain, Austria, and Germany all seem clearly to enforce this lesson. The unloosing of restraint which normally follows upon the downfall of a dictatorship usually calls for some alternative form of strong government. The essential vice of autocracy is that it breaks those habits of compromise and co-operation upon which the successful functioning of democracy depends. Even where, as in Spain and Germany, there is a democratic interlude, the conditions of its continuance seem to be the achievement of a prosperity which enables large reforms to be undertaken without serious cost to established expectations; where these are absent, as they were absent in Spain and Germany, the classes at whose expense large reforms are undertaken are driven into a reaction which becomes impatient with the price they have to pay. The result is that they associate their loss with the democratic system, and this becomes the object of a hatred among the few, and an apathy among the many, which is the direct path to counter-revolution. We then find a drift towards that atmosphere of crisis in which exceptional legislation becomes necessary. If this is enforced, it drives the more reckless opponents of the regime to desperate measures; if it remains unused, it tends, at least, to convince them of the weakness of democracy, and to tempt them, thereby, to sharpen their effort for its overthrow. Few people, I think, can seriously doubt that the tenderness of the Weimar republic to its organized opponents convinced them that its foundations were fragile enough to make overthrow possible. If Ebert and his colleagues had been as firm with the supporters of the Right as they were with those of the Left, the history of German Fascism would have been very different.

Nor need it be the second. Proletarian dictatorship is not an inevitable stage in social evolution. It is not merely the outcome of special economic conditions; it is also the outcome of great leaders who, like Lenin, have the eye to see, and the hand to execute, the requisite strategy at the appropriate moment. The technical conditions under which modern government is carried on make a reversion to barbarism at least as possible an outcome of unsuccessful war as a victory of the working-class. The number of conditions upon which the latter depends are very large. It must be armed. It must be led by a revolutionary party strategically equipped for its task. It must be strong enough not only to overcome the resistance of its opponents, but also to withstand the pressure of foreign intervention, not least, in the modern phase of warfare, from the air. It must be able both to assure its food-supplies, and rapidly to reconstruct the civil administration. From any angle, it is a gigantic task; from any angle its success is hardly less than a miracle. For anyone who reflects on the history of the Russian Revolution can hardly avoid the reflection that its success in establishing a proletarian dictatorship was built above all upon two factors. The first was the weakness of the Russian bourgeoisie, which made its resistance feebler than it would have been in any state of comparable significance. The second was the presence of Lenin not merely as the supreme strategist of the actual seizure of power, but, even more, as the great architect of its consolidation. Revolutions, no doubt, invariably bring men of the first quality to the front; but in the whole of modern history none has produced a man so incomparably fitted as Lenin to the range and intensity of his problems.[1]

V

What, then, is the implication of all this? It seems to me to follow from the analysis I have made that the operations

---

[1] On all this see the admirable discussion by Raymond Postgate, *How to Make a Revolution* (1934), esp. Chaps. II and X.

of the modern state rarely permit of successful revolution. A change in class-relations is only likely, save under the most exceptional circumstances, to be accomplished when the mass of the people is positively convinced of the need for such a change. Unless there is a situation, of which Russia so far affords us the only example in history, where events have given the initiative of action to the opposition, such a change can be effected only by a government which has a strong and determined public opinion behind it. Even then, all the evidence goes to show that it is likely to be challenged; and it is at the best improbable that it will be able, when challenged, to maintain its power by reliance upon the classic technique of democracy. Any overt attack upon it must involve it in a process of controls and repressions which then become the necessary price of its life.

It therefore becomes essential for any party which is seeking to transform the economic foundations of society to maintain as long as it can a constitutional order which permits it openly to recruit its strength. The alternative is its reduction, as in Germany, from a movement to a conspiracy in which its prospects are always a gamble upon the outcome of disaster to the state which has driven it underground. In any case, it will be difficult, in proportion as its success within the framework of constitutionalism is rapid, to prevent its opponents from striking first. Men who see a threat to the foundations of an order in which they believe easily persuade themselves, and, as a rule, sincerely persuade themselves, that they are justified in taking drastic steps to its preservation. The English civil wars were preceded by the eleven years of Charles's personal rule. The threat of the Home Rule Bill produced at once the Ulster Volunteers. It has been the normal history of property to conceive of attack as the best means of defence. And since property, in a capitalist society, has the power of the state in its hands, the opportunity to destroy a democracy which threatens its privileges is both obvious and inviting.

In any event, upon this analysis, the fragile character of the liberty men have so profoundly cherished must be obvious to any observer. Liberty in any society is a function of security; when this is threatened, those who defend the existing order have never had any difficulty in admitting its abrogation. One has only to compare the temper of France in 1789 with its temper in 1792; the political atmosphere in England under Pitt and Sidmouth; the contempt for liberty which characterizes the modern dictatorships, proletarian and Fascist alike, to see that this is the case. Liberty can be maintained when the changes that are proposed are either a matter of general consent, or are sufficiently narrow in character to make those affected feel that peace is preferable to conflict. They have felt this, in general, about piecemeal reforms the outcome of which was small in range and slow in time; they have rarely felt this when the changes made involved the very basis upon which the whole structure of class-relationships has been built.

The inference which is often drawn from this is the simple one that, since liberty depends upon security, the proponents of change, if they care for liberty, must pay the price for it. This consists in guaranteeing to the class which owns the instruments of production the continuance of the privileges such ownership entails for a period at least long enough to reconcile them to the new social order. But it is not a pledge which can easily be made in good faith. It means the creation of a new class of *rentiers* whose claim to their share of the national income is guaranteed by the good faith of the state; and, unless and until national ownership produces the advantages of reorganization, it means the postponement of any improvement in the condition of the workers in an industry taken over by the state except at the expense of the general body of citizens in their capacity either of taxpayers or of consumers. There is everything to be said, on grounds of expediency, against the kind of confiscation which would provoke a possessing-class to conflict; it is amply worth while to pay a considerable price for their willing acceptance of a new social order. But a price which involved loading that order with a new burden of debt which simply perpetuated a regime of privilege in a different and, indeed, a less desirable form than the old, without risk to those who were its beneficiaries, would merely postpone the problem of paying the price without providing a basis upon which it could be creatively solved.

I believe, therefore, that we must anticipate an epoch in which the attitude to liberty characteristic of Western civilization in general, and of Great Britain in particular, during the nineteenth century, will be at a discount. This is a hard saying. That temper bred a habit of tolerance, and indignation against injustice, which were among the major triumphs of the human spirit. There must be few men who can fail to respond, for example, to the poetry in which Byron and Shelley, Heine and Victor Hugo, pled for the emancipation of mankind from its fetters. There must be fewer still who have not felt that events like the freeing of Italy from Austrian tyranny, the Liberal campaign against the Turkish atrocities, the freeing of the slaves in the United States, the entrance of Labour members into the House of Commons, added to the sum of civilized well-being. Yet it is apparent in our own day that the children of the men who accepted these events with enthusiasm are prepared, in the name of the rights of property, to destroy all the advantages of the advance they represent. All over the world, a new barbarism has become our habit which men enforce, as it appears, in the name of principles to which they hold with passion. The suppression by the dictatorships, whether in Russia or Germany or elsewhere, of parties which cannot accept the ideology of those in power; the reduction of the Jews in Germany to the status of an enslaved race; the extent to which political difference involves the infliction of tortures no sensitive person can ever think of without horror; the ease with which these things can be done without arousing even informed opinion from its apathy; the fact that every state can compete with its rivals in the exploitation of methods of warfare which it knows to be incompatible with the decencies of human life; all this suggests the coming of an iron age in which the moral restraints placed by security upon the exercise of power can no longer hope to exert that influence we had come to believe was part of the settled habit of mankind. The murder of Matteotti, with at least the connivance of Mussolini, produced only a momentary revulsion against the Italian dictator. The assassination by Hitler of some of his leading colleagues without trial could be defended by eminent jurists of high academic distinction as the embodiment of the idea of justice. Methods of government, in a word, which we have historically regarded as typical of either an Oriental despot or a mediæval Italian tyrant are deliberately organized by the rulers of Western states of the twentieth century with no obvious feeling of compunction. Terrorism is justified as the high road to power; and power is held to be so supreme a good that the ways of its attainment evoke little protest from the spectators of their barbarities.

When ideas arm themselves for conflict, the voice of reason is unlikely to be heard. When the voice of reason is drowned by the passionate clangor of arms, men have never listened to a plea for freedom. The processes of government by consent are abrogated. Those conquer who have the weapons on their side; and it is not necessarily the case that the possession of the weapons means the better cause. That is the temper which has always developed when a social system is nearing its nadir. The old order fights fiercely for what it has, indifferently to the implications of conflict. So pagan fought Christian in ancient Rome; so Catholic fought Protestant in sixteenth-century Europe; so North fought South in the American Civil War; so Tsarism fought political and social reform in pre-revolutionary Russia. Men holding power, who are habituated to an idea of good, will fight to defend it rather than acknowledge that it no longer suits the needs they confront.

They do not do so from wantonness or insincerity. They do so because their ideas of good and evil are the offspring of their environment, because, in its terms, alien ideas are a threat to foundations they have been taught by their experience to regard as indispensable. They are tolerant, even generous, when alien ideas seem to offer no fear of disturbance to those foundations; when they do, they choose suppression rather than argument as the easiest way of defending themselves. To make a desert and call it peace has always been the method of a threatened social order; and the instrument by which the desert is made has always been the power of the state.

That is why, in an unequal society, the power of the state has always been a means of oppressing those who are excluded from the privileges it protects. That is why, also, those who are excluded must always seek to possess themselves of this power in order to extend their benefits to themselves. But no state, so far in history, has ever been open to such possession merely in terms of a popular will expressed through constitutional forms. Its institutions have always been weighted in the interest of those who own the essential instruments of production in the society. Political forms have always been a mask behind which an owning class has sought to protect from invasion the authority which ownership confers; and, when the political forms have endangered the rights of ownership, the class in possession has always sought to adjust them to its needs. No doubt it has always proffered grounds upon which the attempt might be justified; it has sought to show, like Hitler in Germany, that the adjustment involves the good of the community as a whole. But where the adjustment has been successfully made, as in Italy and Germany in our time, it is clear that, whatever is defended, and however sincerely, the habitual class-relations of the society remain in effective being.

It has been the argument of this book that the essential purpose of the state is always to protect a given system of class-relations. It has been argued that, wherever there is a society divided into economic classes distinguished from one another by ownership in the context of the productive function, the state is a barrier against the movement to the abolition of classes. In a capitalist civilization, therefore, the logic of the state-principle makes it a weapon against the common ownership of the means of production. Where that civilization is wealthy, or expanding, its power to offer concessions to the masses mitigates the antagonism of interests upon which, fundamentally, it is built. But where, as in our time, that civilization encounters crisis, the antagonism becomes stark and decisive, and the state emerges as a sovereign power used to defend the foundations of capitalism from men who seek benefits which involve its transformation.

I have argued here that those who do so use the state do not do so from purely selfish motives. Not less than their opponents, they believe that they are acting for social good; the principles in conflict are in antagonism to each other because the environment and experience interpreted by classes in society lead to interpretations of what social good involves which, in an era of economic decline, become mutually exclusive. When that point emerges in the history of any community, there is always a choice for its members between surrender and social war. So far, on the evidence of history, any class which has sought to re-define its position in the state in any fundamental way has always had to achieve its end by violent revolution. I have argued here that in our time the facts give us no warrant for concluding that our experience will be a different one from that of past ages.

I have denied, indeed, that the high probability of violent revolution means a right to infer a victory for that party which aims at a classless society. Such an inference, I have suggested, depends upon a rare concomitance of circumstances which are not likely to be accessible in most normal situations we can foresee. In particular, I have sought to show that the association of a capitalist society with a democratic form of state offers no certain prospect that the democratic idea will be maintained in an era which tests the validity of capitalist assumptions by crisis. The association, I have argued, has been due to special historical circumstances. The overthrow of the feudal state could only be accomplished, as, most notably, in France and England, by the alliance of the middle- and working-classes; democratic forms were the price paid by the former for that alliance. A long period of expansion made it possible to conceal the divergence of interest between the allies. Now that the epoch of contraction has come, its contradiction is increasingly evident. But I have sought to show that, since the reality of political democracy is limited by its virtually complete absence from the economic sphere—the field not only of essential power, but, also, of predominant middle-class interest—the facts are dissolving into hostility an alliance that has no longer any major functions to fulfil. In the acquisitive society, in short, which capitalist evolution has brought into being, the democratic form of the state, where this exists, merely masks the power of a plutocracy and its dependents who are no longer finding it suitable to the interests they seek to safeguard.

No political philosophy, therefore, can usefully operate with the concept of a state-power which is interpreted as an instrument of the total well-being of the society it controls. So long as the state expresses a society divided into economic classes, it is always the servant of that class which owns, or dominates the ownership of, the instruments of production. The logic of this situation means that no state can secure the total well-being of a society unless the instruments of production are communally owned. Only where this is the case, can the power of the state be devoted to the unbiased protection of the interests of each member of the society. For, in this situation, it is genuinely as an undifferentiated member of a community, and not in the special context of his class-relation to it, that his needs can be considered and secure response. Such a society can be a truly equal society in the vital sense that response to need is organized not in terms of a power to acquire built upon the bare fact of ownership, but upon a service arising from a function measured in terms of its social value. An equal society can plan its life with a view to securing the maximum benefit from its productive resources. In any other form of society, the necessary character of the state bars the way to this achievement.

"A true state," wrote Hegel,[1] "and a true government only appear where there already exists a difference between class, when both riches and poverty are great, and when the situation develops in which a mass of people who once were accustomed to satisfy their needs, find themselves no longer able to do so." Clearly such a state does not, by reason of its origins, transcend this difference between classes; rather its origin drives it to the function of protecting the rich against the poor. "History shows," Professor Jèze has written,[2] "that each social class, as it becomes master of political power, hastens to use it to favour its special interests. No doubt it does so in good faith, which is why it calls the interest of its class the general interest of the community." In any state which is not democratic in form, this is immediately apparent; and, as I have here sought to show, it is true also of the democratic state with the limitation only that this form en-

---

[1] *Philosophy of History* (trans. Sibree, 1894), p. 89.

[2] *Revue politique et parlementaire* (1910), p. 264.

ables those who do not share in the ownership of the means of production to press their claims more strongly than under an alternative political order.

This is the reason why any analysis of the state reveals its essence, whatever its claims, to be coercive authority placed at the service of the holders of economic power. If that power is, as with ourselves, effectively concentrated in the hands of a few, the purpose of the state will be biased also in their interest. For the character of that power, by defining the class-relations of the society, will define also the legal claims of men to their share of the product made by the economic process. No state, in a word, can go very far beyond the implications of its economic postulates. They shape the contours of all its actions in a finally decisive way. The ethic of its conduct will always, in actual life, be bent to the needs those postulates affirm. There can be no essential change in the character of that ethic, whatever be its political form, without a change in the economic postulates of the society.

That change, as I have argued, is the most difficult and delicate of all operations in social history. It involves the profoundest emotions of men. It touches the ultimate roots of their habits, their sense of security, the idea of right to which prescription has accustomed them. To make it in terms of peace involves, in a period of crisis, the conquest of the emotions by reason. There is no experience more rare in the history of the human race. It is unlikely to be our experience where what is affected by the change is the basic factor in all social relationships. The peaceful evolution of institutions depends for its realization upon the ability of men to agree upon the purposes they must have in view; their solidarity is a function of that agreement. And the agreement must be more than a verbal one; it must be daily realized in the lives of average men and women. The signs are about us on every hand that this agreement is no longer possible. We have moved into one of those critical epochs in history where we have to re-define the fundamental objectives of social policy. The traditional habits of the past are breaking down before our eyes; and, with their break-down, there comes an inescapable challenge to the social relationships upon which they were based.

There have been two epochs in modern history where mankind has had to meet a similar challenge. The Reformation broke into pieces the notion of the single Christian commonwealth of the Middle Ages; and with its destruction the theological conception of society was replaced by the secular. Effectively, that change was the reflection of a new system of class-relations born of the inability of the feudal system to realize the potentialities of the latent productive power of society. The Reformation gave the bourgeoisie a foothold within the confines of the new political order that it involved. But the realization of its promise was partial and incomplete. It was not until the end of the eighteenth century that the vast movement we summarize under the name of the French Revolution enabled the middle-class to complete the process of its emancipation. In each case, new economic needs effected a transvaluation of all social values; in each case the price of the effort was violent conflict between the old and the new. It took over three centuries for the order of which we are a part to free itself with any fullness of the categories of the old.

Once more we can see before us the beginnings of a new order. Once more the economic process has become incompatible with the political forms in which it is contained. Once more we have begun that struggle between present fact and historic idea which always involves the remaking of the principles of government.

In such a situation, it is the first duty of political philosophy to examine the character of the state in its actuality rather than in its idea. It is not in what it claims to be, but in what it effectively does, that its real nature lies. Hitherto, for the most part, political philosophy has sought rather to justify than to explain; it has been eager rather to safeguard the past than to make possible the liberation of the future. An adequate theory of politics now must start, as its foundation, with the incompatibility of the sovereign state with the world economic order we require. It must reveal the state as, above all, the guardian of class-relations which deprive us of the richer civilization that might be ours.

It will be a long and arduous task to make the revelation decisive. All institutions whose past has been a majestic one contain, even in their decline, the power to delay the coming of their successors. They are, by our habituation to them, a sort of prison made intimate, and even dear, by the associations of an age-long history. Dwelling therein, to many of us, the prospect without seems vague and doubtful and hard. We weigh uneasily the price of escape from its confines; and the courage to attempt it is rare. But it is only as we make the effort that we can go forward with hope. For in no other fashion can we now add creative dignity to the human adventure.